FIFTEEN
JUDGMENTS

FIFTEEN
JUDGMENTS

CASES THAT SHAPED INDIA'S

FINANCIAL LANDSCAPE

SAURABH KIRPAL

VINTAGE
An imprint of Penguin Random House

VINTAGE

USA | Canada | UK | Ireland | Australia
New Zealand | India | South Africa | China

Vintage is part of the Penguin Random House group of companies
whose addresses can be found at global.penguinrandomhouse.com

Published by Penguin Random House India Pvt. Ltd
4th Floor, Capital Tower 1, MG Road,
Gurugram 122 002, Haryana, India

First published in Vintage by Penguin Random House India 2022

Copyright © Saurabh Kirpal 2022

All rights reserved

10 9 8 7 6 5 4 3 2

The author is a senior advocate practising before the Hon'ble Supreme Court
of India. This book is a work of non-fiction and is a collection of the author's
views and understanding on certain landmark decisions of the Supreme Court.
The views and opinions expressed in the book are those of the author only and
do not reflect or represent the views and opinions held by any other person.
Each chapter reflects the author's own understanding and conception of such
judgments, which are based on materials that can be verified by research.
The objective of this book is not to hurt any sentiments or be biased in favour of or
against any particular person, region, caste, society, gender, creed, nation or religion.

ISBN 9780670096497

Typeset in Garamond by MAP Systems, Bengaluru, India
Printed at Replika Press Pvt. Ltd, India

www.penguin.co.in

Contents

Introduction

The Supreme Court, at times, seems to be running the country. At the very least, it has an outsized role in governance compared to other apex courts around the world.[1] We are all used to waking up in the morning to newspaper headlines telling us what the Court has decided in a particular matter. However, most of this coverage relates to political matters. Newspapers, other than the pink ones, seem disinterested in cases that relate to financial matters unless there is some political link to them. Perhaps the editors feel that cases related purely to finance and economics don't make newspapers sell, which is paradoxical because it is these judgments that often determine the readers' financial health. Since most people get their information from the media, there is a gap in the knowledge of the common person in matters relating to the interaction between the law and finance.

So, how do we remedy this gap in legal awareness? One way to familiarize yourself with the law is to read all the rules, regulations and statutes. However, that is probably a task best left to lawyers, particularly as the draftsmen of most laws seem to almost enjoy using arcane and inaccessible language. A simpler way to learn about the law is to read the judgments in the area of finance. This is so for several reasons. Firstly, a judgment is rendered in a case that has a particular set of facts that can give a context to the issues on hand. We move, so to say, from an abstract discussion of the law to see the practical impact that the law has. Secondly, even though judges are increasingly prolix in their judgments, the language and the reasoning of the Court are far more accessible to the ordinary individual than the actual text of the law. Thirdly, the judgments also give a certain historical context to the social and financial situation at the point of time at which the judgment was delivered. Finally, the cases often prompt a reaction from the Executive, which has a far greater impact on the future than the judgments themselves. For instance, in at least one case that will be discussed in the book, the Parliament felt compelled to amend the Constitution and dilute the right to property.[2] This set in motion a certain disdain for fundamental rights, which ultimately led to the Parliament entirely removing the right to property from the Constitution and setting the course for a socialist economy for some decades.

This book is an endeavour to examine fifteen judgments that have shaped the financial landscape of India and offer an insight into judicial thinking in matters concerning the economy since Independence. The jurisprudence of the Courts going back seventy years is extremely rich and choosing fifteen cases is not a task without controversy. Many judgments can make a claim to influencing the financial destiny of the country as well as that of the common man. In choosing these particular judgments, an attempt has been made to choose those cases that lie on the cusp of law and economic policy. Many judgments of the Courts can affect the financial health of an individual or a family. For instance, cases relating to succession and matters of inheritance will have a greater impact on the affected individuals than a case about telecom licenses.[3] In the larger scheme of things, however, it is judgments that have a macroeconomic dimension which have a long-term impact on the economy of the country.

An attempt has also been made to examine judgments from different times of history to give the reader a flavour of the jurisprudential as well as the political and financial philosophies at different times in the country. In doing so, the aim is to speak to the past as well as the future. It is not possible to fully understand the economic jurisprudence of today without examining the past, i.e., past precedent. Equally, as is said in a rather clichéd manner, those who ignore history are condemned to repeat it. The judgments, and the often knee-jerk reactions opposing them, lay a path for a particular form of economic development. Examining the judgments, as well as the amendments that sought to undo their effect, has a practical impact on determining a future course of action. For instance, is it a good idea to continue to retrospectively alter the tax law after what happened in the Vodafone case?[4]

The fifteen judgments also trace the long path of the economic history of the country. From the almost laissez-faire conception of the economy in the fifties to the socialism of the seventies and eighties; from the recognition of the effects of liberalization in the nineties to the attempt to rein in the perceived excesses of liberalization, the judgments reflect the sentiment of the era that they were delivered in. For instance, fresh with the liberal zeal stemming from a new Constitution, the Courts in the first year of the Constitution passed judgments upholding the right to property of the zamindars.[5] The reaction was swift and stern. The judgments generated a backlash that fundamentally affected the relationship between the State and the individual. The Constitution was amended only fifteen months after it had been promulgated, even before the first election to Parliament had been held[6] under the Constitution. The Parliament was so incensed at the perceived judicial overreach that the infamous Ninth Schedule was inserted into the Constitution—a schedule that made laws immune from judicial scrutiny.[7] Over the years, this schedule has been amended and a host of economic and financial laws have been added to it, leaving the citizen with no legal recourse against unjust laws. The Foreign Exchange Regulation Act, 1973 and the Industries (Development and Regulation Act), 1951 are among some of the pieces of legislation that shackled the Indian economy but were immune from judicial oversight because of their insertion into the Ninth Schedule to the Constitution.

This tension between a free market vision of the Courts, backed by the right to property guaranteed under the Constitution, and the socialist impulses of the Executive continued for a while. The government attempted to nationalize the banks and pay minimal compensation to the shareholders. The Court struck down that action[8] in 1970. In the now familiar manner, the law as well as the Constitution were amended and the road was set for the virtually complete nationalization of the banks, leading to the formation of the large public sector banking system that exists today.

After a tense battle, the winds of judicial opinion shifted. The Courts became more and more socialist in their thinking, giving judgments that were more in tune with the economic philosophy of the government. Some would say that the Courts became more loyal than the queen, with the socialist rhetoric of some judgments exceeding that of the lawyers for the Government. The late seventies and eighties saw a series of judgments where the Courts became more and more Left-leaning.[9] Symptomatic of this ideological shift was the judgment of the Supreme Court in the case of Bangalore Water Supply.[10] The case was, on the face of it, about an arcane interpretation of the word 'industry'. Specifically, the Court was asked to determine which establishments and businesses were covered under the ambit of the Industrial Disputes Act, 1947. In their zeal to cover as many workers as possible, the Court gave an almost impossibly large definition to the term 'industry', including even charitable organizations, professional services like doctors and lawyers, as well as municipal agencies. The discussion in the judgment clearly shows that the judges thought that the function of enterprise was only peripherally to make money.[11] This was in keeping with the increasingly socialist fervour that was evident in the country.

These were the years when the word 'socialist' was introduced in the Constitution[12] and the right to property was formally done away with.[13]

The swing leftwards, both in the politics of the country as well as in the ideology of the judiciary, was like the proverbial pendulum. The license-quota raj and other outmoded laws made the economy of the country weak. The reforms of the nineties commenced, and businesses were slowly freed from their shackles. One of the focal points of liberalization was the process of disinvestment. The government, it was being increasingly felt, had no business to be in business. The large public sector in the country was bloated and often loss-making (no doubt caused in part due to judgments like the *Bangalore Water Supply* case, which made it impossible to restructure loss-making businesses). Accordingly, a process of strategic sales as well as complete privatization of public sector corporations began in the early part of the twenty-first century. One public sector undertaking that was among the first to be sold was Bharat Aluminium Company Ltd (BALCO). The disinvestment was challenged before the Supreme Court and the challenge was rejected in an apparent move away from the socialist ideologies of the seventies and eighties.[14] This judgment led to more privatizations and was part of the opening of the Indian economy.[15]

The Court in BALCO upheld privatization, holding that this was a matter of policy for the government and the Court would not interfere with the sale. This judicial hands-off approach was merely an extension of another well-recognized principle of law, that of the Court's reluctance to enter into matters of economic policy. This is a salutary principle given the lack of democratic participation as well as the competence of the Court in matters of economic policy.

However, the changing nature of economic growth sorely tested this principle of judicial reluctance to enter the policy minefield in at least two fields. This was in the areas of corruption and the environment.

After the telecom revolution of the late nineties and early 2000s, the Indian telecom industry seemed like a cash cow, and everyone wanted a piece of the pie. The dirty underbelly of that, however, was exposed in what has been called the 2G scam. Telecom spectrum, a valuable natural resource, was allegedly given away surreptitiously and corruptly. Criminal prosecutions were begun, ultimately resulting, of course, in the acquittal of all the accused.[16] In the meanwhile, the Supreme Court was moved and decided to hear the matter. The Court ultimately held that the government did not have the liberty to allocate spectrum as part of its economic policy and that it was mandatory to auction it.[17] While holding this, the Court went a step beyond and proceeded to cancel all the licences of the telecom companies, including those that had bought the spectrum in good faith. The judgment had a devastating impact on the companies and the telecom sector as a whole, one that we are still dealing with.

The second area where the Courts did not have their customary reluctance to interfere in executive policy was in the field of the environment. The Courts have been at the forefront, protecting the environment and balancing the claims of industry and those of the citizens. One such stark example was the case of mining in Goa. In 2014, the Supreme Court held that mining leases in Goa were invalid and directed their immediate closure and reauction.[18] The Court also directed that a substantial sum of money be kept aside for the purposes of sustainable development and intergenerational equity. Once the judgment was passed, there was an uproar among the owners of the mines. The government also felt compelled, for some reason, to come to the aid of the owners. Hurriedly, before the new Mines and Minerals Development Act 2014, which mandated auctions, was to come into force, the government renewed the leases of the mine owners. This renewal was challenged afresh in the Court, which struck down the renewals in 2018.[19] The matter is still pending in Court on various issues. This judgment brings into sharp relief the conflict between the demands of the environment and industry and how the judgments of the Court shift the balance between the two demands.

The liberalization of the economy eventually moved the discussion away from the old tropes of communitarianism versus individualism. In the past decade, new issues have engaged the attention of the Courts with substantial implications both for the economy as well as for individual rights, the full impact of which is yet to be fully understood. One example of this is the Aadhaar judgment[20], where the Court upheld the Aadhaar Act and sought to balance the privacy rights of the individual with the interests of the State to acquire biometric data. Of course, it remains to be seen whether the promised revolution based on the JAM[21] model or the apocalyptic data leakages happen first. A more unexamined reason for the failure to grow as rapidly as India's potential has been the inability to increase the participation of women in the workforce. The judgment in *Vishaka v. The State of Rajasthan*[22] went some way to remedy this, but as the chapter discussing the judgment shows, we have a long way to go.

Of course, one reason that the promised explosive economic growth has not happened is because of the precarious state of the financial sector. During the period of rapid economic growth in the early twenty-first century, nationalized banks, among other institutions, lent money recklessly and are now facing crises when the borrowers are unwilling or unable to repay the loans. Parliament has stepped in to try to remedy the problem by enacting the Insolvency and Bankruptcy Code in 2016.[23] The constitutionality of the enactment was challenged before the Supreme Court. The Court, in its judgment in the case of *Swiss Ribbons v. Union of India*[24] upheld the constitutionality of the legislation, harking back to the principles enunciated in the BALCO case—judicial deference to legislative actions. Whether the act has the required effect in improving the precarious financial situation of the banks remains to be seen. What has unfortunately already been seen is repeated amendments to the law. The enactment seems to be amended every time a new issue crops up, showing that either the original law was not drafted properly or that the government is too trigger-happy with amendments. There has been tremendous uncertainty in this branch of the law, which is antithetical to the needs of business. This uncertainty is also manifest in arbitrary policymaking by various regulators. For instance, the Reserve Bank of India (RBI), an otherwise seasoned and well-respected regulator, framed regulations, virtually making it impossible to deal in bitcoins and other cryptocurrencies. The Supreme Court struck down the ban in 2019. Yet, there has been no comprehensive policy surrounding the use of cryptocurrencies. They remain, in a manner of speaking, in virtual limbo.

When Dick the Butcher said, 'The first thing we do, let's kill all the lawyers,' in Shakespeare's *Henry VI*, he wasn't attempting to rid the world of dishonest lawyers. Quite to the contrary, he wanted to overthrow the government and perceived lawyers, and the law in general, as an obstacle to that end. Even if lawyer jokes are only partly in jest, there is a consensus that any modern country has to be governed by predictable, rule-based laws, rather than by discretionary diktats. Economic growth is strongly tied to, and indeed requires, a robust rule of law. Businesses need to have faith in the predictability of the regulatory regimes governing them before making investments. Shareholders require assurance that their investments would be safe from appropriation by the government or a hostile majority. Creditors need to have access to a legal system that allows them to recover their dues from debtors. It is no surprise that the 'ease of doing business' studies published by the World Bank annually ranks countries on parameters that are facets of the country's legal and regulatory regimes. This book is an endeavour to educate the common man and woman about some of the legal issues in the world of finance. After all, the ultimate control on arbitrary power is an informed electorate.

Notes

[1] The Court has been called the most powerful Court in the world, a statement often attributed to George Gadbois in *Supreme Court Decision Making* (1974), *Banaras Law Journal*, Vol. 10, pp. 1–49, though later seemingly debunked in his book *Supreme Court of India; The Beginnings* (ed. Raghavan and Ram, Oxford University Press, 2017). Nevertheless, the phrase has seemingly entered the legal consciousness and has been repeated often, including by Attorney General K.K. Venugopal. See 'SC Most Powerful in World as Govt Has Shown Respect, Says AG KK Venugopal', News18.com, 26 October 2017.

[2] The attack on the right to property started with the very first amendment to the Constitution in June 1951, which diluted Article 31 of the Constitution. The assault on the right to property continued, and the fundamental rights provisions were repeatedly amended and diluted by the 4th, the 24th and the 25th amendment before finally being summarily expunged by the 44th amendment to the Constitution.

[3] For instance, the recent judgment of the Supreme Court giving women the right to family-held property, i.e., a share in the HUF, with retrospective effect, would fundamentally affect the finances of many families. However, that would be a case of distribution of the same asset among the family rather than a fresh creation of wealth. *Vinita Sharma v. Rakesh Sharma* (2020) 9 SCC 1.

[4] *Vodafone International BV v. Union of India* (2012) 6 SCC 613. In 2006, the foreign-owned Hutchison Essar telecom company was purchased by Vodafone. The purchase of Hutchison's shares by Vodafone happened outside India, yet the income tax department sought to tax the transactions in India. The Supreme Court held that no tax liability was attracted. The victory for Vodafone was short-lived because in the next Budget, the law was amended and the tax liability was imposed with retrospective effect. There was an immediate outcry and the effect of the amendment in terms of international perception has been felt by the Indian economy till date.

[5] *Kameshwar Singh v. State of Bihar* AIR 1951 Pat 91.

[6] The first elections to Parliament were held over a time period that exceeds even the prolonged elections held in recent times. The process took four months from 25 October 1951 to 21 February 1952. The first Parliament was constituted in 1952. See General (1st Lok Sabha) Election Results India, elections.in

[7] Article 31-B, inserted by the first amendments with effect from 18 June 1951, provides that 'none of the Acts . . . specified in the Ninth Schedule . . . shall be deemed to be void, or ever to have become void, on the ground that such Act . . . is inconsistent with, or takes away or abridges any of the [fundamental] rights . . .'

[8] *Rustom Cavasjee Cooper v. Union of India* (1970) 1 SCC 248.

[9] Of course, this coincided with the lurch to the Left in the country and the government as a whole, leading one to wonder whether the Court sets or follows public opinion. While there is little empirical evidence to decide this, the situation in the US seems to suggest that the Court tends to follow public opinion. See, for instance, Casillas C.J., 'How Public Opinion Constrains the US Supreme Court', *American Journal of Political Science*, Vol. 55, No. 1 (Jan. 2011), pp. 74–88.

[10] *Bangalore Water Supply & Sewerage Board v. A. Rajappa* (1978) 2 SCC 213.

[11] Even though the days of socialism of the seventies are over, it is important to note that the socialist philosophy has proved hard to extricate from the judicial mindset. Even today, the judgments of the Court often seem to value socialist principles over the rights of business owners. See, for instance, judgments as recent as *Lilavati Kirtilal Mehta Trust v. Unique Shanti Developers* (2020) 2 SCC 265.

[12] Inserted via the 42nd Amendment with effect from 1 February 1977.

[13] Constitution 44th Amendment Act with effect from 30 April 1979.

[14] *BALCO Employees Union v. Union of India* (2002) 2 SCC 233.

[15] Though not without hiccups. The Supreme Court held that the employees who had been hired by NTPC for the purposes of constructing BALCO's plant could not be transferred to BALCO or its private successor. *BCPP Mazdoor Sangh v. NTPC* (2007) 14 SCC 234. In another matter, the Supreme Court also held in the case of the oil companies BPCL and HPCL that the government could not proceed with the disinvestment process without enacting legislation specifically for this purpose. *Centre for Public Interest Litigation v. Union of India* (2003) 7 SCC 532.

[16] All the accused were acquitted by a judgment of the special court in New Delhi on 21 December 2017. *CBI v. A. Raja* case RC No.: 45 (A) 2009.

The government has filed an appeal before the Delhi High Court, which is still pending.

[17] *Centre for Public Interest Litigation v. Union of India* (2012) 3 SCC 1.

[18] *Goa Foundation v. Union of India* (2014) 6 SCC 590.

[19] *Goa Foundation v. Sesa Sterlite Ltd* (2018) 4 SCC 218.

[20] *K.S. Puttaswamy v. Union of India* (2019) 1 SCC 1.

[21] The so-called Jan Dhan Accounts, Aadhaar and Mobile linkage scheme first conceptualized in the economic survey of 2014–15.

[22] (1997) 6 SCC 241.

[23] The Insolvency and Bankruptcy Code, 2016, was an act of Parliament that aimed to make it easier for creditors to recover their money from defaulting companies. Rather than permitting existing promoters to come up with a scheme of repayment, the act envisaged that the management of the debtor companies could be changed, with the new management controlling the company and providing for a scheme for repayment of debts.

[24] (2019) 4 SCC 14.

Chapter 1

The Purloined Constitution

In the first chapter of a book relating to the law and the economy, examining judgments relating to the right to property would seem an obvious choice. After all, it is the right to property, and the corresponding obligation upon the State to respect and protect the right, that forms the bedrock of capitalism. So it may come as a bit of a surprise to learn that our Constitution does not offer any meaningful right to property.[1]

This was not always the case. When the Constitution was first promulgated, it guaranteed many 'fundamental' rights, including the right to property, under Articles 19 and 31. India had finally shed the yoke of colonial oppression in 1947 and the leaders of the Constituent Assembly were keen to adopt a constitution that guaranteed the basic rights of the citizens of the newly born nation. Lofty ideals and inspiring debates often give birth to a host of rights and that is how most constitutions are usually framed. However, the moment the Courts actually started protecting the constitutional right to property, the Executive discovered just how inconvenient this right was.

Relying on the right to property contained in the Constitution, the Bihar High Court struck down laws that had sought to abolish zamindari in India.[2] The reaction to this judgment was swift and decisive. The Indian Constitution was first amended barely a year after it had been promulgated.[3] The amendment was carried out by the very body that had drafted the Constitution—the Constituent Assembly. In light of judgments on various fundamental rights, the amendments were deemed so urgent and necessary, that the Assembly did not even wait for the first elections to Parliament to happen before the amendments were passed.[4]

In a manner that set a pattern for the years to come, faced with judgments that the Executive did not approve of, the Constitution itself was amended and the precious rights of the citizenry were abridged. The first amendment to the Constitution not only diluted the right to property but also laid the groundwork for making a host of anti-business legislation immune from judicial scrutiny. The true story in this chapter, therefore, is not as much about the case that first enforced the right to property, but its aftermath.

I

The Right to Property

The right to property has been said to be the most basic or 'natural right' in treatises[5] and constitutions[6] across the world. To place the right to property at such an exalted position is contentious, but at the very least it is clear that the nature and extent of protection afforded to private property determines the economic model of a state. It is thus not surprising that some of the most pitched battles between courts and legislatures across the world are on matters relating to property rights.[7] The Indian experience has not been different. This chapter deals with a case that enforced the right to property in our fledgling democracy and set off a reaction whose effects can be felt to this day.

India, at the time of Independence, was mired in poverty and deprivation. The Indian economy had been battered by a long period of British rule and was a largely rural economy. A very large number of people worked as landless labourers on estates and lands owned by zamindars.[8] It is estimated that almost half the people working as farmers did not own the land they tilled or owned only a very small tract of land. If the promises of the Independence struggle were to be met, the lot of these agricultural workers had to be improved.

The leaders of the freedom struggle and the members of the Constituent Assembly were of the belief that social justice required redistribution of land to the landless. The zamindari system, where a few families owned and controlled land, which was let out to peasant farmers, was particularly negatively viewed.[9] Virtually the entire discussion in relation to the right to property in the Constituent Assembly was viewed through the lens of compensation to be paid to the zamindars on acquisition of their estates.

Zamindari abolition and the compensation payable to the zamindars had split the Constituent Assembly. On the one hand, there were members who wished that virtually no compensation should be given to zamindars, while there were others who wanted a full and fair market value of the land to be given.[10] Eventually a compromise was reached, which was most closely allied with the view of Sardar Vallabhbhai Patel, arguably the man who commanded the greatest authority in the Constituent Assembly.[11]

The right to property was contained in two articles—Article 19 (1) (f) and Article 31. The sum and substance of the provisions was that property could only be acquired by law. The Constitution also required that the compensation or the principles on which the compensation would be paid were to be expressly laid down in the law that provided for acquisition.[12] It was believed that this right was a fair compromise between the rights of the zamindars to compensation for the expropriation of their lands and the need for social justice and welfare of the landless majority.

It was understood by the framers of the Constitution that the judiciary would keep its hands off the question of compensation to be granted to the zamindars. Pandit Nehru, the prime minister, while moving the motion to accept the article said that 'no Supreme Court and no judiciary can stand in judgement over the sovereign will of Parliament representing the will of the entire community'.[13] He believed that the article provided for just compensation, but the nature and quantum of the compensation was left for Parliament to decide. The role of the judiciary was to be limited. It was believed that the Courts would not rule on the compensation payable to the zamindars but would only step in if there was a 'fraud on the Constitution'.[14] The prime minister felt that the article represented a compromise that 'protects both individual and the community. It gives the final authority to Parliament, subject only to the scrutiny of the superior courts in case of some grave error, in case of contravention of the Constitution or the like, not otherwise.'[15]

This belief in judicial reticence was soon to be proved wrong.

II

The Purloined Constitution

One of the members of the Constituent Assembly who must have been participating in the debates about the right to property with some consternation was Maharajadhiraja Kameshwar Singh of Darbhanga, a zamindar with considerable land holdings in the Mithila region of Bihar. Kameshwar Singh fancied himself a philanthrope.[16] He had once offered his house in Allahabad to the Congress Party to have its session in the face of prohibitory orders of the British government.[17] If he thought that such acts would exempt him from the anti-zamindar sentiment that was raging across the country, he was mistaken. Even while the Constitution was being discussed in the Constituent Assembly, the legislators in the province of Bihar were debating a piece of legislation to do away with the zamindari system.[18] The same discussion was raging across various legislatures around the country.[19]

On 23 April 1950, the Bihar Legislature passed the Bihar Land Reforms Act, 1950. The act abolished most of the zamindaris and allowed the State to take over the proprietorship of the estates.[20] There was an elaborate scheme of compensation that offered a staggered payment to the zamindars in lieu of the loss of their estates. It is important to understand the methodology of compensation only to appreciate just how simple it would have been to tweak it and save the act from being declared unconstitutional. As we shall see, the act was struck down only because of how this computation of compensation worked in practice.

The total compensation payable was dependent on the net income derived from the land. A table was created which gave a graded scale of compensation. Section 24 of the act provided the following table:

	Amount of net income	Rate of compensation payable
(a)	Where the net income so computed does not exceed Rs 500.	Twenty times such net income
(b)	Where the net income so computed exceeds Rs 500 but does not exceed Rs 1250.	Nineteen times such net income but in any case, not less than the maximum amount under item (a) above.
(j)	Where the net income so computed exceeds Rs 20,000 but does not exceed Rs 50,000.	Six times such net income but in any case not less than the maximum amount under item (i) above.
(k)	Where the net income so computed exceeds Rs 50,000 but does not exceed Rs 1,00,000.	Four times such net income but in any case not less than the maximum amount under item (j) above.

(l)	Where the net income so computed exceeds Rs 1,00,000.	Three times such net income but in any case not less than the maximum amount under item (k) above.

The full table has not been reproduced, but it can be seen from the extract above that the higher the income from the land, the lower the compensation to be awarded. The range was from twenty times the value of the net income to only three times the net income for the purposes of compensation.

Unsurprisingly, the act was immediately challenged before the Courts. The matter was heard by a bench of three judges of the Patna High Court. The most senior judge was Justice J.G. Shearer, a British judge who had stayed on in India even after Independence. Justice Shearer was an Indian Civil Service (ICS) officer who, before becoming a judge of the Patna High Court, was a district and sessions judge. It is interesting to note that many high court judges before Independence were civil servants and were intimately tied to the Executive and the bureaucracy.[21] Yet this link did not stop them from acting independently, as in the case of Justice Shearer.

The junior judges were Justice D.A. Reuben and Justice Das. Justice D.A. Reuben was a member of the Bene Israel, a small Jewish community in India. He eventually went on to become the chief justice of the Patna High Court. The third judge was Justice Das, also a former ICS officer, who was later elevated to the Supreme Court of India and also briefly served as the acting chief justice of India.

The matter was heard for over nine days in January and February 1951, a very long hearing for those times. The verdict of the Court was delivered on 12 March 1951. All three judges held that the Land Reforms Act, 1950, was unconstitutional and was to be struck down.

Many grounds were raised when the matter was challenged. It was argued that what the Constitution required was payment of 'compensation', i.e., an amount understood to be something that 'the law regards as compensation' and not some trifling amount or payment. In other words, it was argued that the compensation was 'something which could fairly be said to be equivalent in value to the property taken over by the State'.[22] However, this argument was rejected because of the so-called escape clause contained in Article 31(4) of the Constitution, which prohibited the Court from going into the question of the adequacy of the Constitution.

Ultimately, the Court struck down the law on rather narrow grounds. As the table reproduced above shows, the act provided for differential compensation based solely on the extent of the value of the zamindar's landholding. In the analysis of the Court, all zamindars formed one single class—a class of landholders who earned an income by way of rent from their landholdings. There was nothing in principle to distinguish between a zamindar with a small or a large holding of land as both enjoyed 'unearned income' from the land, i.e., income from receipt of rent rather than tilling and working on the land. To put it more colloquially, a zamindar was a zamindar regardless of the size of his holding.

However, under the act, this single class of zamindars was segregated into separate sub-classes for the purposes of payment of compensation. The larger the piece of land a zamindar owned, the lesser the compensation. As the high court questioned 'on what principle, for instance, ought a proprietor of tenure holder, whose net income is Rs 20,000, to be given eight years' purchase, while a proprietor or tenure holder, whose net income is Rs 20,001 is given only six years' purchase?'[23] In other words, there was no justifiable reason to pay the holder of a larger tract of land less compensation than a holder of a smaller piece of land.

The constitutional basis of this reasoning was the newly minted right to equality contained in Article 14 of the Constitution. The

equality clause in the Constitution allowed lawmakers to make
a differentiation between different classes of people as long as
the classification had a 'reasonable nexus' or relationship with
the object sought to be attained by the legislation. The Court in
the Kameshwar Singh case held that the object of the legislation
was the 'giving of compensation, that is, something which will
represent the value in money of the property which is being
acquired.'[24] A classification that paid twenty times the net income
to a small holder of land and three times the net income to the
holder of a larger piece of land could not be said to have any
reasonable nexus to the object of the act. In other words, if the
purpose of the act was payment of compensation for the taking
over of estates, the differentiation between the large and the small
zamindars was not justified.

Another reason why the act was struck down was because
of the arbitrary nature of the formula used to calculate the 'net
income' of the asset. The zamindars were effectively earning rent
from the land and this rent was the total income from the land.
From this total income, certain deductions were made to account
for management fees and a so-called 'cost of works benefit' to
calculate the 'net income'. The formula provided that the larger
the tract of land, the greater the deduction from the net income.
In other words, if the value of the land was over Rs 20,000, up
to one-third of the income could be discounted from the actual
computed net income. This variability of deductions seems
illogical as management fees cannot vary exponentially depending
on the value of the land. If it is difficult to understand the logic
for this deduction, one can take solace from the fact that the
judges also were puzzled by this approach of reducing income
depending on the value of the land.[25]

Finally, the judgment also noted another pernicious form
of discrimination. The act allowed the government to decide
which zamindaris they wished to take over at any point of time.

They could, in effect, pick and choose between different zamindars and tracts of land. Favoured zamindars would get to retain their land while others would have their estates confiscated on payment of a minuscule compensation. This power to decide which zamindari to acquire was vested in relatively junior government officials and was thus susceptible to rampant abuse. The Court, therefore, held that this provision was also violative of Article 14 of the Constitution. The bench also unanimously decided that the act was not saved by the escape clause, Article 31 (4), which had been incorporated into the Constitution.

III

Outcry and Change

Though the Court did strike down the act, it also held that the legislature was the ultimate judge of the desirability of acquisition of land. The Court held that the judiciary could not second-guess the legislature on this account, and it was to be presumed that 'the scheme imbued in the impugned Act [was] a scheme intended to benefit the public.'[26] It thus appeared that all the government had to do was to tweak the act with regard to the mode and quantum of determining the compensation payable. These amendments to the act could presumably have saved the act from being declared unconstitutional. In fact, the Allahabad High Court[27] and the Nagpur High Court had already upheld acts with very similar provisions to the Bihar Land Reforms Act.

However, there was outrage in Delhi as well as in Patna that the pioneering piece of legislation for improving the lot of landless labourers had been struck down by the Court. In fact, at that time the government probably felt besieged, because relying on the fundamental rights allegedly entrenched in the Constitution a large number of adverse judgments were passed against it. For instance, various high courts set aside orders that were restrictive of free speech[28] while the Supreme Court struck down restrictions on free speech imposed on both the Left[29] and the Right.[30] The Madras High Court struck down a significant part of the affirmative action policy of the then government, which had provided for caste-based reservations.[31]

One would have thought that the leaders of the Constituent Assembly would have welcomed these judgments after having suffered the denial of their liberties by the British. But it appeared that the new rulers were a lot like their old masters.

A drastic solution was proposed to solve the pesky decisions by the Court upholding the rights of the citizens of India. Two new articles were proposed to be added to the Constitution, Article 31A and 31B. Article 31A would provide that 'no law providing for the acquisition by the State of any estate or of any rights therein or for the extinguishment or modification of any such rights shall be deemed to be void on the ground that it is inconsistent with, or takes away or abridges any of the rights conferred by' the fundamental rights. Effectively, laws relating to the zamindari abolition were rendered immune from judicial review even if they contravened the fundamental rights of citizens.

Though Article 31A was broadly worded, the far more dangerous insertion was Article 31B. It provided for the insertion of a Ninth Schedule to the Constitution and stated that 'none of the Acts and Regulations specified in the Ninth Schedule nor any of the provisions thereof shall be deemed to be void, or ever to have become void, on the ground that such Act, Regulation or provision is inconsistent with, or takes away or abridges any of the rights conferred by, any provisions of this Part, and notwithstanding any judgment, decree or order of any court or tribunal to the contrary, each of the said Acts and Regulations shall, subject to the power of any competent Legislature to repeal or amend it, continue in force.'

This article was like an omnibus escape clause. The legislature could determine which law it wanted to protect and then insert in the Ninth Schedule to the Constitution. Any law that was inserted into the Schedule would not have to be tested on the anvil of fundamental rights. It would be as though for the purposes of the acts included in the schedule, the fundamental rights did not exist! It is said that this amendment prompted Chief Justice P.B. Gajendragadkar to say that the Indian Constitution was the only one that contained a provision providing for protection against itself.[32]

The Constitution no longer had a fundamental right to property. By virtue of the newly inserted articles, rights could be diminished, and the Courts had no power to intercede. It is important to remember that the Constitution had given the Courts the power to strike down laws that abridged fundamental rights specifically to protect citizens from the tyranny of the majority. After these amendments, this was no longer the case.

However, the judiciary still had other ideas. When the appeal from the Patna High Court reached the Supreme Court,[33] it was heard by a bench of five judges. While the Bihar Zamindari Abolition Act was upheld, certain provisions of the act were still struck down even though Articles 31A and 31B had been inserted in the Constitution. Three of the five judges ruled that notwithstanding the new amendments, the principles in relation to the determination of compensation were incorrect. They did this by interpreting an entry in the Concurrent List (i.e. the list by which the powers of the legislatures are defined) rather than relying on the fundamental rights provisions. However, in spite of this act of judicial calisthenics, it was now clear. The right to property had been dealt a severe blow.

It is also of interest to note that one of the lawyers who appeared before the Supreme Court challenging the act was

Dr B.R. Ambedkar. Dr Ambedkar had not only been the architect of the Constitution and the fundamental rights, but he was also the law minister when the First Amendment, which abridged the right to property, was passed. He had famously given a two-hour-long speech in Parliament defending the amendment.[34] However, when the matter came to the Supreme Court, he was decidedly in a different camp. As is recorded in the judgment of the Supreme Court, he argued that 'a constitutional prohibition against compulsory acquisition of property without public necessity and payment of compensation was deducible from what he called the "spirit of the Constitution"', which, according to him, was a valid test for judging the constitutionality of a statute. 'The Constitution, being avowedly one for establishing liberty, justice, equality and a government of a free people with only limited powers, must be held to contain an implied prohibition against the taking of private property without just compensation and in the absence of a public purpose.' In other words, he felt that even though Article 31A and 31B had been included in the Constitution, the adequacy of compensation was still open to be determined by the Court. Of course, this immediately led to the question as to why these articles had been inserted if a law could still be challenged on more or less the same grounds as the ones before their insertion, i.e., on the grounds of adequacy of compensation.

This appeal to the spirit of the Constitution was soundly rejected by the Supreme Court. Noting the amendments to the Constitution, the Supreme Court largely upheld the Bihar Land Reforms Act. In fact, a close reading of the judgment may lead one to believe that the Court would have upheld large parts of the act even without the amendments.[35] This shows that the wholesale amendments to the Constitution were probably premature. However, this was now a fait accompli. Articles 31A and 31B were now part of the Indian Constitution.

IV

Impact of the First Amendment on Economic Policy

The effect of the first amendment to the Constitution has been felt across the entire range of economic legislation in India. When the Constitution was first amended, it was only to protect laws in relation to land reforms and abolition of zamindaris. However, the language of the amendment was broad enough to protect a whole range of legislation from judicial review. It was thus only a matter of time before the genie was let out of the bottle. Over the course of the next several decades, the Ninth Schedule was expanded as an ever-increasing number of enactments, which had nothing whatsoever to do with land reforms, were inserted in it. Many of these insertions were part of the socialist agenda of the government of the seventies.

The notorious Foreign Exchange Regulation Act, 1973 ('FERA'), the Essential Commodities Act (EC Act), 1955 , the Industries (Regulation and Development) Act, 1951 as well as a large number of acts that provided for nationalization of industries were included in the Ninth Schedule. Once the safeguard of judicial review was eliminated, the legislature found it convenient to render various laws immune from judicial scrutiny by including them in the Ninth Schedule. This attitude altered the constitutional balance and diminished the sanctity of the fundamental rights. In particular, the right to property was dealt a severe blow. With each inclusion of a legislation in the Ninth Schedule, the effect of the right was increasingly attenuated. Ultimately, the legislature performed the formal final rites of the right to property and deleted it as a fundamental right altogether. An Indian citizen holding property was now fully at the mercy of the Executive.

In fact, the First Amendment also altered the balance of between the legislature and the Courts. Given the constit immunity to certain legislative acts, the power of judicial review has effectively been taken away.[36] Laws like FERA and the EC Act, which are vestiges of an extreme form of Indian socialism might well have been struck down but for the protection granted to them by the First Amendment. The balance of power decisively tilts towards the legislature in such cases, with the Courts often being mute spectators even in the face of laws that would otherwise violate fundamental rights.

Conclusion

A country is often born into innocence but matures, over time, to accommodate social and economic realities. In India's case, the break from innocence was rather rapid. Fresh from the freedom struggle, we, the people, gave ourselves a Constitution full of hope for the future and a promise to redeem the sins of the past. It was a liberal document that seemed way ahead of its time. It was as if the rights promised were too good to last, and in true form, they didn't.

Over three centuries ago, Thomas Muller said, 'Be ye never so high, the law is above you.' The phrase has been used rather often and seems trite, but it embodies a powerful concept of limiting Executive power through law. Protection from arbitrary State action and access to the justice system is an essential ingredient of the rule of law that enables businesses to thrive. The story of the *Kameshwar Prasad* case shows how even constitutional protections may prove unable to control the Executive in the face of a strong parliamentary majority.

Notes

[1] The right to property now contained in Article 300A of the Constitution merely states that 'No person shall be deprived of his property save by authority of law'. There is, as can be seen, no mention of the extent of compensation to be awarded in case of any compulsory acquisition.

[2] *Kameshwar Singh v. State of Bihar* ILR (1951) 30 Pat.

[3] The First Amendment also amended other parts of the Constitution. For instance, Article 19 (1) (a) was amended to undo the effect of the judgment of the Supreme Court in the case of *Romesh Thappar v. State of Madras* AIR 1950 SC 124. Article 15 (4) was introduced to counter the striking down of the reservation policy in the case of *State of Madras v. Shrimati Champaknam Dorairajan* AIR 1951 SC 226. The portion relating to the amendment of the right to property, however, was clearly attributable to the judgment referred to below.

[4] President Rajendra Prasad was reluctant to sign the Amendment Act on the ground that he felt it necessary for the amendment to be made by a duly elected Parliament. See Granville Austin, *Working a Democratic Constitution: A History of the Indian Experience*, Oxford University Press (1999), pp. 89–90.

[5] See Locke, John (1689), *Two Treatises of Government* and Jean Jacques Rousseau (1755) *Discours sur l'origine de l'inegalité*, (*Discourse on the Origin of Inequality*).

[6] Though the US Constitution declares the 'pursuit of happiness' as an unalienable right, it is clear that the foundational documents for the Constitution considered the right to property as a natural right bestowed upon persons when they 'enter into a state of society'. See the Virginia Declaration of Rights (1776), Article I: 'That all men are by nature equally free and independent and have certain inherent rights, of which, when they enter into a state of society, they cannot, by any compact, deprive or divest their posterity; namely, the enjoyment of life and liberty, with the means of acquiring and possessing property, and pursuing and obtaining happiness and safety.' This discourse follows the idea of social contract theory propounded by Locke.

[7] In a famous example, the US Supreme Court declared a host of welfare legislation during the 'New Deal' era as unconstitutional. The Executive, led by President Franklin D. Roosevelt, threatened to pack the Supreme Court with its own nominees as judges by introducing the Judiciary Reorganization Bill, 1937. This plan was never effected as one judge, Justice Owen Roberts, altered his judicial opinion in three New Deal cases and upheld the welfare legislation. It is said that this was a 'switch in time that saved nine', attributed to humorist Carl Tinney in 1937.

[8] Tirthankar Roy. *The Economic History of India 1857–1947* (Oxford University Press, 2006).

[9] *The Constituent Assembly Debates*, Vol. III, p. 511 onwards.

[10] Dr B.R. Ambedkar noted that there were three factions in the Congress Party. Sardar Vallabhbhai Patel believed in full compensation, Pandit Nehru was

against compensation and G.B. Pant wanted the protection of the Zamindari
Abolition Bill that was passing through the United Provinces Legislature at
this point of time. See Parliamentary Debates, Rajya Sabha, Official Report,
Vol. IX, No. 19, 19 March 1955, p. 2452.

[11] Granville Austin. *The Indian Constitution: Cornerstone of a Nation*, (1972), p. 117.

[12] This Article was closely fashioned after Section 299 of the Government of
India Act, 1935.

[13] The Constituent Assembly Debates, 10 September 1949, Vol. IX, p. 1197.

[14] This was to cover a case where the compensation was so low as to be illusory
or meaningless. See also in this regard, the statement of K.M. Munshi in the
Constituent Assembly. Constituent Assembly Debates, 10 September 1949,
Vol. IX, p. 1299.

[15] The Constituent Assembly Debates, 10 September 1949, Volume IX, p. 1198.

[16] He was the pro-vice chancellor of the Benares Hindu University and in 1930
had donated Rs 1 lakh twenty thousand to the University of Patna.

[17] Amarkant Mishra. *Ruling Dynasty of Mithila: Dr Sir Kameshwar Singh* (Notion
Press, 2018).

[18] On 6 July 1949, even before the promulgation of the Constitution, the
governor general gave his assent to the Bihar Abolition of Zamindaris Act,
1948. This act empowered the provincial government to deprive proprietors
and tenure holders of their estates and tenures. It also provided, or purported
to provide, for the payment of compensation. However, before it could be
implemented, it was repealed, and a more comprehensive piece of legislation
was enacted.

[19] Uttar Pradesh, Madras, Madhya Pradesh, Assam and Bombay also had state
zamindari abolition bills.

[20] Another piece of expropriatory legislation had been passed by the Bihar
Legislature prior to the enactment of the Land Reforms Act. An act titled
the Bihar Management of Estates and Tenures Act, 1949, had been enacted
which left the ostensible ownership of the lands in the hands of the zamindars
but took over the management and possession of the estates without payment
of compensation. The act was challenged before the Patna High Court,
which ruled on its validity on the touchstone of the unamended Article 31.
This is because the amendment had not been notified as on the date of the
judgment, i.e., 5 June 1950. The Court struck down the act, holding it to be
an expropriatory piece of legislation that was not saved by Article 19 (5) of

31 (6) of the unamended Constitution. See *MD Sir Kameshwar Singh v. State of Bihar* ILR 1950 (29) Patna 79.

[21] George Gadbois. *Judges of the Supreme Court of India,* 1950–89 (Oxford University Press, 2011).

[22] p. 473–74.

[23] p. 477.

[24] p. 528

[25] See, for instance, the judgment of Reuben J. at page 531.

[26] p. 476

[27] *Raja Suriyapal Singh v. The UP Govt* AIR 1951 All 674.

[28] In re Bharti Press AIR 1951 Pat 21.

[29] *Romesh Thappar v. State of Madras* 1950 SCR 594.

[30] *Brij Bhushan v. State of Delhi* AIR 1950 SC 129.

[31] *Champakam Dorairajan v. The State of Madras* AIR 1951 Mad 120.

[32] Granville Austin. *Working a Democratic Constitution: A History of the Indian Experience* (New Delhi: Oxford University Press, 1999).

[33] *State of Bihar v. Maharajadhiraja Sir Kameshwar Singh of Darbhanga and Ors* AIR 1952 SC 252.

[34] Tripurdaman Singh. *Sixteen Stormy Days* (Penguin, 2020), p. 150–51.

[35] For instance, Patanjali Sastri C.J. repelled many contentions as to the nature and quantum of compensation relying on the unamended Article 31 (4).

[36] One such instance is the judgment which upheld the validity of the Conservation of Foreign Exchange and Prevention of Smuggling Activities Act, 1974, and the Smugglers and Foreign Exchange Manipulators (Forfeiture of Property) Act, 1976. In the case of *AG v. Amritlal Prajivandas* (1994) 5 SCC 54, a nine-judge bench relied on the 40th amendment to the Constitution whereby these acts had been inserted into the Ninth Schedule to the Constitution. The Court held that the impugned acts could not be tested on the grounds of violation of one of the most sacrosanct rights in the Constitution, i.e., Article 22, which provides for protection against arrest and detention in certain cases.

Chapter 2

Garibi Hatao: The Case for Bank Nationalization

The financial crises of the last decade have established the crucial role of banks in the economic system of a country. In the Indian context, rising bad debts and NPAs have hobbled the banking industry. While the entire banking ecosystem is under stress, it has been the public sector banks that have suffered particularly acutely in this time of crisis. It is often said that this is because of the comparatively poorer management of public sector banks compared to those in the private sector.[1] Whether or not that explanation is true, it cannot be denied that the public sector banks (PSU Banks) routinely perform worse than their private-sector counterparts.

Given the starkly different performance metrics of the two sets of banks, it is only logical to question the utility of PSU banks. After all, why should valuable capital be locked up in banks that have proved themselves comparatively inefficient? However, this query overlooks a vital social role that is allegedly performed by PSU banks. It is argued that private sector banks run purely for profit are unlikely to advance the vital social functions a bank is supposed to offer. For instance, a private sector bank may not be interested in setting up branches in far-flung locations as the profitability of such branches would be low. This would lead to a situation where vast swathes of rural India would be unbanked or underbanked. Similarly, private banks would prefer to lend money to industries that offer a quick and high return on profits as opposed to sectors like agriculture, which are comparatively riskier and offer less return on capital.

It is precisely these kinds of 'social control' arguments that had been used in the fifties and sixties to argue for the wholesale nationalization of banks. After an initially tepid attempt at tinkering with the banking sector, the government of the day took the plunge and proceeded to nationalize fourteen of the largest private sector banks. Unsurprisingly, the matter found its way to the Supreme Court. In a stunning verdict, in *R.C. Cooper v. Union of India*,[2] colloquially referred to as the 'Bank Nationalization Case', the Court struck down the attempt at nationalization.

It was not merely the striking down of the law that caused great discomfiture to the establishment. Even the reasoning employed by the Court seemed to indicate its willingness to ensure that the government pay full compensation to persons whose property was being taken over. Given the scant resources of the government of the time, such an approach would have rung a death knell for the policy of acquisition and centralization of the economy.

So, in a practice that has now become all too common, the government promptly proceeded to enact fresh legislation to remove the basis of the judgment of the Supreme Court. More importantly, the judgment spurred further constitutional amendments, which empowered Parliament to abridge fundamental rights. In the field of finance, however, the legacy of nationalization is felt even today. This chapter will trace the path leading to the nationalization of banks, the impact of the judgment and then examine how successful the nationalization experiment has been in the Indian context.

I

The Build-Up

The history of the bank nationalization case shows that economic decisions are often predicated on political compulsions. There was an undoubtedly leftward lurch in Indian politics soon after Independence, as has been noted in the previous chapter. This was part of the general Nehruvian ideological drift away from free market economics.[3] Indeed, some part of this socialist ideology found its way into the Constitution itself. For instance, the Constitution cast an obligation on the State to ensure that 'the ownership and control of the material resources of the community are so distributed as best to subserve the common good'—a distinctly socialist ideal.

As far back as 1948, the All-India Congress Committee's (AICC) Economic Programme Committee had recommended that the businesses of banking and insurance be nationalized.[4] While this was not immediately acted upon, Parliament enacted the Banking Companies Act, 1949[5] giving the newly nationalized Reserve Bank of India substantial powers of superintendence over the banking industry. As part of the effort to bring the banking sector in line with the ideology of the government, the Imperial Bank was nationalized in 1953 and thus the State Bank of India was born.

In spite of the general inclination of social control over the banking sector, there was no immediate push towards nationalization. This was in part due to the belief that the compensation that would have to be paid to the banks for their acquisition could be used more productively elsewhere. Implicit in this belief was the acknowledgement that banks would have to be paid just compensation in case of acquisition. The ultimate cause for the enactment of legislation nationalizing banks was the internal political working of the Congress Party and not the result of any particular ideological inevitability. In fact, it was only once Indira Gandhi came to the helm that the talk of nationalization became more strident.

After the sudden death of Lal Bahadur Shastri, the Congress Party was split as to the choice of the next prime minister. While the most powerful contender for the post was probably Morarji Desai, he was not favoured by the top bosses of the Congress Party who were called the 'Syndicate'.[6] Given the fiscal conservatism of Morarji Desai, India's economic history might have been very different had he become prime minister.

In the end, the syndicate chose Indira Gandhi to be the prime minister after Shastri. The party bosses , who were all men, wanted to retain their stranglehold over the party and decided to elevate Gandhi as prime minister as they believed she would be much easier to manipulate compared to Desai. This was initially the case and for the first year of her premiership, Mrs Gandhi largely toed the line of the party bosses. However, the political winds were shifting and, in the elections held in 1967, the position of both Mrs Gandhi as well as that of the members of the Syndicate were weakened.[7] The Congress Party's majority in Parliament was greatly reduced and it lost a large number of provincial elections. While this might have been debilitating for the newly installed prime minister, it helped her that a large number of party bosses also suffered personal defeats. The leader of the Syndicate, K. Kamraj, lost the elections as did several other leaders. With both sides weakened, there began a tussle for control over the party.

II

The Ordinance and the Law

As the power and influence of the Syndicate were on the decline, there arose another grouping that was in the political ascendancy—the so-called 'Young Turks'. These were a group of young politicians, all of whom were far more to the Left than the mainstream Congress Party. In fact, one of its most prominent members, Mohan Kumaramangalam, had been a member of the Communist Party before he joined the Congress Party.

This group, which also included Chandra Shekhar, who eventually went on to become prime minister himself, favoured nationalization of a large number of industries. Whether Mrs Gandhi herself held the same economic view is uncertain (given the fact that she had earlier demurred in not nationalizing the banks). However, political compulsions weighed in favour of her siding with the left wing of the party. The mood in the country, as apparent from the election of left-wing governments in provincial assemblies, was increasingly moving to the Left. A more cynical yet pragmatic reason was perhaps that Mrs Gandhi wished to split the powerful Syndicate on ideological lines so that they would not be able to present a united force against her.

The Young Turks were thus mobilized and they in turn recruited some economists to submit a report that gave a picture of the banking industry. While the report was criticized for lacking empirical data, it did contain certain incontrovertible and uncomfortable facts. About half the shareholding of the banks was owned by 3 per cent of its shareholders, or even more tellingly, the top 1 per cent of the shareholders held as much as 36 per cent of the shares.[8] While such statistics may not shock the reader of today, this was certainly an argument to show that 'the ownership and control of the material resources of the community' were not so 'distributed as best to subserve the common good.'[9] Even more troublesome than the shareholding of the bank was the way credit was distributed across sectors. In the case of agriculture, the share of the credit had declined from 3.8 per cent in 1953 to only 0.2 per cent in 1965. This was in spite of the fact that the vast majority of the country was involved in agriculture and almost 50 per cent of the GDP of the time and almost 40 per cent of exports were attributable to the agricultural sector. The position was similarly stark in the case of the small-scale sector. Even though the sector employed 35 per cent of all factory employment, its share in credit was only 5.7 per cent.

It was also equally clear that the incremental attempts to reform the banking industry were not having their desired effect. There had been two main attempts to remedy the problems highlighted in the report mentioned above. The Banking Regulation Act was amended to provide for a more professional management by technocrats and bankers as opposed to industrialists. The act also restricted the banks from lending to their own directors. However, the act failed in its ultimate purpose as the provisions were easily bypassed through the use of a well-established 'old-boys' network.

The second attempt was to create a National Credit Council (NCC), which was a high-powered body chaired by the finance minister, meant to ensure an equitable distribution of credit across various sectors of the economy.[10] Here too, even though there was some initial success, the measure failed to achieve its ultimate goal of equitable credit to all sectors of the economy.

This concentration of power in the hands of a few industrialists had generated a clear anti-banking sentiment in the country. In an attempt to ride the populist feelings of the time, Mrs Gandhi set about an ambitious agenda. First, she removed Morarji Desai as finance minister, though she retained him as her deputy. Miffed at the removal of the important portfolio, Morarji Desai promptly resigned from the Union Cabinet. Mrs Gandhi accepted the resignation and became the finance minister herself, becoming in the process the first female finance minister of the country.[11]

The same day she asked the acting president, V.V. Giri, to promulgate an ordinance taking over the banks. The acting president willingly obliged and signed the Banking Companies

(Acquisition and Transfer of Undertakings) Ordinance, 1969, into law on 19 July 1969. The very next day he resigned so as to run for the office of President.[12]

III

The Judgment

The ordinance was immediately challenged by way of a petition filed directly before the Supreme Court. The lead petition was filed by one Rustom Cowasji Cooper, who was a shareholder of one of the banks that had been nationalized. Cooper also happened to be the general secretary of the Swatantrata Party. Some other petitions were also filed, including those by Minoo Masani and Balraj Madhok of the Jana Sangh. The fact that petitions were filed by members of the Swatantrata Party and the Jana Sangh highlights the fact that the nationalization of banks was an issue that was political at its core. These were the only two parties that opposed the nationalization in Parliament. Otherwise, there was an almost total consensus in Parliament about the need for nationalization.

This political consensus in favour of nationalization met with an opposite consensus from the Supreme Court. The very next day after the ordinance was promulgated, a bench of eight judges of the Court effectively granted a stay on its operation.[13]

Even though the challenge to the ordinance was pending in Court, Parliament went ahead and enacted the Banking Companies (Acquisition and Transfer of Undertakings) Act 22 of 1969, an act to replace the ordinance. The act was challenged by the petitioners asking the Supreme Court to rule on the constitutionality of nationalization primarily on the grounds of violation of the petitioners' fundamental rights guaranteed by Articles 14, 19 and 31.

A bench of eleven judges was constituted to hear the matter. Interestingly, Chief Justice M. Hidayatullah did not sit on the bench. The chief justice had to recuse himself as he, in his capacity as acting president, had signed the act into law. The bench was instead presided over by the next senior justice in the Court, Justice J.C. Shah.

The judgment was nearly a unanimous one. Of the eleven judges who were on the bench, ten agreed on a common judgment that was authored by Justice J.C. Shah. The lone dissenter was Justice A.N. Ray.

The judgment of the Court laid down a new constitutional path. For the first time the Court expressly held that different fundamental rights were not mutually exclusive. Prior to the judgment, the predominant view in the Court was that each fundamental right was protected by a specific provision in the Constitution. The various articles of the Constitution were, effectively, watertight compartments. The net result was that if a particular right was covered by one provision, it could be limited in the manner specified in the provision. The validity of the limitation was not to be tested against any other fundamental right in the Constitution.

This seems to be an abstract proposition, but in the constitutional scheme, it had a great impact. If each right was protected only by one article, the scope of protection of the right was greatly diminished. This was because most fundamental rights had many facets, only some of which could be protected and covered by one article. Other facets of the right, not covered by the 'main' right, which might otherwise have been covered by other 'ancillary' articles, were not protected. This issue can be better understood with reference to the right in question in the nationalization case—the right to property.

The government argued that the property rights of the shareholders of the banks were governed solely by Article 31, while the counsel for the banks argued that the rights were also protected by Articles 14 and 19 of the Constitution. Article

31 (1) of the Constitution impliedly guaranteed the right to property and stated that the right could only be taken away by the authority of law. In other words, the article provided that the right to property could be abridged by an act of Parliament or some other instrument having the force of law. What could be the permissible contours of the law abridging the right were governed by Article 31 (2), which stated that the law was required to contain provisions fixing or providing for the determination and payment of compensation. Article 31 (4) further debarred the Court from going into the adequacy of the compensation. Relying on this scheme of the article, the government argued that once there was a law (the nationalization act), which provided for principles for the determination of compensation, the scope of judicial inquiry was to be over. The Court could not go into the question of whether the act imposed any restrictions on the right to property that were not reasonable.

The Court disagreed with this interpretation of the Constitution and held that 'formal compliance with the conditions under Article 31 (2) is not sufficient to negative the protection of the guarantee of the right to property. Acquisition must be under the authority of a law and the expression "law" means a law which is within the competence of the Legislature and does not impair the guarantee of the rights in [the fundamental rights chapter].' The Court essentially held that any attempt to nationalize the bank and take over their business would impair the right to property, which was also guaranteed by Article 19 (1) (f) of the Constitution. Therefore, the law would have to be tested on the grounds specified by Article 19 (5), more particularly that the restrictions on the right had to be reasonable.

The sum and substance of this ruling was that the right of the shareholder to her shares was protected not just by Article 31, but also by the other rights which she would have, namely Articles 14 and 19. This increased the petitioners' arsenal of constitutional protections. Correspondingly, this imposed a greater responsibility on the part of the government to justify its actions. Most importantly, this gave far greater power to the Court to scrutinize the actions of the government.

Having held that the act had to pass the constitutional test of different fundamental rights, the Court proceeded to hold that each of these rights had been violated by the impugned act.

The equality clause contained in Article 14 was violated because there was no justification for singling out the fourteen banks for nationalization while leaving out all the other private sector banks. The explanation offered by the government was that the banks that were sought to be nationalized were the larger banks, each of which had deposits of over Rs 50 crore. The Court summarily rejected this explanation. The constitutional test required that in any classification exercise, the classification made must at the least have a nexus with the object sought to be achieved by the law. The object of the Nationalization Act was ostensibly to serve the needs of the development of the economy. The Court noticed that even if the banks were nationalized, the total deposit would be 83 per cent of all the deposits, which would still not 'meet wholly or even substantially the needs of development of the economy'.

The second ground for striking down the act was its violation of the compendiously termed 'right to freedom'. Article 19 (1) (f) of the Constitution guaranteed citizens the right to acquire, hold or dispose of property while Article 19 (1) (g) assured the right to carry on business. These rights were subject to the limitations prescribed by Article 19 (5) and (6) of the Constitution, which permitted the State to impose reasonable restrictions in the interest of the general public. To satisfy this test, the government would have to show that any curtailment of the fundamental rights was genuinely required in the larger public interest and that the infringement of the right was not broader than absolutely necessary.

However, in the case of the Nationalization Act, the Court held that both the right to carry on business and the right to hold property were breached. The Nationalization Act had only barred the companies from carrying out any banking business in future but had permitted them to carry on other non-banking businesses. On the face of it, therefore, the companies' rights to carry on business, albeit in a truncated manner, was permitted. However, the Court held that this right to carry on non-banking business was merely illusory. The act prohibited the companies from using their name, and hence, the goodwill attached to it. The compensation was payable in the distant future and thus the companies would not have any asset with which to carry on the business. While theoretically possible, carrying on non-banking business was a practical impossibility. The Court held that 'where restrictions imposed upon the carrying on of a business are so stringent that the business in practice cannot be carried on, the Court will regard the imposition of the restriction as unreasonable'.

The most controversial grounds for striking down the act was the alleged violation of Article 31. Article 31 (2) of the Constitution required the law providing for acquisition 'must again either fix the amount of compensation or specify the principles upon which, and the manner in which, the compensation is to be determined and given'. If the principles employed for determining compensation were entirely irrelevant, the acquisition was liable to be set aside.

Upon a consideration of the provisions of the act, the Court held that the principles for determining compensation were completely arbitrary. For instance, the act did not provide for the valuation of the goodwill of the bank, which was one of its most important assets. The act also did not accord any value to the unexpired leases held by a bank. The valuation on the buildings was made on a basis that could not possibly reflect their true value. All these facts led the Court to hold that the principles for determination of compensation were irrelevant and arbitrary, and therefore violative of Article 31 of the Constitution.

There were, however, certain observations of the Court that must have deeply troubled the government. It may be recollected that the First and the Fourth Amendment to the Constitution had sought to exclude an examination of the adequacy, or otherwise of compensation, from the purview of the court. Yet, relying on the meaning of the term compensation, the Court held that 'compensation being the equivalent in terms of money of the property compulsorily acquired, the principle for determination of compensation is intended to award to the expropriated owner the value of the property acquired'. The Court reiterated that 'the broad object underlying the principle of valuation is to award to the owner the equivalent of his property with its existing advantages and its potentialities'. In effect, the Court turned to the definition of the term 'compensation' to rule that any owner of property was entitled to the full value of the expropriated property. This judicial sleight of hand implied that the amount of compensation payable would have to be equivalent to the approximate value of the property acquired.

In fact, it is just these observations that stung the government. In a scathing article,[14] Mohan Kumaramangalam said that the Court had usurped the role of determining compensation and that the judgment amounted to undoing all parliamentary efforts to promote the Directive Principles of State Policy. In what seems like a challenge to the authority of the Court (or indeed the Constitution), he wrote that 'to permit the present decision of the Supreme Court to remain as the law of the land would mean giving the Courts a power that would block any possibility of building a socialist economy within the framework of the present Constitution. It would compel any sincere and devoted adherent of socialism to decide that to work for the establishment of socialism in India involves working out-side the Constitution and in defiance of it, as the Courts by their judicial pronouncements have made impossible the use of this Constitution for the achievement of a socialist order.'

There was the slightest silver lining for the government, though. In a portent of things to come, Justice Ray dissented with the majority and agreed with the arguments of the government on virtually every point. This was the first of a triumvirate of cases where Justice Ray disagreed with the majority of the Supreme Court and sided with the government of the day. The other two cases were the privy purses case[15] and the fundamental rights case.[16] As a reward for such loyalty to the government, Justice Ray was made chief justice superseding three other senior judges of the Court in April 1973. The former Attorney General of India, C.K. Daphtary, is rumoured to have said, 'The boy who wrote the best essay won the first prize.'[17] Just to put a seal on the ignominy of his judicial career, Justice Ray also headed the infamous ADM Jabalpur case where the Supreme Court held that all fundamental rights, including the right to life, were suspended during the Emergency.

Conclusion

The judgment came as a severe blow to the government. However, rather than backing down from the confrontation with the Court, the Parliament enacted another law, which provided for taking over the banks. This time, the Parliament took care to avoid the constitutional pitfalls noted in the judgment. So, rather than determining the principles of compensation, the new act provided for the payment of a fixed amount of compensation. By one estimate, this payment was around Rs 87 crore, which would be almost Rs 4000 crore in today's money!

The banks were thus nationalized and the banking sector was brought in line with the ideological predilections of the day. It cannot be denied that the nationalization did have a direct and beneficial impact on increasing penetration of the formal banking sector into rural areas. Also, the banking sector started to lend to the priority sectors, or at least those sectors that were considered to be important by the government of the day. Of course, the question remains as to whether market forces would have caused this move to have happened in any case. However, that point became moot once the Parliament took matters into its own hands and imposed 'social control' on the banks.

On a more personal note, R.C. Cooper received his share of the compensation and eventually moved to Singapore where he set up a flourishing economic consultancy. He lived till the ripe old age of ninety, the last six years of which were spent living permanently in the Shangri-La Hotel in Singapore. His party, the Swatantrata Party, did not have such a happy ending. After its founder, C. Rajagopalachari, the first Indian Governor General, died in 1972, the party fell into radical decline and was dissolved in 1972. The other party that had opposed nationalization, the Jana Sangh, eventually morphed into the Bharatiya Janata Party (BJP).

The lasting legacy of Cooper's case, however, is in an area more than just finance and economics. It is in the sphere of constitutional adjudication and the interpretation of fundamental rights. The Supreme Court held that the fundamental rights were to be read holistically. They were not to be dissected and emasculated, but to be read expansively. The fundamental rights were rather like the individual in whom they inured—they had different facets and dimensions, none of which could be divorced from the other and each of which deserved to be protected. This interpretation of the Constitution has permitted the Court to exert far greater control over the actions of the government than would otherwise have been possible.

Notes

[1] 'Private Sector Banks Are Better Money Managers, State Owned Lenders Grow Faster' *Business Standard*, 23 June 2022.

[2] 1970 AIR SC 564.

[3] Nehru believed in the socialization of essential services and basic industries within the framework of parliamentary government as the best means of eliminating poverty, a British socialist ideology developed by the Fabian Society. See H. Venkatasubbiah, 'Nehru's Economic Philosophy', *The Hindu*, 29 May 1964.

[4] The Reserve Bank of India, Vol. 3, 1967–81 (2005), p. 14.

[5] The act has now been rechristened as the Banking Regulation Act, 1949 w.e.f. 1 March 1966.

[6] Michelguglielmo Torri. 'Factional Politics and Economic Policy: The Case of India's Bank Nationalization,' *Asian Survey*, vol. 15, no. 12 (1975), pp. 1077–96.

[7] Ibid.

[8] Ibid.

[9] It can be argued that ownership of shares in an industry is not a community resource. However, there exists a body of jurisprudence in the Indian Courts which holds just that. [*See Sanjeev Coke Manufacturing Co. v. Bharat Coking Coal Ltd (1983) 1 SCC 147* and *Mafatlal Industries Ltd v. Union of India (1997) 5 SCC 536*].

[10] Michelguglielmo Torri. 'Factional Politics and Economic Policy: The Case of India's Bank Nationalization', p. 1084.

[11] Granville Austin. *Working a Democratic Constitution: A History of the Indian Experience* (Oxford University Press, 1999).

[12] The president, Dr Zakir Hussain, passed away in May 1969. Sensing an opportunity to deal a body blow to the Syndicate, Mrs Gandhi promoted her own nominee rather than the official nominee of the party. In the presidential elections that followed, her nominee, V.V. Giri, was elected as the President of India. Not only did this weaken and demoralize the Syndicate, it also empowered Mrs Gandhi, as she now had a President who was distinctly more likely to be friendly to her.

[13] Tamal Bandyopadhyaya. 'Life of Banks after Five Decades of Nationalization', Livemint, 16 July 2018 for details of the stay as well as the hurried circumstances in which the ordinance came to be promulgated.

[14] Mohan S. Kumaramangalam. 'Slide-Back on Compensation: Bank Nationalisation Judgment', *Economic and Political Weekly*, Vol. 5, no. 8 (1970), pp. 356–58A.

[15] *H.H. Maharajadhiraja Madhav Rao v. Union Of India* 1971 AIR 530.

[16] *Kesavananda Bharati Sripadagalvaru & Ors. v. State of Kerala & Anr.* AIR 1973 SC 1461.

[17] Granville Austin. *Working a Democratic Constitution: A History of the Indian Experience* (Oxford University Press, 1999), p. 282.

Chapter 3

The Sweat and Toil of Workers

One of India's greatest economic strengths is also its weakness. The country has a largely young population, which should provide human capital to drive industry. We are at the stage of our developmental growth where we should be able to reap this demographic dividend and propel ourselves on the road to growth before the population starts ageing. However, this large population also constitutes a problem if the youth are unemployed or underemployed. Inability to generate adequate employment will not only make India miss the benefit of the dividend, but also sow seeds of social, political and economic unrest. Further, the resources required to ensure social security for the population would divert resources away from those required for infrastructure and industry.

The question then arises as to whether the large amount of employable but underemployed population is the cause or the consequence of the slowdown of economic growth. There are inadequate resources to ensure the optimum health and education of such a large population, as also observed by the Supreme Court.[1] Thus, a large part of the workforce is extremely low-skilled and unable to fully engage in the economic development of the country. On the other hand, if there booming industrial growth, that itself would generate employment and ensure improvement in the quality of life of the workers.

In this circle of cause and effect, it is undoubtedly the laws regulating industries that have a major role to play. It is the law that draws a balance between the needs of industries to structure its workforce to maximize efficiency and the demands of workers for fair conditions of work and pay. Among all of these considerations there is, of course, the question of the unorganized sector, which is often left out of the protection of the law altogether.[2]

One of the first attempts of the law to deal with this problem was through the enactment of the Industrial Disputes Act, 1947. This chapter deals with the interpretation given to the act by a bench of seven judges at a time when the flag of socialism flew firmly on the Indian economic firmament in *Bangalore Water Supply & Sewerage Board v. A. Rajappa*.[3] The judges expanded the scope of the act to extend its protection to vast categories of employees who would probably find it a surprise to know that they were 'workers' in an 'industry'. In expanding the scope of industry, the judgment had the practical impact of increasing protection of many classes of workers and imposing the corresponding costs on organizations. More than just this practical impact, the judgment showed the sharp leftward turn of the jurisprudence of the Supreme Court, the effects of which are felt even till today.

I

The Industrial Disputes Act

During colonial rule in India, the ethos of industry was distinctly laissez-faire. There were very few laws that protected the rights of workers. In case of any violation of their rights, workers had to move the regular courts of law. This would presumably have entailed a significant expense, rendering such remedies virtually illusory for workers being paid paltry wages. To remedy this situation, in 1920, the Trade Disputes Act was enacted, which set up courts of inquiry and conciliation boards. Though ostensibly enacted to provide for the redressal of industrial disputes, the act's main intent seemed to be to make strikes and lockouts illegal. The Trade Disputes Act, 1920, was, in turn, replaced by the Trade Disputes Act, 1929. However, it was noticed that even this act was rarely used since 'the Government policy at that time continued to be one of *laissez faire* and selective intervention'.[4]

After the outbreak of the Second World War the government of the day promulgated the Defence of India Rules under which industrial tribunals were set up as specialist bodies to resolve disputes. It is quite telling that labour disputes were seen as requiring intervention under an act that gave emergency powers to the colonial overlords. It was presumably understood even then, that industrial disputes could seriously undermine the economic security of the country and therefore needed to be dealt with as such.

Even though the value of governmental intervention to solve workers' disputes had been recognized, not much was done to ameliorate the lot of industrial workers. It was only around the time of Independence that the attitude of the governing classes towards workers underwent a change. The Industrial Disputes Act, 1947, was passed by the Central Legislative Assembly in March 1947 and became law with effect from 1 April 1947.

The philosophy underpinning the Industrial Disputes Act can be traced back to Nehruvian socialism, which itself was deeply influenced by Fabian socialism. Fabian socialism was a political and economic philosophy that believed in moving from a capitalist model to a socialist model incrementally.[5] The underlying belief was in having a socialist economy where large industries were owned and controlled by the government while remaining a democracy. There was also a great emphasis on workers' participation in industry.

This protectionist philosophy found many expressions in the Constitution. For instance, the Directive Principles of State Policy require that the State has to direct its policies so as to ensure that citizens 'have the right to an adequate means of livelihood' and that they should not be 'forced by economic necessity to enter avocations unsuited to their age and strength'. In particular, the State is to ensure that the 'operation of the economic system does not result in the concentration of wealth and means of production to the common detriment'. It has been argued that the labour laws that were promulgated as part of this philosophy are what have led to India's 'sclerotic growth'.[6]

It was with this socialist spirit that the Industrial Disputes Act, 1947 was enacted.[7] The act provided not only for the settlement of disputes by conciliation or by industrial tribunals, but also gave the workers a huge number of important rights. For instance, in 1953, a new Chapter VA was inserted into the act providing for compensation in case of lay-offs and retrenchments.[8] That amendment also provided that, in case any establishment was to be closed, a sixty-day notice was to be given along with compensation to the workers.

The act was made even more stringent in 1976 with the insertion of a new Chapter VB. This chapter strictly curtailed the rights of employers to lay off or retrench workers, even after the payment of compensation. The act required any industry to seek the permission of the government if it wished to close an industry. Originally, this provision empowered the government to refuse to give permission without according any reasons and did not give the owners of the factories any legal recourse to challenge the rejection. The employers would be forced to carry on paying wages to employees even if they did not have any resources. This provision was challenged before the Supreme Court and even with the socialist fervour of the day, this provision was difficult to accept for the Court. The section was struck down by holding that the right to run an industry included the right to close it down.[9] Failure to give reasons or any legal recourse amounted to a violation of an industrialist's right to trade and business guaranteed by Article 19 (1) (g) of the Constitution. The reprieve, however, was short-lived. The Parliament amended the law shortly after this judgment by the Industrial Disputes (Amendment) Act, 1982, which inserted an amended Section 25-O. The amendment retained the core of the provision but tinkered only with the procedural provisions. This time, the Court upheld the provision.[10]

II

The Law Before the Judgment

Since the act was extremely expansive in its scope, the natural attempt for any business was to try to avoid the application of the act to itself. The simplest way was for a business to argue that it was not an 'industry' within the meaning of the act. This is because the act did not apply to all commercial (or indeed governmental) enterprises, but only to certain industrial establishments.[11]

Hence, if businesses could convince Courts that their enterprises were not covered by the definition of the word 'industry' as contemplated by the act, they could escape the rigours of the act. This led to a large amount of litigation in the Courts, with industries pleading that the scope of the definition was narrow. On the other hand, workers urged that the term 'industry' was of a very wide amplitude and that they would be entitled to the various protections guaranteed under the act. These disputes often found their way to the Supreme Court, which issued a series of judgments on this vexed question of law.

One of the first cases where this dispute arose was in what has been come to be known as the *Bannerji* case.[12] Praful Chandra Mitra was the head clerk, and Phanindra Nath Ghose, the sanitary inspector of the Budge Municipality in the state of West Bengal. They were also members of the Municipal Workers' Union, something which may well have caused the municipality to view them less than favourably. On the receipt of complaints against them for negligence, insubordination and indiscipline, they were dismissed by the municipality. At the instance of the Municipal Workers' Union, who questioned the propriety of the dismissal, the matter was referred to the industrial tribunal for adjudication under the act. The tribunal ruled in the employees' favour and decided that their suspension and punishment was a case of victimization. The tribunal also directed their reinstatement.

The dispute ultimately reached the Supreme Court where a perturbed municipality urged that it was a government agency exercising sovereign functions and it could not thus be understood to be an industry in any sense of the word. Unfortunately for the municipality, the Court ruled that it was indeed an industry, at least under the provisions of the act. The Court noticed that the ordinary definition of industry would not include a municipality, but it was always possible for the legislature to give an artificial and expansive definition of that term. The definition of the term, and hence the scope of the application of the act, would depend on a particular time and context in the country's development.

The Court thus held that 'it is obvious that the limited concept of what an industry meant in early times must now yield place to an enormously wider concept so as to take in various and varied forms of industry, so that disputes arising in connection with them might be settled quickly without much dislocation and disorganization of the needs of society and in a manner more adapted to conciliation and settlement than a determination of the respective rights and liabilities according to strict legal procedure and principles. The conflicts between capital and labour have now to be determined more from the standpoint of status than of contract.' The Court, in this passage, was saying that the contractual agreements between employers and employees did not determine whether a particular undertaking was an industry. What mattered was 'status', i.e., the relative position between the two, rather than the formal terms of the 'contract'. The reason behind this expansion of the term 'industry' was also because the Court saw the Act as providing an alternate mechanism for resolving labour disputes. The wider the definition of the term 'industry', the greater the number of disputes that could be resolved through the process of conciliation (rather than litigation) as mandated by the act.

Round one of the litigation in relation to the definition of industry seemed to have gone in favour of the workers. However, this was soon to change. Shortly after the *Bannerji* case, other matters reached the Supreme Court where the Court took a decidedly different approach. For instance, the Court held that the Madras Gymkhana Club[13] and the Cricket Club of India[14] were not industries. Similarly, the Court ruled that the so-called 'liberal professions' like a firm of solicitors[15] or even universities[16] could not be held to be industries. Most importantly, a six-judge bench in the case of Safdarjung Hospital[17] held that hospitals were also not industries under the act.

In the *Safdarjung* case, the Court referred to the definition of the term 'industry' under the act. Section 2 (j) of the act defined industry thus: 'Industry means any business, trade, undertaking, manufacture or calling of employers and includes any calling, service, employment, handicraft or industrial occupation or avocation of workmen.'

This was a peculiarly framed definition. The first part of the section referred to the status of the employer, i.e., the employer had to be engaged in any 'business, trade, undertaking, manufacture or calling'. However, the sting was in the second part of the definition, which referred to the nature of work of the employees. In the *Safdarjung* case, the employees argued that this implied that regardless of who the employer was, if there was any employee who undertook work, the establishment where she worked would be deemed to be an industry regardless of what activity was being undertaken by the establishment. This suggestion was rejected by the Court as being overly expansive. The Supreme Court ruled that the real test was whether the employers were engaged in some activity that could be described as an industry. The judgment recorded that it was not necessary for an industry to have a profit element, but 'the enterprise must be analogous to trade or business in the commercial sense'.

There were now two inconsistent lines of judgment. One line of judgment referred to the role of the employers, while the other looked to the nature of the employees' work to determine whether a particular enterprise was an industry. The result of all these judgments was that the law was in a state of flux and was entirely unpredictable. Conflicting judgments gave rise to uncertainty in the applicability of the law, which was harmful to industry since predictability is one of the core requirements of business. Therefore, when the matter relating to the *Bangalore Water Supply* case reached the Supreme Court, the matter was referred to a bench of seven judges so that the judgment in the *Safdarjung* case could be reconsidered.

III

The Judgment and the Judges

The matter was heard by a bench of seven judges resulting in 5–2 split verdict.[18] The majority judgment was delivered in three concurring judgments while the minority was a short, pithy judgment by two judges.

Interestingly, two of the majority concurring judgments were delivered by two separate chief justices of the same Court. The judgment was originally pronounced on 21 February 1978, when Justice M.H. Beg was the chief justice of India. On that date, Justice Chandrachud merely recorded his concurrence with the judgment but noted that he would give detailed reasons

later. By the time he gave his reasons on 7 April 1978, Justice
Beg had retired and Justice Chandrachud was the chief justice.
Therefore, the second judgment was also by a chief justice of the
Supreme Court.

The main judgment, however, was that of Justice Krishna
Iyer. In fact, it had been Justice Krishna Iyer who had doubted
the correctness of the *Safdarjung* case and referred the matter
to a bench of seven judges. Given this fact, it would not come
as a surprise to people aware of legal history that the majority
proceeded to overrule the *Safdarjung* case and come down heavily
in favour of workers' rights. This was so because by this time
Justice Krishna Iyer had established his reputation as the bulwark
of the Court's left wing.

Justice Krishna Iyer had been an avowed communist all
his life. He had been briefly jailed in May 1948 for aiding and
abetting violent communists by providing them shelter. As has
been noticed, 'he was the only Supreme Court judge to have
been jailed by his own countrymen'.[19] After this incident, he
got involved with politics and stood for elections to the Madras
Legislative Assembly. After the carving out of the state of Kerala,
he was elected to the State Assembly in 1957. The first elected
communist government of E.M.S. Namboodiripad was formed,
and Krishna Iyer was made a minister in his cabinet.

One would have thought that a person who had been a
minister in a communist government, and one with extremely
strong socialist views, would never be sent to the Supreme Court.
However, given the wave of socialism that was ruling the country
at that time, this was precisely what happened. Even though he
was a relatively junior judge, he was elevated to the Supreme Court
in 1973, just five years after his appointment to the High Court
of Kerala. His appointment was met by trenchant criticism on
the ground that he was a Marxist. However, this criticism never

fazed Justice Krishna Iyer and he proceeded to deliver a series of judgments, each of them propelling the Court further to the Left.

So, it was entirely expected that the judgment would side with the workers and give an extremely expansive definition of the term 'industry'. And indeed, this was just what happened. The judgment solemnly declared that it was better to be 'ultimately right than consistently wrong' and proceeded to overrule a host of cases mentioned above. Private members' clubs, universities, hospitals, law firms and even cooperative societies and charitable institutions were declared to be 'industries'. The crux of the argument was that if there was an establishment that engaged the services of employees, that establishment was deemed to be an industry! The judgment laid down a 'triple test' to determine whether an establishment was an industry or not. The Court held that:

(a) Where (*i*) systematic activity, (*ii*) organized by co-operation between employer and employee (the direct and substantial element is chimerical) (*iii*) for the production and/or distribution of goods and services calculated to satisfy human wants and wishes (not spiritual or religious but inclusive of material things or services geared to celestial bliss e.g. making, on a large scale *prasad* or food), prima facie, there is an 'industry' in that enterprise.

(b) Absence of profit motive or gainful objective is irrelevant, be the venture in the public, joint, private or other sector.

(c) The true focus is functional and the decisive test is the nature of the activity with special emphasis on the employer–employee relations.

(d) If the organization is a trade or business it does not cease to be one because of philanthropy animating the undertaking.

A close perusal of the so-called 'triple test' would reveal that virtually every enterprise would be covered by this definition. All that was required was that the establishment should have some paid employees who engaged in what was euphemistically called 'systematic activity'. The definition of 'industry' was so wide that even the relatively socialist government of the day had trouble accepting it.[20]

However, more interesting than the explicit text of the judgement, was the subtext. The ethos of the judgment was decidedly socialist. This was expressly stated in the judgment when the Court held that 'the mechanism of the Act is geared to conferment of regulated benefits to workmen and resolution, according to a sympathetic rule of law, of the conflicts, actual or potential, between managements and workmen. Its goal is amelioration of the conditions of workers, tempered by a sense of peaceful co-existence, to the benefit of both—not a neutral position but restraints on laissez faire and concern for the welfare of the weaker lot'. This statement indicated that the Court could not abide a hands-off approach to disputes between workers and their employers. The tilt was clearly in favour of the workers since the Court believed that the mandate of the law was for it to intervene on their behalf because they were the 'weaker lot'. At another point, the judge even held that 'in trade and business, goods and services are for the community, not for self-consumption'. The true purport of this statement was that the judges viewed industry through the lens of a communist.

Of course, another explanation for these puzzling statements was that Justice Krishna Iyer was fond of a rather florid writing style. For instance, without any apparent sense of irony, the judge wrote, 'Esoterica is anathema for law affecting the common man in the commerce of life, and so the starting point of our discussion is the determination to go by the plain, not the possible, sense of the words used in the definition, informed by the context and purpose of the statute, illuminated by its scheme and setting and conceptually coloured by what is an industry at the current developmental stage in our country.'

This effectively incomprehensible statement (to people other than lawyers) was a hallmark of the learned judge, whose undoubted erudition was often masked by made-up words. Unfortunately, a large number of judgments from that time seem to have copied the style rather than the substance of the judgments.

IV

The Aftermath

The judgment sent shivers down the spine of not only industries, as classically understood, but virtually any economic venture. Compliance with India's notoriously complex labour laws was not easy for a profit-making business enterprise. Now, all sorts of other players had been included in the dragnet of 'industry'. As has been noted, the absence of a profit motive made even charitable enterprises industries. A large number of voluntary welfare schemes were abandoned due to their inclusion as industries.[21]

The judgment had exhorted Parliament to pass a law clarifying the definition of industry. This would have been the ideal time to pass a legislation undoing the excessively broad definition of industry. However, this was not to be. In 1982, Parliament did, in fact, pass a law redefining industry so as to mitigate the impact of the Bangalore Water Supply judgment. However, this amendment remained a dead letter as it was never notified and brought into force by the government.

Even though the government did not think it fit to revisit the definition of industry, the Court certainly had second thoughts about the Bangalore Water Supply judgment. Judicial unease at the width of the judgment had been expressed in several judgments.[22] In 1998, a bench of two judges felt that the case needed a relook and referred the matter to the chief justice for the constitution of a larger bench.

A larger bench was constituted only in 2005, some eight years after the reference. By this time, the effects of liberalization had begun to be felt in virtually every sector of the economy. Socialism was no longer the orthodoxy. Possibly because of this, the judges made the most trenchant comments about the judgment. A unanimous bench of five judges (interestingly the same number of judges who formed the majority in the *Bangalore Water Supply* case) held that the case was wrongly decided.[23] It was held that the experience of the past had shown that awarding huge sums of money to employees in fact had a counter-productive effect. Industries had to be shut down, thereby hurting other employees, just for an employer to be able to make the payment awarded under the act.

In an attempt to walk back from the protectionist aspects of the act, the Court specifically held that 'Exploitation of workers and the employers has to be equally checked. Law and particularly industrial law needs to be so interpreted as to ensure that neither the employers nor the employees are in a position to dominate the other. Both should be able to cooperate for their mutual benefit in the growth of industry and thereby serve public good. An overexpansive interpretation of the definition of "industry" might be a deterrent to private enterprise in India where public employment opportunities are scarce. The people should, therefore, be encouraged towards self-employment.'

The judgment ended with a veiled criticism of the government for not notifying the amendment to the act even though '23 long years' had passed since the amendment. Unfortunately, the Court could not put its own house in order. While there was clear Executive dithering in the matter of notifying the amendment, it was not as though the judicial process was lightning fast. It took another twelve years for the larger bench to be constituted. A seven-judge bench was constituted in 2017, which again referred the matter to a bench of nine judges.[24] The matter rests there and that bench of nine judges has not been constituted till date!

Conclusion

The Bangalore Water Supply judgment marked a turning point for the jurisprudence of the Court. The Court had been moving to the Left for quite some time, partly as a result of governmental efforts to have a 'committed judiciary'. This judgment, and the series of cases relating to workers' rights that followed it, firmly put the Court on a socialist trajectory. However, this case demonstrates more than just the Court's ideological shift. It also demonstrates the political compulsions in matters of industrial relations. The definition of industry was amended by Parliament nearly forty years ago and yet the government has not notified the amendment to bring it into force. This, in spite of the near total judicial consensus that the Court may have overreached itself in the Bangalore Water Supply judgment. The Court has also not covered itself with glory, failing to constitute a bench that could reconsider the judgment, even though forty-five years have passed after its pronouncement.

In the meanwhile, there is nearly uniform consensus that the Indian labour law regime has ossified and has been a significant drag on economic productivity. Various commissions and task forces have been constituted, which have recommended making labour laws less onerous to comply with to make industry more agile and better suited to be able to deal with a rapidly changing economic environment.

It cannot be denied that labour market reform is needed; the only question is how best to achieve this. To the extent that an argument can be raised that greater regulation is needed to protect workmen, this ignores that stark reality that the present statutory framework covers a shockingly low proportion of the workforce. The proportion of the organized sector workforce in the total workforce has never been above 8 per cent and has, in fact, been falling consistently. This suggests that industry is either seeking ways to hire informal labour or that industrialization is not happening at the pace at which it is required in a country such as ours. On the other hand, a return to a laissez-faire policy is also deeply unsatisfactory.[25]

The only hope for change seems to be for Parliament to enact a whole new labour code. In doing so, the interests of workers and industries would have to be recalibrated. Excessive faith in market mechanisms resulting in complete deregulation of the labour markets would probably be misplaced, both politically and economically.[26] Equally, the current status quo with an almost Marxist regime of regulation is unsustainable. It remains to be seen whether India can find the balance that will propel its huge and impatient workforce towards a better future.

In this backdrop, Parliament has enacted four separate sets of laws seeking to codify, regulate and amend the entire gamut of labour laws in India. The Code on Industrial Relations, the Code on Wages, the Code on Social Security and the Code on Occupational Safety, Health and Working Conditions have been enacted in 2020. While these laws will certainly revolutionize the employment sector in India, we may have to wait a while to see their impact. This is not because the laws will take time to make an impact, but because, in the time-honoured tradition of this area of the law, the laws have yet to be operationalized and brought into force. One can only hope that these laws do not become another statistic in the list of reforms that could have been accomplished but never were.

Notes

[1] *T.M.A Pai Foundation v. State of Karnataka* (2002) 8 SCC 481.

[2] Though Parliament enacted a piece of legislation titled 'The Unorganized Workers Social Security Act' in 2008, it has not been effectively implemented.

[3] (1978) 2 SCC 213.

[4] O.P. Malhotra. *The Law of Industrial Disputes* (Universal, (5th edn.), p.1.

[5] Margaret Cole. *The Story of Fabian Socialism* (Stanford University Press, 1961).

[6] B.E. Kaufman. *Labor Law Reform in India: Insights from Tangled Legacy of Sidney & Beatrice Webb, Indian Journal of Industrial Relations*, 50(1) (2014), p.20.

[7] Even though the Industrial Disputes Act, 1947, was enacted prior to coming into the force of the Constitution, the Directive Principles of State Policy had already found expression in the Report of the Rights Sub-Committee. See Granville Austin. *The Indian Constitution* (Oxford University Press, 2019), p. 101.

[8] The Industrial Disputes (Amendment) Act, 1953.

[9] *Excel Wear v. Union of India*, (1978) 4 SCC 224.

[10] *Orissa Textile and Steel Ltd v. State of Orissa* (2002) 2 SCC 578.

[11] Section 25K—Application of Chapter VB:

(1) *The provisions of this chapter shall apply to an industrial establishment (not being an establishment of a seasonal character or in which work is performed only intermittently) in which not less than one hundred workmen were employed on an average per working day for the preceding twelve months.*

(2) *If a question arises whether an industrial establishment is of a seasonal character or whether work is performed therein only intermittently, the decision of the appropriate Government thereon shall be final.*

As an aside, this obsession with protecting the rights of workers only in the large formal industrial sector has been a hallmark of India's labour policy. The effect of this is that the condition of workers in the large informal sector is largely ignored.

[12] *D.N. Banerji v. P.R. Mukherjee* AIR 1953 SC 58.

[13] Secretary, *Madras Gymkhana Club Employees Union v. Management of the Gymkhana Club* (1968) 1 SCR 742.

[14] *Cricket Club of India v. Bombay Labour Union* (1969) 1 SCR 600.

[15] *National Union of Commercial Employees v. M.R. Meher*, Industrial Tribunal Bombay AIR 1962 SC 1080.

[16] *University of Delhi v. Ram Nath* AIR 1963 SC 1873.

[17] *Safdarjung Hospital v. Kuldip Singh Sethi* (1970) 1 SCC 735.

[18] *Bangalore Water Supply & Sewerage Board v. A. Rajappa* (1978) 2 SCC 213.

[19] George H. Gadbois. *Judges of the Supreme Court of India 1950-1989* (Oxford University Press, 2011).

[20] In fact, it may be noted that only one appeal of the many cases that were heard together that was actually disposed of was that of the Bangalore Water Supply and Sewerage Board (Civil Appeal 753/1975). The Attorney General

for India, S.V. Gupte, appeared in the appeal and sought to convince the Court that the board was not an industry. The Court rejected this submission and ruled against the government.

[21] As noticed in *Coir Board, Ernakulam v. Indira Devi P.S.* (1998) 3 SCC 259.

[22] *Sub-Divisional Inspector of Post v. Theyyam Joseph* (1996) 8 SCC 489 and *Bombay Telephone Canteen Employees Assn. v. Union of India* (1997) 6 SCC 723. However, these judgments were overruled in *General Manager, Telecom v. A. Srinivasa Rao* (1997) 8 SCC 767.

[23] *State of UP v. Jai Bir Singh* (2005) 5 SCC 1.

[24] (2017) 3 SCC 311

[25] For an excellent argument against laissez-faire liberalization, see Anamitra Roychowdhury. *Labour Law Reforms in India: All in the Name of Jobs* (Routledge 2018), Chapter 8.

[26] Simon F. Deakin and Antara Haldar. 'How Should India Reform Its Labour Laws?', University of Cambridge Faculty of Law, Research Paper No. 25/2015, 31 March 2015.

Chapter 4

Needling the Shareholders:
Oppression and Mismanagement

One of the greatest innovations in law was the creation of the limited liability company. It was a juristic entity distinct from its shareholders. Over the years, the form of a company has transformed the way that business is conducted. Most of the larger businesses function through a corporate structure rather than as partnerships or proprietorships. For instance, all the entities listed on the National Stock Exchange or the Bombay Stock Exchange are companies. There are many reasons why companies are the preferred route to operate businesses, including the concept of limited liability where individual shareholders are not saddled with all the losses that any business may incur. There is another advantage that a corporate structure brings and that is the flexibility in the change of ownership. The company is effectively owned by its shareholders.[1] Whenever a company needs fresh capital, it can issue fresh shares to new (or existing) shareholders. In most companies, shareholders can sell their shares to other people and thus bring about a change in ownership of the company.[2] Of course, the moment there are multiple owners, there is also a possibility of dispute between them. This chapter examines how the Courts have attempted to resolve some of these conflicts.

Some publicly listed companies have millions of shareholders. These shareholders have a common interest in the well-being of the company in which they hold shares. They may also have differences on many issues, including how the company should be run. For instance, some shareholders may prefer that profits earned by the company be distributed to them as dividends, while other shareholders may wish that the profits be re-invested by the company to secure future growth. The question then arises as to how differences between the shareholders in a company are to be resolved.

In this regard the company is not too different from a democratic country. In a democracy, once a government has been elected through the voting process, it has the right to govern the country for the period of its elected term. However, modern democracies are not merely elective dictatorships where all the decisions are taken solely as per the commands of the majority. If the government were to be run solely as per the wishes of the majority, there is the possibility that minorities, or those who disagree with the majority, would be subjected to oppressive behaviour. Most modern democracies thus have special provisions, in their constitutions or otherwise, that afford additional protection to minorities. These rights are enforced through the Courts, which are meant to be immune from the whims of popular opinion and are thus in a position to safeguard the interests of minorities.

Companies are very similarly run. The shareholders of the company have the right to 'elect' the board of directors that runs a company, in a manner very similar to how voters elect their members of Parliament (and indirectly the cabinet).[3] The board has substantial powers of governance and is answerable to the entire body of shareholders. In this manner, the company is also bound by the will of the majority of its shareholders. However, there may be some minority shareholders who may not be able to get their nominees elected to the board. The board may also act in a manner oppressive to the minority shareholders since they may be beholden to the majority shareholders who voted for them. In such a situation, the Companies Act has special provisions that permit the Courts to intervene and protect the interests of the minority shareholders.

This chapter concerns itself with the saga of a company that manufactured needles used to play gramophones, the Needle Industries (India) Pvt. Ltd ('Needle Industries'). The company was the subsidiary of a British company but was also partly owned by certain Indian promoters. There were thus two groups in the company: the foreign shareholders and the domestic ones. The foreign shareholders alleged that the domestic group acted in a manner that was oppressive to them. The British parent company claimed that its rights as a shareholder had been significantly undermined by concerted actions of the domestic shareholders.

The dispute eventually reached the Supreme Court where a three-judge panel gave a verdict siding with the Indian shareholders in the case titled *Needle Industries (India) Ltd v. Needle Industries Newey (India) Holding Ltd* ('the Needle Industries judgment').[4] The Court examined the allegations of the foreign shareholders in light of the provisions of the law that permitted a member to complain that the 'affairs of the company [were] being conducted prejudicial to the public interest or in a manner oppressive to the member' and came to a conclusion that there was no oppression. However, in doing so, the Court laid down the tests of what would constitute oppression of shareholders of a company, a test that has been applied in most similar cases.[5] Over the years, this judgment has become the leading one of the field and has shaped how far the majority may dictate the functioning of a company before falling foul of the law. The Needle Industries judgment has also determined many other areas of company law and has thus shaped the development of the Indian financial sector by regulating how its most important engine, the company, operates.

I

The Gramophone Needle

Needle Industries had been set up shortly after Independence in 1949 and manufactured needles used to play gramophones. The factory of the company was set up high in the mountains, in the Ketty valley in the Nilgiri mountains of Tamil Nadu. This was because gramophone needles were made of unplated steel and could not afford to get rusted as they would not otherwise fit the grooves of the 78 rpm disc to play music.[6] The dry and rarefied mountain air allowed the manufacture of a world-class product that was exported around the world.

Needle Industries was an Indian success story, albeit with a bit of mixed parentage. At the time of its incorporation, it was a wholly-owned subsidiary of a British holding company. However, at that time, it had given an undertaking to the Government of India that it would eventually induct more Indian shareholders. The government also issued directions asking foreign shareholders to sell their shares to Indian citizens so as to achieve 'Indianization' of certain foreign-held companies.[7] Over the years, the foreign shareholders diluted their shares so that by 1971 some 40 per cent of the company was owned by the employees of Needle Industries as well as by one T.A. Devagnanam and his family. Devagnanam had been appointed as a director in Needle Industries in 1956 and was made its managing director in 1961.

Even though the company had been substantially owned by foreign entities, the management was entirely in Indian hands. The holding company had only one director whom it had nominated to the board, one N.T. Sanders. Sanders lived in England and rarely attended the board meetings of Needle Industries. The Indian management then had a free rein over running the company, with the tacit approval of the British holding company. This bonhomie continued till two events occurred in the early seventies.

In 1972, a company called Coats Patons Ltd, Glasgow ('Coats') bought 50 per cent of the shares of the British holding company. Since the holding company at this point in time held about 60 per cent of Needle Industries, this gave Coats indirect ownership of 30 per cent of the company. By this point in time, Needle Industries had expanded its business from purely domestic consumption to exports to a large number of companies. It had also grown significantly with its turnover increasing from Rs 2.8 lakh in 1953 to Rs 150 lakh by 1972. Devagnanam was a shrewd businessman who saw the potential in the company and wished for it to grow even further.

Coats was a giant multinational and was a competitor of Needle Industries since it too manufactured and sold needles for various uses. As the Supreme Court noted, 'It is plain business, involving no moral turpitude as far as business ethics go, that Coats could not have welcomed competition from [Needle Industries] with their world interests.'[8] After Coats came into part ownership of the company, there was increasing friction between the holding company and the Indian management.

The second event that upset the apple cart was the enactment of the draconian FERA in 1973. FERA was an act that had been enacted in the socialist fervour of the early seventies, shortly after Indira Gandhi defeated the opposing forces within the Congress Party.[9] The purpose of FERA, as per its long title, was to regulate 'for the conservation of the foreign exchange resources of the country and the proper utilisation thereof in the interests of the economic development of the country'. The act made it extremely difficult for foreign entities to own and operate businesses in India. Section 29 of FERA prohibited any non-resident from owning more than 40 per cent of a company that carried on business in India without seeking the permission of the Reserve Bank of India (RBI). Since 60 per cent of Needle Industries was owned by foreign entities, the company had a six-month period within which it had to approach RBI to get the permission to carry on with its business.[10] An application was made in terms of the act, which was allowed by RBI. However, RBI imposed some conditions that were required to be fulfilled. One condition was that the extent of the foreign shareholding had to be brought down from 60 per cent to 40 per cent. A one-year limit was prescribed for this, a period that would expire by 17 May 1977.

Faced with this requirement to 'Indianize' the company, disputes broke out among the shareholders as how best to achieve this. Initially, Devagnanam wanted to sell the shares to another Indian investor, one Mr Khaitan who had considerable clout in the industry. Khaitan also ran businesses that were closely allied to Needle Industries. However, this proposal met with stiff resistance from Coats. Coats was alarmed at the prospect of selling the company to Khaitan, who was viewed as a possible competitor in its international markets.

Given this opposition, it was decided that the shares of the holding company would be sold to some other Indian entity. This was where the differences became even more acute. Coats wanted to sell its shares to another Indian entity—Madura Coats—which was another subsidiary of Coats. This would have allowed Coats to retain substantial control over Needle Industries even after the divestment of its shares. On the other hand, Devagnanam was of the view, as per their Articles of Association, that the shares in Needle Industries could only be sold to existing shareholders and not to any third party. This was not acceptable to Coats as it would give the Indian shareholders control of over 60 per cent of the company and 'carried in the long run too great a risk to their world trade.'[11]

There was a stalemate and the deadline set by RBI to Indianize the company, being 17 May 1977, was fast approaching. It was at this point that the board of directors of Needle Industries swung into action. A meeting of the board was convened on 6 April 1977, with the agenda item of 'Indianization'. It was decided in the meeting that the company would increase its capital by issuing an extra 16,000 shares at par value (which was Rs 100). These shares would be offered to all the shareholders in proportion to their existing shareholding. If a shareholder did not respond to the offer within sixteen days from the date on which it was made, it would be deemed to have been refused by the shareholder.

If each existing shareholder had purchased the shares as per their rights, the overall percentage of the shareholding would not have been altered. Thus it was not clear as to how this proposal to issue extra shares, and that too at par value, would have resulted in any Indianization. Perhaps it was felt that the holding company would be legally barred from purchasing the extra shares in view of the provisions of FERA, or that they may be compelled to permit an Indian nominee of theirs to purchase the shares. However, such an eventuality never transpired. The offer to purchase shares was made by a letter dated 14 April 1977.[12] However, this was posted from Chennai only on 27 April 1977 (as shown by the postmark) and received by Coats on 2 May 1977. This was after the last date by which Coats could have possibly accepted the offer made by it and thus, in effect, it was denied the opportunity to subscribe to the shares as a result of the delayed posting of the offer letter.

As if to add insult to injury, the board of directors issued a notice on 19 April 1977, proposing to call another meeting on 2 May 1977. The agenda of this meeting was also Indianization and the allotment of shares. However, even this notice was posted from Chennai only on 27 April and received by Coats on 2 May 1977, i.e., the day of the meeting! Thus there was no earthly way that Coats could have attended the meeting. Even though the representatives of the holding company sent a telex on 2 May to Devagnanam complaining about the inadequacy of the notice, the board of directors went ahead with the meeting anyway. At that meeting, the board noted that only certain Indian shareholders had accepted the offer for purchasing the extra shares as per the rights issue. This was hardly surprising, given the paucity of time that the holding company had in purchasing their portion of the rights issue. Nevertheless, the board went ahead and confirmed the allotment of 11,734 shares to Devagnanam and his family. This way the shareholding of the Indian shareholders went above the 60 per cent threshold mandated by RBI.

This was extremely problematic for the holding company. First, their share in Needle Industries was diluted without them having had adequate time to exercise their right to subscribe to the shares. Secondly, the shares had been issued at par, i.e., at a value of Rs 100 per share, even though the actual worth of the shares was much more, around Rs 190 per share. Thus the Indian shareholders were given the shares of the company at a value lower than the market price.

These actions compelled the holding company to move the Madras High Court. A petition was filed under Section 387 and 398 of the Indian Companies Act, 1956, alleging oppression and mismanagement by the board of directors of Needle Industries.[13] The single judge of the high court held that there indeed had been oppression of the foreign shareholders, but felt that the situation could be remedied by the award of compensation. The single judge directed that Needle Industries would simply pay a sum of Rs 8,54,550 as damages to the holding company to recompense them for their loss. Aggrieved by this decision, the holding company filed an appeal before the division bench of two honourable judges of the high court. The bench decided that there indeed had been oppression but agreed with the foreign shareholders that damages were not an adequate remedy. The bench went ahead and directed that the board of directors of the company be superseded, Devagnanam be removed from the board and that the rights issue of 2 May 1977 be cancelled.[14]

II

The Judgment

Needle Industries appealed against this decision by the division bench of the high court. The matter thus reached the Supreme Court. The matter was initially heard by a bench of two judges of the Supreme Court who disagreed about how the case should be decided.[15] The case was therefore placed before a bench of three judges, headed by Justice Y.V. Chandrachud. The other judges on the bench were P.N. Bhagwati and E.S. Venkataramaiah. Each of the three judges went on to become chief justices of India.

The judgment conducted an exhaustive survey of company law across India and the UK. This was so because the Indian Companies Act, 1956, was closely modelled after the English Companies Act, 1948. Indian Courts also looked to decisions of the UK Courts for guidance as some of the concepts involved the 'common law'. Common law is that corpus of case law that is made by judicial pronouncements rather than by any legislature. It is, so to say, judge-made law, where any new matter is decided based upon the principles deducible from the previously decided cases. Judgment proceeds on analogical reasoning and extension of the principles laid down in prior decided cases. This reference to the common law was necessary to decide which conduct was 'oppressive to any member' of the company.

The Court relied on prior decided cases to rule that 'the true position is that an isolated act, which is contrary to law, may not necessarily and by itself support the inference that the law was violated with a mala fide intention or that such violation was burdensome, harsh and wrongful. But a series of illegal acts following upon one another can, in the context, lead justifiably to the conclusion that they are a part of the same transaction, of which the object is to cause or commit the oppression of persons against whom those acts are directed.'[16]

In effect, the Court decided that in order to invoke the jurisdiction of the Court on the grounds of oppression, any shareholder had to establish that the conduct of the board of directors was not in good faith. In determining this, simply pointing out that some decision of the board was illegal was not sufficient. An illegal act could even be taken for the larger benefit of the company rather than with any desire to oppress any shareholder.[17] However, when the board took illegal decisions multiple times, it was quite likely that the decisions were taken in bad faith with the intention of acting against the interests of a particular shareholder or a class of shareholders.

Isolated instances of disagreements between the majority and minority shareholder groups were not sufficient to invoke the jurisdiction of the Company Court. 'The person complaining of oppression must show that he has been constrained to submit to a conduct which lacks in probity, conduct which is unfair to him and which causes prejudice to him in the exercise of his legal and proprietary rights as a shareholder.'[18] This is a high threshold to clear. But the reason for requiring this is obvious. First, this difficult standard is a natural consequence of how a company is structured and secondly, is a result of the limited expertise of the court.

In a company, as in a democracy, there are bound to be disagreements between the majority and the minority group. Every time a majority overrules the minority, it could not be said that there is any oppression. This would simply be the consequence of corporate democracy in action. A company is a distinct juristic entity but is a fictional one. The power and authority to run a company vests with its board of directors, who are normally elected by the majority of the shareholders. The minority thus cannot normally claim to represent or act on behalf of the company, because that is the right given to the majority. In fact, there is a law of great antiquity that lays down the principle that a minority shareholder cannot file any case on behalf of the company against the majority.[19] This right belongs solely to the company, as represented through the will of the majority. The very concept of democracy would militate against giving the minority shareholders the power to move court at every instance of perceived illegality, a result which could bring the functioning of the company to a virtual standstill.

The second reason for this judicial reticence to intervene at the behest of a disgruntled shareholder is because the Court lacks the expertise to take commercial decisions on behalf of the company. Several actions that appear prejudicial to a minority shareholder might be bona fide commercial decisions taken by the company. The Court does not have the wherewithal to determine whether these decisions are for the corporate good or not. The Courts have always been loath to intervene in matters pertaining to the commercial wisdom of the shareholders or the board of directors of the company.[20]

These reasons explain why the Court laid down a difficult test that a shareholder had to comply with before it could establish any cause of action. The right of a shareholder to sue the company for oppression is an exception to the general rule of corporate decision-making. When there are repeated illegal acts or actions taken with the clear intention of acting against the interest of the minority, and that too with a mala fide intent, the jurisdiction of the Courts could be invoked. However, in most other cases, the Court would have a hands-off approach when it came to the rights of a majority to run a company.

On the facts of the case, the Court ruled that the conduct of neither Devagnanam nor Coats was entirely honourable. But if a comparison were to be done of the conduct of the parties, Coats would emerge as the larger villain. This was because their sole intention appeared to be to weaken the Indian company so as to further their international business. These actions also included an attempt to pirate the trademarks owned by Needle Industries. In the words of the Court, the actions of Coats was 'unethical'[21] and it acted in a 'high and mighty'[22] manner. After examining all the evidence in the matter,[23] the Court came to the conclusion that there was no oppression of the foreign shareholders. The holding company had no option but to sell its shares since that was the mandate of the law, i.e., the provisions of FERA and the directives of RBI.

The actions of the Devagnanam group were explained with reference to the fact that they had been undertaken to safeguard the interests of the company rather than any hostile view towards the holding company. The Court ruled that 'what the Directors did was clearly in the larger interests of the Company and in obedience to their duty to comply with the law of the land.'[24]

But it was not as though the Devagnanam group got a clean chit. The fact that both the notice of the meeting dated 16 April and the offer letter dated 14 April were posted only on 27 April, was held not to be a coincidence, but a deliberate act by the group to disable the foreign shareholders from exercising their rights to subscribe to the rights issue. The Court used a rather colourful metaphor to explain what it felt about this explanation. It ruled that 'what is naively sought to be explained as a mere coincidence reminds one of the Brides in the Bath Tub case: The death of the first bride in the bath tub may pass off as an accident and of the second as suicide but when, in identical circumstances, the third bride dies of asphyxia in the bath tub, the conclusion becomes compelling, even applying the rule of circumstantial evidence, that she died a homicidal death.'[25]

Having held that neither party was free from blame, but that there was no oppression in terms of the Companies Act, the

Court could simply have allowed the appeals and dismissed the action on behalf of the holding company.[26] However, the Court did not do so. Perhaps the conscience of the Court was pricked sufficiently so that it could not simply let the actions of the Devagnanam group go unrebuked. Accordingly, the Court invoked its constitutional power under Article 142 of the Constitution and directed Devagnanam and other Indian shareholders to pay compensation to the holding company for their portion of the shares that they were entitled to as per the rights issue, but could not purchase because of the delayed posting of the offer letter.

Conclusion

This decision of the Court has laid the foundations for corporate governance in the country by laying down the tests for when it would intervene at the instance of a shareholder alleging oppression by the majority. However, this is not the only reason why this decision is relevant. For one, in this case, it was the majority shareholder, i.e., the holding company, that claimed that the board of directors acting on behalf of the minority Devagnanam group had acted oppressively towards it. The Court exercised its constitutional powers to direct the minority to pay compensation to the majority. Another reason why this judgment is of relevance is that the Court granted some relief to the majority shareholder, even though it came to the conclusion that there was no oppression.

This brings one to the question of whether the high threshold set by the Court before it intervenes in an alleged act of oppression is justified. The judgment laid down the principles that an action under Section 397 would be maintainable only when the actions of the company were harsh, burdensome or wrong. These are elastic terms and have received substantial judicial interpretation since the Needle Industries judgment.[27] Nevertheless, it is accepted that the test is fairly rigorous and a tough one to meet. In laying down such a stringent set of conditions, the Court has impliedly given the majority shareholders of a company the right to run it with substantial freedom.[28] The judgment is also a virtual carte blanche for incompetent directors when it rules that 'unwise, inefficient or careless conduct of a Director in the performance of his duties cannot give rise to a claim for relief under that section.'[29] Such freedom to the majority as well as the directors of a company may itself be unwise in a country where corporate governance as well as regulatory controls are lax. Minority shareholders in India, like minorities in civil society, need greater protection from the law.

Notes

[1] This is, of course, a colloquialism. Strictly speaking, the shareholders do not own any asset of the company but merely own their shares. See *Bacha Guzdar v. CIT* (1955) 1 SCR 876. Shares confer certain rights through which they can, if sufficient, control the operations of the company.

[2] Many private limited companies have restrictions that regulate how and whether a shareholder can transfer her shares to a person. However, publicly-listed companies do not have such restrictions.

[3] For a discussion on the rights of a shareholder in the company, see the case of *Vodafone International Holdings v. UOI* (2012) 6 SCC 613, which has also been discussed in another chapter of the book.

[4] (1981) 3 SCC 333.

[5] See, for instance, the judgment of the Court in *Dale & Carrington v. PK Prathapan* (2005) 1 SCC 212. Even the recent dispute between the Mistrys and Tatas relied heavily on the Needle Industries judgment. See *Tata Consultancy Services v. Cyrus Investments (P) Ltd* (2021) 9 SCC 449.

[6] Allan Lasrado. 'Haberdasher to the World', *The Hindu Business Line*, 19 November 2019.

[7] Para 4 of the *Needle Industries* case.

[8] Para 7 of the *Needle Industries* case.

[9] See Chapter 2 titled 'Garibi Hatao: The Case for Bank Nationalization'.

[10] Section 29 (2) (a).

[11] Para 16 of the Needle Industries judgment.

[12] As per the resolution, the holding company would have sixteen days to accept this offer, i.e., to decide by 1 May 1977.

[13] Section 397 of the Companies Act, 1956 reads:

(I) Any members of a company who complain that the affairs of the company are being conducted in a manner prejudicial to public interest or in a manner oppressive to any member or members (including any one or more of themselves) may apply to the court for an order under this section: provided such members have a right so to apply in virtue of Section 399.

(2) If, on any application under sub-section (I), the court is of the opinion:

(a) that the company's affairs are being conducted in a manner prejudicial to public interest or in a manner oppressive to any member or members; and

(b) that to wind up the company would unfairly prejudice such member or members, but that otherwise the facts would justify the making of a winding up order on the ground that it was just and equitable that the company should be wound up;

the court may, with a view to bringing to an end the matters complained of, make such order as it thinks fit.

[14] Para 37 of the Needle Industries judgment.

[15] Para 38 of the Needle Industries judgment.

[16] Para 49 of the Needle Industries judgment.

[17] See, for instance, *Seth Mohanlal Ganpatram v. Sayaji Jubilee Cotton* (1964) 34 Company Cases 777.

[18] Para 52 of the Needle Industries judgment.

[19] *Foss v. Harbottle* (1843) 2 Hare 461.

[20] See, for instance, *Miheer Mafatlal v. Mafatlal Industries* (1997) 1 SCC 579.

[21] Para 76 of the Needle Industries judgment.

[22] Para 78 of the Needle Industries judgment.

[23] An argument was raised by the counsel for the appellant that in matters of determining mala fide, evidence by way of affidavits alone should not be relied upon and that there ought to be oral testimony with the possibility of cross-examination. However, this submission was rejected by the Court. See Paragraph 65 of the judgment.

[24] Para 107 of the Needle Industries judgment.

[25] Paragraph 123 of the Needle Industries judgment.

[26] The judgment also decided an interesting question as to the status of a private company that became a deemed public company by operation of law. Analysing the Articles of Association as well as the provisions of the Companies Act, 1956, the Court ruled that the holding company could not be

permitted to sell the shares falling to its share under the rights issue to a third
party, i.e., to a person who was not already a member of the company. Para
169 of the Needle Industries judgment.

[27] See, for instance, *Sangramsinh P. Gaekwad v. Shantadevi P. Gaekwad* (2005) 11
SCC 314 and *Dale & Carrington v. PK Prathapan.*

[28] Though the *Needle Industries* case was one of majority oppression, this is
generally a rare phenomenon. It is usually the majority that has the power to
oppress the minority.

[29] Para 52 of the Needle Industries judgment.

Chapter 5

Swashbuckling Takeovers

Hostile takeovers are the stuff of movie legends. Marauding corporate raiders attempting to take over family-owned businesses only to sell their assets have us on the edge of our seats.[1] While life rarely mimics cinema, the case of Swaraj Paul's attempted takeover of two large Indian conglomerates in the 1980s is one such exception. Business, politics and law made a potent cocktail; resulting in a landmark judgment of the Supreme Court in the case of *Life Insurance Corporation v. Escorts Ltd* ('the LIC case').[2]

The case concerned a failed attempt by a non-resident Indian (NRI) investor to take over the rather sleepy businesses of the day. The matter saw many ups and downs. The government was split down the middle, with some institutions favouring Swaraj Paul while other authorities and politicians took a protectionist line, seeking to safeguard the interests of Indian-owned businesses. Even the courts were divided. The Bombay High Court initially handed a big win to the Indian owners. However, when the matter was carried to the Supreme Court, a bench of five judges unanimously held in favour of Paul. This was, however, to prove to be a pyrrhic victory, as ultimately, the takeovers fell through.

While the takeover was unsuccessful eventually, the legacy of the judgment is being felt even today. The LIC judgment has enshrined the principles of shareholder democracy, defined the

concept of corporate personality and clarified the role of the
Reserve Bank of India and financial institutions. These principles,
which form the bedrock of corporate governance, are deployed
to date, including, most recently, in the fight between Cyrus Mistry
and the Tata Group. Hence, while the history of the dispute does
make for a tantalizing read, a careful examination of the LIC
judgment would prove to be far more beneficial to any student
of law and industry.

I

The Economic Crisis

The first attempt at liberalization of the economy was not in 1991
but in the early eighties. As in the nineties, the need for reform
was necessitated by a balance of payments crisis. Decades of
nationalization and a license-permit raj had brought the economy
to dire straits by the early eighties. This was further compounded by
the agitation in Assam in 1980–81 because of which oil production
from those fields was affected with a corresponding need to import
expensive oil into the country. That year, India's import bill rose to
about Rs 11,000 crore, while the receipt of foreign currency through
exports was only about Rs 7000 crore. Even after accounting for
the roughly Rs 2000 crore of remittances by NRIs, the country
faced a balance of payments shortage of Rs 2000 crore. This was
projected to go up even further in the year 1981–82.[3]

It was with this background that India was forced to approach
the International Monetary Fund (IMF) for a loan. The then
finance minister, R. Venkataraman, who later went on to become
the President of India, sought and obtained a loan of 5 billion
Special Drawing Rights (SDR), or about Rs 5000 crore from
the IMF. This amount came up to more than twice the amount
India had borrowed from Independence in 1947 until then. The
IMF loans were also given with a slew of conditionalities that

would have required significant restructuring of the economy. These included the liberalization of imports, a cut in food and agricultural subsidies and a reduction in the regulation of private industry.[4]

Naturally, the issue was a political hot potato with protests in Parliament. Sensing that the situation was getting untenable, the prime minister moved R. Venkataraman to the defence ministry and appointed Pranab Mukherjee, another minister who went on to become the President of India, to the post of finance minister. It seems that after some money was drawn from the IMF, the balance of payments position eased a bit. India did not take the final tranche of 1.1 billion SDR from the IMF.

Nevertheless, the crisis highlighted the urgent need to reform the economy, in particular the need to draw in foreign capital. This had so far been an anathema to the protectionist ideology of the country. In fact, just a few years earlier, Coca-Cola and IBM had left the country rather than continue operating with diluted ownership as required by the draconian FERA, 1973. The eighties crisis was, however, a wake-up call.

The new finance minister decided to explore different ways to shore up India's precariously low foreign exchange reserves. Pranab Mukherjee thought it a good idea to cast the net to entice the large number of NRI businessmen he had met in his travels abroad. It had been estimated that a large sum of money, around USD 20–25 billion, was available from this source, i.e., NRIs.[5] Though the government had started a deposit scheme for NRIs, the so-called Foreign Currency Non-Resident (FCNR) deposit scheme, it had not proved to be sufficient to attract investments into the country. Accordingly, a committee headed by R.N. Malhotra, who went on to become the governor of the Reserve Bank of India, was set up to tap into this resource.

The committee gave a report[6] recommending that companies substantially owned and controlled by Indians residing abroad, or by foreign nationals of Indian origin, should be allowed to invest into domestic companies. The government accepted this recommendation and in the budget speech for that year, the finance minister announced a liberalized scheme to encourage foreign investors to invest in Indian companies. The speech gave the following rights to NRIs:

> 'Any investment, without repatriation rights, made by non-residents of Indian origin, so long as it is not for transactions in commercial property and land, will be treated on the same footing as investments of resident Indian nationals. They will be allowed to invest, with repatriation rights, in any new or existing company up to 40 per cent of the capital issued by such a company. They can now purchase shares of companies quoted on the stock exchanges subject to specified limits . . .'[7]

This statement in the speech was operationalized through the issuance of several RBI circulars. The net effect of all the circulars issued up till 15 May 1983 was that foreign companies were allowed to purchase up to 1 per cent of the shares of any listed company, provided that 60 per cent of such a company was owned by an Indian national or a person of Indian origin living abroad. The circulars did not prohibit members of any one family or even related group companies from acquiring shares of the same company. In effect, family members and companies controlled by them could buy the entire shareholding of a company, provided that the ownership of any one entity was restricted to 1 per cent. This was a loophole that Swaraj Paul was about to exploit.

II

The Battle for Control

Faced with dwindling foreign exchange, the government had brought into force the notorious FERA in 1973. The idea was to

'Indianize' industry and to ensure foreigners could not own vital sectors of the economy. Coupled with the licensing regime, the economic environment of India was anything but free. One natural effect of this was that the Indian companies that did manage to survive faced virtually no competition and were mollycoddled. Promoters of large concerns, facing no competition, diluted their equity. Large portions of the equity were held by public financial institutions. Promoters could, with the tacit consent of the institution, run large industrial conglomerates with equity of as low as 5 per cent. This cozy arrangement between the promoters and the financial institutions was soon to be shaken by the new legal regime.

Two Delhi-based conglomerates were particularly vulnerable because of the low promoter holding. The first was Delhi Cloth and General Mills (DCGM), which was founded by Lala Sri Ram. A self-made man, Lala Sri Ram made the company grow from owning just a cloth mill to a large conglomerate having interests in sugar, chemicals, machine parts and many other areas. In 1980, its turnover was a staggering Rs 420 crore,[8] the equivalent in today's money of about Rs 8000 crore. However, the family owned only about 10 per cent of the total equity in the company. The rest was either publicly held or owned by the institutional investors.

The other corporation was Escorts Ltd, promoted and controlled by the family of H.P. Nanda. Escorts, at that time, was a giant in the manufacture of tractors and other industrial equipment. Even though its turnover was around Rs 240 crore, worth about Rs 4500 crore today, its promoters owned only 5 per cent of its shares!

Sensing the frailty of DCGM and Escorts, the wily NRI investor, Swaraj Paul, decided to move in. Swaraj Paul was born in Jalandhar but had moved to the UK where he had made a large fortune with his Caparo group of industries. Paul decided to use the new regime to take over the companies and

appointed Punjab National Bank as his bankers. He instructed
the bank to write to RBI seeking its approval for the opening of
thirteen non-resident external (NRE) accounts for the purposes
of 'conducting investment operations in India'. These thirteen
companies were fully owned by one Caparo Group Ltd.[9] 61.6 per
cent of the Caparo Group Ltd was, in turn, owned by the Swaraj
Paul family trust. In a strict understanding of the law, therefore,
the conditions of the circular had been complied with, with NRIs
owning over 60 per cent of the shares of the companies through
which investments were made.

Swaraj Paul also appointed one Raja Ram Bhasin & Co. as his
stockbroker in the Delhi Stock Exchange. The Caparo companies
gave instructions in January to the brokers to commence purchase
of shares of DCGM. Similarly, the Caparo companies started
buying the shares of Escorts around February. Paul had begun his
attempted takeover of the companies even before RBI permission
had been formally obtained.

The promoters of DCGM and Escorts would initially have
been unaware of this attempted takeover. It was only when the
share prices of the two companies started surging that there was
some concern. The prices of DCGM shares surged from about
Rs 35 at the end of January to almost Rs 80 by the end of April, a
rise of 130 per cent. The case was similar in the case of Escorts,
whose share prices rose from about Rs 40 to Rs 70 in the same
period, a rise of about 75 per cent.[10]

The two industrialists were probably surprised at this abrupt
and unusual rise in their share prices. They made inquiries about
this sharp rise, only to discover that Swaraj Paul had begun buying
large chunks of their companies' shares. Not ones to simply cede
control over their companies, the promoters began to push back,
by taking recourse to both political as well as legal avenues.

The first few rounds seemed to have gone the way of the
Indian promoters. Under the Companies Act, 1956, the board

of directors of any company had the power to refuse to register shares. When Swaraj Paul asked for his shares to be registered, the two companies called for board meetings. At the meetings, the boards claimed that the shares had been bought in contravention of Indian laws and that there were serious irregularities involved in their purchase. The boards accordingly refused to register the shares. The nominee directors of the financial institutions either abstained in the vote or did not attend the meeting. Clearly, this could not have been done without at least some tacit support from the institutions.

Even the government appeared to initially support Indian industry. A group of industrialists went and met the finance minister and asked him to intercede in the ongoing battle. Captains of industry, including J.R.D. Tata, had a meeting with Pranab Mukherjee in April 1983 shortly whereafter even Rajiv Gandhi made a statement in favour of Indian industry,[11] saying that NRIs should be prevented from actions that might destabilize well-run Indian industries.

The appeal appears to have had an effect. The government stepped in and sought to limit the amount of shareholding Swaraj Paul could buy. On 16 May, RBI issued a fresh circular.[12] The effect of this circular was to put a cap on the total shareholding that could be acquired through the portfolio investment scheme at 5 per cent of the total paid-up equity capital of the company. Paul could not acquire more shares of the company to overtake the shareholding of the promoters. The only question was whether he had already managed to purchase sufficient shares in the companies to make the ban moot.

While this round seemed to have gone the way of the industrial houses, the next victory would be that of Swaraj Paul. Sensing that things were not going his way, Paul made a visit to India in July where he addressed large crowds of the then social influencers—stockbrokers, investors, journalists and members of

Parliament. His argument was persuasive as it was based on sound economic policy. He pointed out that by refusing to transfer the shares in his name, the owners of large companies had created a virtual fiefdom for themselves. The reins of management passed down from generation to generation even though the owners had virtually no stock holding themselves. He also accused the managements of using public sector funds to bolster their own positions.[13]

This push by Paul, coupled with backroom lobbying, had its desired effect. The presidents of the four major stock exchanges wrote to the finance ministry, seeking its intervention to ensure the registration of shares in Paul's favour. Even in the government, the winds were shifting in favour of Paul. Stung by the accusations that they had been siding with Indian companies, the public financial institutions decided to change course. They requisitioned a meeting with the express aim of removing the non-executive directors of the companies. Since they held over 50 per cent of the shares of the company, the institutions would have been able to replace nine of the total of fifteen on the board of directors with their own nominees. The reconstituted board would then, presumably, proceed to register the shares of Swaraj Paul and potentially hand over the management of the companies to him.[14]

III

The Judgment

Faced with an imminent boardroom coup by the financial institutions, H.P. Nanda and his company filed a writ petition before the Bombay High Court.[15] The matter was argued at length and ultimately a thumping judgment in favour of the Nandas was delivered by the Bombay High Court. The high court held[16] that RBI permission was to be mandatorily taken prior to any purchase of shares. Since that had not been done in this case, the purchase of shares by Swaraj Paul was void. Even more stinging was the Courts' rebuke to LIC. The Court ruled that their attempt to hold the meeting and to replace a majority of the directors amounted to a virtual takeover of the company. This, the Court held, was not permissible for LIC. It could only attempt a change of management if its investment was in any way threatened and for no other reason. It was stated that a 'statutory corporation such as the LIC cannot be permitted to take any step for taking over the management of another company like the petitioner-company'. This was not the only decision regarding the rights of LIC. The Court also went on to hold that when it requisitioned a meeting, it was required to give reasons and those reasons were subject to judicial review.

In effect, the Court held that even though LIC was an investor, its hands were tied and that it could not act like any normal investor. Each of its actions could be examined by the Court on the touchstone of Article 14. In other words, LIC was required to act in a non-arbitrary and rational manner. In effect, this would give the Courts the ultimate veto power on LIC's business decisions!

However, even before the Nandas could begin to savour the taste of victory, LIC swung into action. The judgment of the Court was delivered on a Friday. It appears that the lawyers of Escorts apprehended that LIC may file an appeal before the Supreme Court and pursued their own legal strategy. They approached the Supreme Court on Monday to file a caveat, which would have ensured that no appeal could be filed without prior notice to them. However, they were to be surprised when they learnt that LIC had beat them to it and had already filed a voluminous appeal before they had even filed the caveat.[17]

The matter was eventually heard by a bench of five judges of the Supreme Court, given the importance of the various issues at stake. The unanimous verdict of the Supreme Court was delivered in December 1985. The judgment allowed LIC's appeal and set aside the verdict of the Bombay High Court. It was a massive win for the government, though whether this was also a win for Swaraj Paul was a slightly more complicated question, as we shall see later in the chapter.

IV

Foreign Exchange and the Role of RBI

One of the principal questions that arose in the case was the role of RBI. In particular, the question was whether any prior permission was required from RBI before a foreign investor could purchase the shares of an Indian company.

The stance of RBI had been, to say the least, equivocal. When Punjab National Bank (PNB) first wrote to RBI seeking approval of purchase of shares, RBI had appeared to take a stand contrary to that of Swaraj Paul. The view within RBI was that the scheme did not permit companies that were only indirectly owned by NRIs or persons of Indian origin (PIOs) to invest in shares of Indian companies. It wrote to the government seeking approval of this position. The government, however, was not so keen to oblige.

This disagreement may also have had to do something with the personnel who were in charge of the decision-making within RBI and the government: Manmohan Singh, the then RBI governor, and Pranab Mukherjee, the finance minister. As noted by Manmohan Singh, there was a disagreement between himself and Pranab Mukherjee. He is quoted as having said, 'Sometimes there was tension. For instance, there was that famous case of Swaraj Paul's investments.'[18] Pranab Mukherjee acknowledged this but said that the disagreement was never personal. He said, 'At times, the Government takes decisions based on considerations which may not be available or evident to RBI. If the Government announces a scheme and obtains the approval of Parliament, it is only natural that it tried every means possible, within the law, to ensure its success.'[19]

It appears that while RBI was going strictly by the letter of the law, the government was keener to take a softer stance as its intention was to shore up foreign exchange reserves. Therefore, the government took the position, which was eventually backed up by an opinion obtained from the attorney general, that indirect holding of shares was permitted. RBI, being subservient to the government, had no choice but to comply. In September 1983, RBI gave ex-post facto approval to the Swaraj Paul companies for the purchase of shares.

The high court had held that RBI could not give post facto permission, and that any permission had to be taken prior to the purchase of the shares. The Supreme Court reversed this finding and held that RBI could, under the terms of Section 29 of FERA, also give subsequent permission.[20] The Court held that RBI had been given the flexibility to determine whether to give permission to purchase the shares. There was no explicit or implicit restriction in giving this permission subsequent to the actual event, i.e., after the shares were purchased. In case RBI gave such permission, it would relate back to the date of the application.

In effect, the Court held that the purchase by Swaraj Paul had been legal and not in violation of FERA. This finding effectively was sufficient to remove the underlying basis for Escorts to refuse to register the shares. However, Escorts had a large number of legal arguments up its sleeve, defended as it was by the very able Fali S. Nariman.

V

Piercing the Veil

The main plank, at least initially, of both Escorts and RBI had been that the thirteen companies purchasing the shares were all held ultimately by Swaraj Paul and his family. In effect, it was alleged, one person was buying more than the permitted 1 per cent per person limit that the scheme had imposed. The structuring of the companies was merely a stratagem designed to defeat this limit. At the heart of this argument was an exception to one of the fundamental tenets of company law.

The law had always recognized a company as a juristic entity separate from its shareholders. This had originally been a device that had been developed to ensure that liability did not fall personally on the shareholders of the company in case the company went bankrupt or incurred losses. The losses of the company would be that of the company alone and not that of the shareholder. The liability of the shareholder would be limited to the extent of her value of her shareholding in the company. There was a straightforward economic reason to develop this theory—to ensure that shareholders were encouraged to invest in potentially risky businesses without the fear of having their entire assets taken over in case of losses.

Of course, this was a legal fiction, as in reality there were shareholders who were behind the company. In certain instances, the law allowed the Court to peek behind the veil of the corporate entity to determine who the actual owners (i.e., the shareholders) were. However, this exception had to be exercised rarely since its overuse would render the distinct corporate identity of the company meaningless. Escorts argued that the case required the Court to 'lift the corporate veil'[21] because the use of the companies to purchase the shares was only a device meant to circumvent the law. This, it was argued, ought not to be permitted.

The Court rejected this request holding that the scheme itself permitted the piercing of the veil to determine the nationality of the shareholders, but not their identity. Some broad parameters for piercing of the veil were given, which included whether the scheme or the statute itself permitted the lifting of the veil, or where 'fraud or improper conduct is intended to be prevented, or a taxing statute or a beneficent statute is sought to be evaded or where associated companies are inextricably connected as to be part of one concern'.[22]

Once the scheme permitted the lifting for a limited purpose, it had to be restricted to that purpose and no other. In other words, under the scheme, the lifting of the veil was permissible to the extent of determining the origin or nationality of the shareholders, but not their identity. The Court felt that it would be an impermissible exercise of judicial power to lift the veil to determine the identity when the Executive itself had not thought it fit to do so in the scheme itself.

The fundamental principle the Court upheld was that the company was distinct from its shareholders. This, of course, begged the question as to what the role and the rights of the shareholder were. This issue also directly arose in the case since it was the rights of LIC as a shareholder that had been whittled down by the high court.

VI

Shareholder Democracy

One of the most important reasons why LIC had filed an appeal was because its attempt to call for a meeting to replace the directors on the board of Escorts had been rebuffed. The high court had held that LIC, being a statutory corporation, was not entitled to requisition meetings without giving reasons. Further, the Court had held that LIC could not use its voting power to take over the management of the company. The effect of this, of course, was to virtually entrench the existing management of the company. Two separate classes of shareholders were created—the promoters on the one hand, and the public financial institutions on the other. This, the Supreme Court held, was an anathema to the very concept of shareholding as well as to the idea of a shareholder democracy.

Shares in a company and the nature of a shareholder's interest in the company and its assets had been the subject matter of several judgments. Indeed, even the Escorts judgment held that the company was distinct from its shareholders. Earlier judgments had also held that the shareholder had no direct interest in the assets of the company.[23] What, however, was the exact nature of the rights of a shareholder? After a comprehensive examination of the law, the Court laid down certain principles of shareholding which hold good till date.

The Court ruled that a 'share is movable property, with all the attributes of such property. The rights of a shareholder are (i) to elect directors and thus to participate in the management through them; (ii) to vote on resolutions at meetings of the company; (iii) to enjoy the profits of the company in the shape of dividends; (iv) to apply to the court for relief in the case of oppression; (v) to apply to the court for relief in the case of mismanagement; (vi) to apply to the court for winding up of the company; (vii) to share in the surplus on winding up'.[24]

These rights of the shareholder were recognized by statute, i.e., the Companies Act, 1956. They were also recognized under the common law—i.e., the system of precedents and judgments that predated the Companies Act.

After holding that the shareholder had a right to vote on a resolution of a company and to elect its directors, it was clear that the judgment of the High Court was erroneous. LIC, even though it was a statutory corporation, was first and foremost a shareholder in Escorts and had all the rights a shareholder normally has. Under the law, the only way a shareholder could direct the management of the company was through the appointment of a director. Therefore, if the majority shareholders wished to call for a meeting and proceed to appoint their nominee directors, this was their right under the Companies Act and no Court could injunct the exercise of this right.

Thus, the appeal of LIC and RBI was allowed by all five judges of the Court in a single judgment authored by one of the most learned and erudite judges of the Supreme Court— Justice O. Chinnappa Reddy. The judgment held in favour of the government on virtually every point that had been raised in the case. But that would not be enough to hand over the victory to Swaraj Paul. There was, so to say, a sting in the tail of the judgment.

VII

Sting in the Tail

A most curious feature of the judgment was that Swaraj Paul, the dramatis personae of the case, did not appear before any Indian court during this battle. His entire case was fought, as if by proxy, by LIC, RBI and the Government of India. This led the Court to conclude that it was apparent 'from the beginning that if there was much front-line battle strategy, there was considerably more backstage "diplomatic" manoeuvring, as may be expected when financial giants clash, though we are afraid neither giant was greatly concerned for justice or the public interest. For both of them the courtroom was just another arena for their war, except that one of the giants carefully kept himself at the back behind a screen. One was reminded of the Mahabharata war where Arjuna kept Shikhandi in front of him while fighting Bhishma, not that either of the warriors in this case can be compared with Bhishma or Arjuna nor can the Government of India and Reserve Bank of India be downgraded as Shikhandis.'[25]

Clearly, the conduct of Swaraj Paul had not appealed to the judges. Indeed, even though the judgment was in favour of the government on questions of law, the Court clearly thought

Swaraj Paul to be a most unsavoury character, and recorded in its judgment that 'Mr Swaraj Paul was also reported to have said that the Governor of the Reserve Bank (Dr Manmohan Singh, a highly respected civil servant of our country) was applying double standards and was feeding wrong information to the Union Finance Minister. If the reported statement is correct, we can only characterise it as saucy, rude and impudent coming as it does from a foreign national seeking the permission of the Reserve Bank to invest in shares of Indian companies. Perhaps those are the ways of the markets in which he operates. People afflicted with double vision are ready to see double standards in others. We appreciate neither his conduct nor his statements.'[26]

This disdain for Swaraj Paul was coupled with consternation at the actions of PNB. The Court held that PNB had not been diligent in its role as an authorized dealer under the provisions of FERA, 1973 and directed RBI to conduct an inquiry into its conduct. Perhaps it was for this reason that even though the judgment was in favour of LIC and the government, Swaraj Paul did not get the immediate benefit of it. Noticing certain irregularities in relation to the purchase of shares, the Court directed RBI to conduct a fresh inquiry into the purchase of shares and accord fresh approval if necessary. This inquiry was to be conducted in a period of three months.

RBI duly conducted this inquiry and gave Swaraj Paul a clean chit. However, this lapse of time had given the promoters of the companies enough time to marshal their defences and they slowly increased their shareholding in their companies. More importantly, they had also been able to do backroom negotiations with the powers that be. Virtually pushed by the government, Swaraj Paul agreed to sell his shares to the nominees of the Indian promoters. It is reported that Paul got 15 per cent interest on the value of his investment, but some of that profit was set off because of the fall in the value of the Indian rupee as well as capital gains.[27] All in all, Swaraj Paul walked out of the field without having gained or lost any money.

The promoters of the companies managed to hold on to their companies. However, the rot in the system that had been exposed by the Swaraj Paul affair in part contributed to the downfall of these companies. DCGM, once a giant conglomerate, suffered multiple bouts of infighting between its promoters and is now merely a rump of the giant it once was. Escorts also teetered on the brink of virtual bankruptcy before stabilizing its position somewhat more recently.[28] It is still a much smaller concern than other businesses of its time.[29]

Conclusion

The Swaraj Paul affair was not the first takeover attempt of an Indian company nor was it the last. However, it exposed the vulnerabilities of the Indian corporate set-up at the time. The licence-permit raj regime had ossified Indian business. Companies were incapable of being nimble to face any form of challenge to their mode of doing business. As Swaraj Paul has been famously quoted as saying, 'I never imagined that a mere 13 crores could shake up the whole of India's industry.'[30] Indian business did ultimately reform itself, forced as it was by the liberalization of the nineties.

Nevertheless, it was not merely the psychological impact that the Swaraj Paul affair had on Indian industry that makes the case noteworthy. The verdict was pathbreaking in the effect it had on the development of company law. The judgment read like a charter of rights for the shareholder, cementing her position in the governance of the company. More importantly, it laid down the contours of the law relating to the corporate personality, i.e., the instances when the Court permitted itself to look at the shareholders who owned the shares of the company. The judgment held that this 'piercing' could happen only in exceptional circumstances and thus set the precedent for many other cases, including the Vodafone case about which we shall read more in the chapter relating to that case.

Notes

[1] Often the value of a company as a going concern is less than the worth of the individual assets owned by it. In such circumstances, a hostile takeover may happen where the acquirer has no interest in running the company. The company is bought only for it to be would up and individual assets sold, resulting in a cessation of its business and the laying off of all the workmen. The plot of the Hollywood film *Pretty Woman* comes to mind.

[2] AIR 1986 SC 1370.

[3] 'Has Finance Minister Ramaswami Venkataraman Bungled the IMF Loan?', *India Today*, 31 October 1981.

[4] 'IMF Grants India Its Largest Ever Loan of Rs. 5000 Crores, Sets off Heated Debate', *India Today*, 15 December 1981.

[5] Pranab Mukherjee. *The Turbulent Years 1980–1996* (Rupa Publications India, 2016).

[6] Government of India (1994), Report of the Committee on Reforms in the Insurance Sector (Malhotra Report), Ministry of Finance, New Delhi.

[7] Budget speech of 1982–83, para 27.

[8] 'Indian Industries Face Takeover Scare by NRI Investors', *India Today*, 15 May 1983.

[9] Caparo was a private limited company owned by Swaraj Paul and his family members and was incorporated in the UK. Twelve companies were fully owned by the Caparo Group Ltd and the thirteenth company was 98 per cent owned by Caparo.

[10] 'Indian Industries Face Takeover Scare by NRI Investors', *India Today*.

[11] Mukherjee. *The Turbulent Years*.

[12] Para 31 of the LIC judgement.

[13] 'Swaraj Paul Carries His Battle for Control of DCM and Escorts into the Enemy Camp', *India Today*, 31 August 1983.

[14] 'LIC Plans to Sack Majority of Escorts Directors, Replace Them with its Own Nominees', *India Today*, 15 March 1984.

[15] The petition had been filed in the high court earlier challenging, among others, certain circulars issued by RBI. However, when LIC requisitioned

the meeting on 13 February 1984, the petition was amended to challenge this meeting as well.

[16] *Escorts Ltd And Another v. Union Of India* 1985 57 CompCas 241 Bom.

[17] 'Bombay High Court Declares Swaraj Paul's Investment in Escorts Illegal, LIC's Role Unconstitutional', *India Today*, 15 December 1984.

[18] Daman Singh. *Strictly Personal: Manmohan and Gursharan* (HarperCollins India, 2014).

[19] Mukherjee, *The Turbulent Years*, p. 56.

[20] Para 70, LIC judgment.

[21] Lifting the corporate veil is a legal tool employed by the Courts to enable them to examine who the shareholders of the company are. The 'veil' or the legal fiction of the distinct corporate identity of the company is cast aside and the Court proceeds to focus its attention on the shareholders of the company. See *DDA v. Skipper* (1996) 4 SCC 622.

[22] Para 90 of the judgment.

[23] *Bacha F. Guzdar v. Commissioner of Income-Tax* AIR 1955 SC 740.

[24] Para 84 of the judgment.

[25] Para 3 of the judgment.

[26] Para 57 of the judgment.

[27] 'London-based Corporate Raider Swraj Paul Finally Agrees to Sell His Shares in Escorts, DCM', *India Today*, 30 June 1986.

[28] Sharad Gupta. *Back from the Brink: Turning Escorts Around* (Harper Business, 2020).

[29] H.P. Nanda was one of just two first-generation entrepreneurs—the other being Dhirubhai Ambani—to be counted among the country's business elite. See 'The Escorts Story: Can It Be Saved', Rediff.com, 15 September 2005.

[30] 'Swaraj Paul Carries His Battle for Control of DCM and Escorts into the Enemy Camp', *India Today*, 31 August 1983.

Chapter 6

Government Tenders and State Largesse

Tenders in India have become ubiquitous. One only has to open the pages of a daily newspaper to see just how prevalent tenders have become since this is the method through which most government procurement happens. The purpose behind the tendering process is presumably to bring transparency into the system. It is believed that an open system of tendering, where different bidders make a bid, will automatically root out any form of corruption or arbitrariness.[1] Unfortunately, this faith is often misplaced. The process is often subverted by officials, either through the rigging of eligibility conditions or other manipulations. In such a case, the losing bidder has no option but to move the Court seeking redressal. However, the Court has taken a view that it should have a 'hands-off' approach in such cases. In the famous case of Tata Cellular,[2] the Court ruled that in matters relating to tenders, the Court would exercise only a minimal form of judicial oversight. It decided that public authorities would have full freedom to determine the terms and conditions of the tender and that the Court would only supervise the 'tendering process'.

The net result of this judicial reticence is that rather than being a means for bringing transparency into the system, the tendering process has become a virtual 'black box'. The Court, if it satisfies itself that the procurement process has been made through

86

tendering, does not examine any other potential arbitrariness. This self-imposed limitation by the Court has been detrimental to the cause of transparency. Given that public procurement is such an important part of commerce engaged in the country, the judgment has had a dramatic impact on the relationship between private entities and public agencies.

Since the Court has been unwilling to call government agencies to account, some other systems that can check potential abuses have to be urgently put in place. That, however, appears to be a distant dream since virtually no government is ever keen to put any regulatory control over its own dealing. The net result is that one of the largest sectors in the country with the greatest potential for corruption has been virtually excluded from any form of scrutiny. This chapter examines just how this anomalous judgment came to be passed and what its lasting consequences have been.

I

Telecom Policy and the Initial Bidding Process

The early nineties saw the shift from landline telephones to the emerging new technology of wireless telephony. The Government of India also sought to bring this nascent technology into India and floated a tender for the provision of cellular services. In this tendering process, thirty Indian companies submitted their bids, which were all opened on 30 March 1992. Normally, the bids ought to have been evaluated and awarded to the lowest bidder. However, it appears that the tender documents did not clearly specify the process of how the tenders would be adjudged. Thus began a labyrinthine procedure of bid evaluation. A short summary of the process is necessary only to see how often changes were made while the process was being conducted, with the tacit understanding that each change could be the result of bureaucratic or political manipulations.

The bid was a two-stage process, comprising evaluation of tenders on technical criteria and thereafter on financial criteria. As regards the technical criteria, the bids were initially sent to a Tender Evaluation Committee (the TEC). The TEC, after some tweaking of the tender conditions,[3] shortlisted twelve companies. This shortlist was approved by the Telecom Commission and referred to a so-called 'Selection Committee' headed by the Minister.[4] This committee shortlisted fourteen different bidders, though why the recommendations of the TEC were given a go-by is not exactly clear.

In the second stage, the fourteen shortlisted companies then submitted financial bids. These bids were examined by another TEC who then made certain recommendations. However, the government changed the financial criteria and referred the matter back to the second TEC. This TEC then took another look at the bids as per the revised criteria and made fresh recommendations. As in the case of the technical bid, the matter ought to have been referred to the Selection Committee. This, it appears, was not done and the minister proceeded to finalize the bids at the level of the government itself. In the end, two bidders were selected for the provision of cellular services in the four metro cities—Delhi, Bombay, Calcutta and Chennai.

Some bidders who had been excluded through this process challenged the finalization of the bids before the Delhi High Court. In a lengthy and elaborate decision, the high court upheld the tendering process, holding that Courts did not have the requisite knowledge to examine decisions taken by experts in the field. A disturbing statement of the law was also made. The high court[5] held that:

'The process of selection and the considerations taken into account at the stage of final selection cannot be pre-determined and it was neither necessary nor possible to pre-determine the exact method of comparative evaluation, or to disclose the same to the bidders in advance . . . In a case like this also there could not be any declared policy as to how different bids were to be evaluated.'

This finding effectively meant that in case of complex tenders, the authorities could proceed to evolve different criteria during the process of evaluation. Needless to state, this would seriously undermine the fairness in the process. After all, it was necessary for bidders to know which criteria would be relevant before they prepared their bids. This also left open the possibility of manipulation of the criteria. Given the insidious nature of corruption, it was also possible that these hidden criteria would remain hidden. This is because even a biased decision could be justified on some technical grounds and thereafter shielded from examination by giving it the cloak of 'complexity'.

Eventually, the high court dismissed virtually all challenges to the tendering process. Given the stakes involved, it is not surprising that the matter was then appealed before the Supreme Court.

II

The Supreme Court Judgment

The appellants, led by a Tata group company, moved the Supreme Court asking it to interfere in the tendering process. It was argued that in matters of government procurement, where there was little other scrutiny, the Courts ought to step in to make sure that the entire procedure was fair and transparent. The appellants pointed to the arbitrariness of the tendering process and asked the Court to intervene.

The only way it was possible for the Supreme Court to have interfered in the tender was if it took an expansive view of its jurisdiction. Given the evolving jurisprudence of the Court, it was quite possible for the Court to have flexed its judicial muscle and demand greater accountability in the tendering process. After all, in the decade or so before this case, the Court had expanded the boundaries of judicial review of administrative action in matters of both procedure and substance.

The field of administrative law in India, where the Courts scrutinize actions of the government, had so far developed very differently from Britain and other common law countries. Those countries had much older legal systems that were more concerned with procedure than substance. They had archaic rules that limited judicial intervention, depending on the form of petition that had been filed in court.[6] Similarly, the rules of natural justice, like hearing a person before taking a decision that affected them, were dependent upon whether the Executive action taken was deemed to be 'administrative' or 'quasi-judicial'. The difference between the two forms of Executive action was hardly apparent, even to the most legally trained mind. Similarly, the rule of *locus standi* (or standing), which permitted only persons who had a personal interest in any matter to approach the Court, was very strictly applied.

Most importantly, the foreign Courts gave great deference to the decisions of the government and interfered only when the decision was arbitrary to the extreme, i.e., when the Executive took a decision that no reasonable person in their right mind could ever have taken. The juristic foundation of this was the so-called ultra vires principle. This was a legal fiction as per which it would be presumed that Parliament could never have intended for the Executive to act in such an unreasonable manner. Therefore, so went the theory, when the Executive acted unreasonably, it went against the will of Parliament. Thus the Courts had the duty as well as the jurisdiction to intervene and set aside such action.

The Indian Courts, on the other hand, had taken a completely different trajectory. Relying on the provisions under the Indian Constitution, they adopted a far more expansive role for themselves. The rules of standing had virtually withered away with the advent of public interest litigation. The technicalities of the procedure had also been abandoned, almost with the commencement of the Constitution.

However, the greatest jurisprudential move was to shift the basis of administrative law from the ultra vires principle to the demands of Article 14 of the Constitution. In a landmark case,[7] the Supreme Court noted, rather poetically, that 'Equality is a dynamic concept with many aspects and dimensions and it cannot be "cribbed, cabined and confined" within traditional and doctrinaire limits. From a positivistic point of view, equality is antithetic to arbitrariness. In fact, equality and arbitrariness are sworn enemies; one belongs to the rule of law in a republic while the other, to the whim and caprice of an absolute monarch. Where an act is arbitrary, it is implicit in it that it is unequal both according to political logic and constitutional law and is therefore violative of Article 14.'

Effectively what the Court said was that whenever the State acted arbitrarily, it implied that it acted unreasonably, i.e., without any valid reason or justification. The essence of equality was that all State action must treat all people equally. The only time when a set of people (or even one person) could be treated differently was when there was a valid justification to do so. To put it in almost mathematical terms, arbitrariness implied unreasonableness, which implied inequality. Since the Constitution forbade inequality, it followed that the Constitution also forbade arbitrariness.[8]

Using this newly forged constitutional tool, the Court proceeded to put a range of government action under its lens. The Court held that even in areas of contract, the State could not act as though it were a private entity. It had to abide by the rules of reasonableness that would be strictly enforced by the Court. Thus, a government could not fire its lawyers without reason[9] or evict a person from its premises without good reason.[10]

The Court also forayed into the area of government procurement contracts. In a series of judgments, the Court established that the government could not enter a contract with whomsoever it wanted.[11] There had to be a reasonable procedure to select the contractor and the decision could not be left to the unbridled discretion of the government.

Given this background, it was hoped that the Court would forge a new path demanding greater accountability and transparency. These hopes, however, were dashed when the judgment was pronounced. The Supreme Court essentially upheld the judgment of the high court. More importantly, the Court also indicated that henceforth any examination of tenders would be extremely limited. In a famous passage,[12] the Court decided that:

(1) The modern trend points to judicial restraint in administrative action.

(2) The court does not sit as a court of appeal but merely reviews the manner in which the decision was made.

(3) The court does not have the expertise to correct the administrative decision. If a review of the administrative decision is permitted, it will be substituting its own decision, without the necessary expertise, which itself may be fallible.

(4) The terms of *the invitation to tender* cannot be open to judicial scrutiny because the invitation to tender is in the realm of contract. Normally speaking, the decision to accept the tender or award the contract is reached by the process of negotiations through several tiers. More often than not, such decisions are made qualitatively by experts.

(5) The government must have freedom of contract. In other words, a fair play in the joints is a necessary concomitant for an administrative body functioning in an administrative sphere or quasi-administrative sphere. However, the decision must not only be tested by the application of the Wednesbury

principle of reasonableness (including its other facts pointed out above) but must be free from arbitrariness not affected by bias or actuated by mala fides.

(6) Quashing decisions may impose heavy administrative burden on the administration and lead to increased and unbudgeted expenditure.

The judgment read like a textbook of foreign case law. Virtually all the cases cited were of British or American provenance.[13] The Indian cases were referred to almost as afterthoughts. In fact, most of the cases mentioned earlier in this chapter were not even cited. In doing so, the crucial differences between India and the other countries were papered over. Ours is a country with a robust constitutional framework and a rather bloated public sector. This is not the case in Britain and the US. Ignoring these differences, the Court allowed a virtual free pass to the government and in the process, effectively froze future development of the law on tenders in India.

The Court gave two reasons as to why it would give the government almost a free run in matters relating to tenders. First, the Court felt that the government was entitled to conduct its business affairs freely, without being overly controlled by any outside authority such as the Court. Secondly, the Court felt that it had limited expertise to be able to supervise complex tendering processes. These were, so to say, reasons relating to confidence and competence, i.e., confidence in the government's ability to manage its own affairs and a belief in the Court's own lack of competence.

Both these justifications need to be examined in much greater detail than the Court did. Is it really true that the government is free to act like any other commercial entity? Is it really the case that the Court does not have the necessary competence to examine the terms of a tender?

III

Is the Government Entitled to a Free Play in the Joints?

The Court said that they would only examine the decision-making process and not the merits of the actual decision itself. This was, ostensibly, because the government deserved a 'free play in the joints'. As per the Court, the government had special expertise in matters of economic policy and thus had to be allowed to exercise its own discretion in matters relating to contracts that it entered into.

But this judicial hands-off approach overestimates the competence of government in the contractual field. It is correct that the government is answerable to the people and the ultimate check on a failed economic policy is through the conduct of regular elections. Courts should keep their hands off in matters of economic policy since they do not have the necessary democratic input and legitimacy.[14] However, when the government enters the field of contract, and that too in areas relating to matters that might otherwise be served by the private sector, this no longer holds.

The Indian experience has shown that high hopes and greater investment do not lead to better outcomes, both in the public[15] as well as the private sphere. If we were to keep aside the social justifications for a public sector, it can confidently be said that the public sector has been a laggard in economic growth. There are multiple reasons for this, but one of the most important causes is that the personnel put in charge of the management of the PSUs are often bureaucrats rather than managerial experts. If that is the case, it is difficult to accord much deference to the so-called expertise of the government. There is no basis in principle or in law to accord the same sanctity to the decision of the same bureaucrat when she is exercising jurisdiction over a purely administrative act or deciding the terms of a tender. To equate economic policy with efficiency in running a business is an error. As C. Rajagopalachari said,[16] 'When the State trespasses beyond what is legitimately within its province, it just hands over the management from those who are interested in frugal and efficient management to bureaucracy, which is untrained and uninterested except in its own survival.'

Therefore, it is somewhat hard to understand why any special deference is shown to the government when it acts in the private sphere. Virtually all the committees in the *Tata Cellular* case were manned by bureaucrats. As the high court itself noted, the ultimate decision was that of the central government and even the so-called Selection Committee only had a recommendatory role. If that be the case, it is difficult to accept any alleged expertise on the part of the government and accord it any extra degree of deference.

Even assuming that the government has some special expertise, it cannot be forgotten that the matters ultimately relate to public funds. As the Court noted in *Tata Cellular*: 'Government is guardian of finance of the State. It is expected to protect the financial interest of the State.' In fact, when the government deals with public money it acts as a trustee of public funds.[17] As a trustee, the Executive is expected to act in the utmost good faith— i.e., with greater than normal caution.[18] This greater responsibility surely cannot be without greater scrutiny. The Courts must, as in the case of any other trust, ensure that the trustees act for the benefit of the beneficiaries, i.e., the people of India. In the dispute between the comparative competence of government and the Court, it appears that the Court forgot to examine the impact its decision would have on the general populace.

IV

Does the Court Lack Competence to Decide Issues Relating to Tenders?

The other reason offered by the Court to exercise a limited review of the tendering system was its own limited expertise in fiscal matters. Yet, even this claim may not fully hold up to scrutiny.

Judges are trained in the law, but they are routinely asked to compare opinions of different experts. This is part of the judicial process and is engrafted statutorily in the Indian Evidence Act, 1872. While judges may not be experts themselves, they certainly have the training to be able to determine whether the decision of an expert is correct or not. It is also interesting to see that the claimed lack of expertise is in contractual matters. This is completely counter-intuitive. After all, judges are more accustomed to deciding matters relating to commercial issues and almost any other matter.

In fact, the same Court that claims that it does not have competence to interfere in matters of commerce routinely passes judgments and orders in a host of matters where it does not have traditional competence. This is not a bad thing. It is necessary for the Court to oversee the decisions of so-called experts when public health, the environment or public finances are concerned. Courts are the ultimate guardians of fundamental rights. If the government acts arbitrarily in any manner, it is no defence to say that the Court should let that constitutional infraction be, since it lacks the requisite expertise. It ought not to be necessary for arbitrariness to rise to the level of absurdity before the Court intervenes. After all, our constitutional rights are not meant to be infringed—until the point that the Court can no longer sit as a mute spectator!

While arguing for a more robust intervention by the Court, one must add a caveat. The court system itself is notoriously slow. Further, quashing the tendering process also leads to administrative delay, which might result in increasing the costs of a project. Therefore, it might be necessary to have a mechanism to ensure that frivolous challenges to tenders are weeded out. Also, matters of such public interest must be accorded greater priority than other regular commercial matters. This requires a rethink, and a possible rehaul of the way the legal system functions. Investment in the legal system may be necessary to ensure an expeditious disposal not only of matters relating to tenders and public finance, but also a whole host of other areas where substantial public interest is involved.

V

Impact of the Judgment on Public Procurement in India

The Court has said that it would not examine the merits of the decision, but only examine the 'decision-making process.' In particular, it has said that the terms of the tender will not be examined by it unless they are so clearly 'tailor-made' so as to suit only one party to the exclusion of all others. Presumably, what the Court means is that they will not examine what the rules of the game are; they will only ensure that the rules are fairly applied to all the players.

This lack of scrutiny of the terms and conditions of the tender have had a direct impact on the economy. It is said that public procurement constitutes almost one-fourth of India's GDP.[19] Hence, hindrance in competing for the 'public procurement pie' would directly affect the growth of companies and also have a direct effect on the competition. Companies that are unreasonably excluded would not be able to grow, given the size of the government sector. As a corollary, the government would have fewer bidders competing for projects.

The question thus arises as to how these hindrances are put in place in a system that is supposed to be facially neutral. The most common method is through the drafting of the eligibility conditions. These are criteria that any bidder must fulfil before they are allowed to even put in an offer. For instance, there may be a requirement for the bidder to have a certain annual turnover or a specified net worth, or for it to have performed similar works in the past three to five years. The stated purpose behind these conditions is to weed out firms that may not have the necessary expertise to be able to perform the contract if it is awarded to them. Since these eligibility conditions form part of what the Court considers the 'terms of the tender', they are not subject to any meaningful judicial scrutiny.

In an interesting study, it has been found that these terms have created such high entry barriers that small and medium-sized firms are often unable to meet these eligibility criteria.[20] These criteria include the requirement of a bid security or earnest money deposit that is unreasonably high or a turnover requirement that has no relation to the size of the project at hand. Effectively, micro, small and medium enterprises (MSMEs) and small-scale firms are excluded from the larger tenders, which in turn ends up creating virtual monopolies.

The same study also noted another area where there was scope for manipulation. All tenders give a window of time from when they are advertised to when the bid is supposed to be submitted. This period is intended to give the bidders the time to prepare the bid papers. The longer the period, the more time the bidders would have to prepare the bid. As a corollary, if the period provided is very short, a large number of bidders may not have the time or the resources to prepare the bid. The study noted that in cases of large contracts, providing for a very short window within which to make the bid also 'favour[ed] a few large firms that have already had experience in preparing numerous applications and possibly in discussing upcoming projects with government officials. Small firms with few resources cannot manage tender documentation because they cannot afford to have a dedicated team preparing bids all year round.' As the period within which a bid is to be made is also a term of the contract, the same is exempt from judicial scrutiny.

The net result of the manipulation of these terms is that certain large companies get entrenched and form virtual monopolies, or at least some form of oligarchies. This comes at a great cost to the public exchequer. Further, the big monopolistic contractors have to endure certain costs to 'pay' for their monopolies. This could either be legal (i.e., keeping a large workforce ready to bid for tenders as and when they are announced) or not (corruption or payments to secure access to the powers that be). Either way, these costs are passed on to the government and eventually the people. These costs are incurred only because the terms of the tenders are virtually sacrosanct. This unusual abdication of judicial responsibility has built up a culture of impunity whose ultimate losers are the citizens of the country.

Conclusion

Since the government is such a large purchaser of goods and services, it is surprising that there is no formal legislation in place regulating public procurement. In the absence of any meaningful judicial oversight of the procurement process, there is a crying need for legislation, or at the very least, a set of rules applicable to government procurement. Unfortunately, there is no such law, at least at the central level. Each department of the government develops its own methodology without reference to any standardized system. A Public Procurement Bill had been cleared by the Lok Sabha in 2012, but was never passed by the Rajya Sabha and it hence lapsed. In this case it is the states that have taken the lead. Many have passed laws dealing with public procurement[21] but these are not as comprehensive as the Public Procurement Bill would have been. Perhaps, one alternative could have been to adopt the UNCITRAL[22] model law on public procurement, which provides a challenge procedure not only to the tendering process, but also to the terms and conditions of the tender.[23]

Of course, laws alone cannot be sufficient in controlling corruption in the procurement process.[24] In a detailed survey conducted under the aegis of the United Nations Office on Drugs and Crime, various officials gave a host of methods through which even the most regulated process could be subverted.[25] The report gave some instances of this:

> 'Objective laws being interpreted subjectively in practice; inconsistencies in vocabulary and lack of standardization of key definitions and terms; winners identified before procurement process; subversion of procedures under the excuse of "suitable bidders not available"; partiality and laxity in establishing specifications to suit specific bidders; bribing, collusion, cartel formation to suppress competition and other coercive practices; limited skills of consultants or personnel to detect corrupt practices and limited liability; low integrity of external consultants; loopholes and vulnerability to corruption in project implementation stages and challenges arising from mergers and acquisitions.'

This shows that even the most robust laws can be circumvented. What is required is that the personnel enforcing the laws should be honest, efficient and compliant. While recruitment and training of government officials will go some way to ensure this, the most obvious method is to have some form of an oversight mechanism. Since the Courts have washed their hands of this, there is a need to have some external regulator or an ombudsman to ensure that public money is well spent. Perhaps one day, the Supreme Court will revisit the Tata Cellular decision and allow for greater scrutiny of public procurement.

Notes

1. This could be a form of the Rawlsian imperfect procedural justice.
2. (1994) 6 SCC 651.
3. *India Telecomp Limited v. Union of India* 50 (1993) DLT 117.
4. This selection committee was not statutory, but an advisory body created by the minister. See *India Telecomp Ltd v. Union of India*, p. 9.

[5] *India Telecomp Limited v. Union of India* 50 (1993) DLT 117, p. 21.

[6] The English Courts recognized different kinds of writs for different kinds of relief. For instance, in case of a challenge to a decision of the government, the writ of certiorari was issued while in the case of directing the government to do an act, a writ of mandamus was issued. Each of these writs had stringent procedural requirements that imposed a limit on the powers of the Court to grant effective relief. The Indian Constitution did away with such technicalities by using much broader words. Article 226 empowers the high courts to issue 'orders or writs' for the enforcement of fundamental rights or for any other purpose. This is extremely wide language and has greatly contributed to the powers of the Court to intervene effectively in matters.

[7] *E.P. Royappa v. State of Tamil Nadu* 1974 SCR (2) 348.

[8] *Shayara Bano v. Union of India* (2017) 9 SCC 1.

[9] *Shrilekha Vidyarthi v. State of Uttar Pradesh* (1991) 1 SCC 212.

[10] *Dwarkadas Marfatia and Sons v. Board of Trustees of the Port of Bombay* (1989) 3 SCC 293.

[11] *Ramana Dayaram Shetty v. International Airport Authority of India* (1979) 3 SCC 489.

[12] Para 94.

[13] Reliance on foreign jurisprudence is a divisive issue for the Court, with judges often taking different views on the merits (or demerits) of relying on foreign case law. For instance, in the matter of reading down Section 377 of the Indian Penal Court, a bench of two judges of the Supreme Court refused to follow foreign precedent. See *Suresh Kumar Koushal v. Naz Foundation* (2014) 1 SCC 1. The same issue was viewed completely differently by a larger bench of the Court in the case of *Navtej Singh Johar v. UOI* (2018) 10 SCC 1. In this judgment, the Court relied extensively on the constitutional jurisprudence of countries across the globe.

[14] Subject to the caveat that even matters of policy are subject to challenge if any fundamental rights are violated. See the case of *DDA v. Joint Action Committee, Allottee of SFS Flats,* (2008) 2 SCC 672.

[15] For instance, expenditure per student in government schools rose from Rs 2455 in 2010 to Rs 4385 in 2016, but the learning outcomes fell in the same period. See Vijay Kelkar and Ajay Shah. *In Service of the Republic: The Art and Science of Economic Policy* (Allen Lane Publishers, 2019), p. 26.

[16] 'Why Swatantra?', from the pamphlet 'Why Swatantra' published by the Swatantra Party, National Headquarters, April 1973.

[17] The public trust doctrine was most used in environmental jurisprudence, where the Court held that the government was a trustee of natural resources

and held them for the greater common good, i.e., as a trustee for the people of India. See *M.C. Mehta v. Kamal Nath* (1997) 1 SCC 388.

[18] This concept is well known in the law of trusts or insurance contracts. A duty is cast upon the trustee (or a person seeking insurance coverage) not merely to act with prudence. A much-higher standard is demanded, one of the utmost good faith. See *Hanil Era Textiles v. Oriental Insurance* (2001) 1 SCC 269.

[19] 'India Seeks Fair Play in Public Procurement', Livemint, 5 November 2018.

[20] Yugank Goyal. 'How Governments Promote Monopolies: Public Procurement in India', *American Journal of Economics and Sociology*, Vol. 78, Issue 5 (2019), p. 1135–69.

[21] For instance, the state of Karnataka has enacted The Karnataka Transparency in Public Procurement Act, 1999. Similar laws have also been passed by other state governments like Rajasthan, Tamil Nadu, Assam and Punjab.

[22] United Nations Commission on International Trade Law.

[23] UNCITRAL Model Law on Public Procurement, 2014.

[24] One method of reducing corruption may be to eliminate any contact that a bidder might have with potentially corrupt officials; for instance, through the method of e-procurement. However, the impact of this might also be limited. In an interesting study, it has been noticed that e-procurement did not lead to any price reduction or reduction in delays. However, it did have an impact on improving the quality of the works. Sean Lewis-Faupel, Yusuf Neggers, Benjamin A. Olken, and Rohini Pande. 'Can Electronic Procurement Improve Infrastructure Provision? Evidence from Public Works in India and Indonesia', *American Economic Journal: Economic Policy*, 8 (3) (2016), pp. 258-83.

[25] India: Probity in Public Procurement, UNODC, 2013.

Chapter 7

Women in the Workplace

2021 was a year of many firsts, including the first time that women outnumbered men in India.[1] The improving sex ratio was widely celebrated, with government officials saying that this was the result of the increasing financial inclusion of women in the Indian economy.[2] Unfortunately, despite this talk of financial empowerment, the reality is that female workforce participation has been steadily falling in India,[3] in spite of rising wages and a growing economy. In fact, Indian women's participation in the workforce is among the worst in the world, save for certain parts of the Arab world.[4] This rather dismal figure is the result of many systemic disadvantages faced by women, with sexual harassment at the workplace being one of the major contributors.

Sexual harassment, of course, is not a new invention, and has been endemic to the workplace for centuries.[5] In spite of being such a drag on the economic empowerment of women, the Indian Parliament had not thought it necessary to intervene with any legislation to prohibit any form of sexual harassment at the workplace. This chapter is the story of how the Supreme Court of India, faced with the inaction of the government, intervened to curb the menace of harassment at a time when the government had little interest in securing the rights of women. The judgment of the Court in the case of *Vishaka v. State of Rajasthan*[6] was a pathbreaking one where the Court forged innovative, though controversial, legal techniques to come to the aid of women. A robust system of prevention and prohibition of sexual harassment at the workplace was put in place via judicial diktat rather than through any legislation.

Whether the judgment actually improved the financial empowerment of women generally is debatable. However, at the very least, the verdict shone a light on an obvious but often ignored fact that the financial well-being of a country cannot improve if more than half of its population cannot even work without fear.

I

Women and the Workforce

The economic costs of sexual harassment can be of many types and have a negative financial impact on both the organization as well as the employee. The company will be directly impacted by way of lost productivity since a harassed employee may take time off resulting in absenteeism or may be less productive at work if she is forced to work in a threatening environment.[7] There would also be administrative and opportunity costs involved in dealing with the complaints made to the management. Setting up of committees to investigate and adjudicate on allegations of sexual harassment takes the time of senior management as well as direct costs.

Then there are the indirect costs to the organization in the form of the tarnishing of the company's reputation both in the eyes of prospective employees as well as the general public. Companies would find it harder to attract fresh and competent talent, since prospective employees may not want to work in an organization that has gained notoriety for the wrong reasons. In any event, they would have to pay a premium to employees who would be willing to work in a firm with such a poor corporate culture of harassment. Equally, an increasingly aware public could well choose to punish an errant firm by boycotting the purchase of its goods. In the net result, the inherent value of the firm, including the return on equity for its investors, suffers in companies where the culture of sexual harassment is prevalent.[8]

Similarly, the costs to the employee can be direct as well as indirect. There is a direct financial impact to the employee in cases where she is dismissed or is denied promotions, or other modes of career advancement. There are also indirect costs which are not so readily quantifiable. For instance, the victim may have to quit a higher paying job where she is harassed to take on a safer but lower paying job. Or the woman may quit working altogether, losing not only her income but all the other statutory and ancillary benefits.[9] It has also been shown that workplace harassment has a clearly detrimental effect on the health of women.[10]

While the exact mode, manner and quantification of the costs of sexual harassment may be debated, what cannot be disputed is that it imposes potent costs on both the employer and the employees. This provides an economic, apart from the obvious moral[11] justification to attempt to curb the practice.[12] Given the financial impact, it is surprising that this issue has not been given the consideration that it deserves by organizations, particularly in the private sector. One possible reason could be that the work of women is generally undervalued and hence the economic costs are also underplayed. Another possible reason is that sexual harassment is the result of a toxic work culture where the male superiors are the perpetrators of the harassment and therefore see no reason to clamp down on it. In such a work environment, sexual harassment could simply be one of many other forms of harassment—for instance, creating spaces where jealousies and non-productive competition is encouraged. It has been posited that all these instances of unacceptable workplace behaviour stems from an imbalance of power and the desire (and ability) of the superior to exert his power over a subordinate. As the authors of a study point out, 'It is often assumed that sex is the primary motive in incidents of sexual harassment. However, sexual harassment actually has a strong power component, which is often reflected in the elements of hostility and aggression that characterize such incidents.'[13]

The roots of sexual harassment thus lie not only in sex, but in an abuse of power. In a society such as ours, with its entrenched patriarchy and enormous differences in the access to power and authority, it is not surprising that the problem of sexual harassment is so acute. It is also not surprising that it was with this toxic mix of power and patriarchy that the story of India's fight against sexual harassment began.

II

Bhanwari Devi and the Vishaka Guidelines

The battle against sexual harassment in India did not begin from the corporate powerhouses situated in any of the metros. Instead, the first mover was a humble social worker in the state of Rajasthan. Faced with the problem of child marriages, the Government of Rajasthan decided to hire female social workers whose job it was to try to convince families to refrain from this practice. Bhanwari Devi, a potter from the village of Bhateri in Rajasthan, enrolled as a volunteer in the programme, to speak to the local residents.[14] In the course of her employment, it came to her notice that some families were organizing child marriages, including the wedding of a nine-month-old infant. She tried to speak to the families and convince them against going ahead with the marriages, but to no avail. The marriages happened, just at a different venue from where they had been originally planned.

Even though the marriage had taken place, the members of the families, who were Gujjars, were livid at the fact that Bhanwari Devi had dared to interfere. The panchayat first directed an economic boycott of Bhanwari Devi, so her produce was not purchased by anyone and the vegetables on her plot of land were destroyed. But it seems this was not sufficient revenge. One morning in September 1992, five men accosted Bhanwari Devi and her husband when they were out in their fields. Her husband was held down by three of them while the other two men raped her in his presence.

Then started the typical rigmarole of police inaction and incompetence in matters relating to sexual violence against women. When Bhanwari Devi sought to file a complaint at the police station, she was informed that she would have to undergo a medical examination before any FIR would be registered. She went to the local health centre only to find that the woman doctor was not on duty. Bhanwari Devi and her husband had to take a bus all the way to Jaipur. When they reached Jaipur, the magistrate on duty who was to approve the medical examination said that it was past his working hours. The victim of a brutal sexual assault then had to wait till the next morning, some fifty-two hours after the incident, to be medically examined.

The injustices did not stop there. Even though the men were belatedly arrested and their bail petitions dismissed, they were acquitted by the trial court on what appear to be wholly tenuous reasons. The Court held that as the accused were upper caste men, the rape could not have taken place.[15] The verdict sparked an outrage and prompted a number of women's groups to move the Supreme Court seeking the establishment of a set of guidelines in case of sexual harassment.

Some might ask what the tragic reality of rape of women by upper caste men in rural India has to do with sexual harassment. But the clear answer is that Bhanwari Devi was assaulted not for just any reason but because she was simply trying to do her job. While it was not a case of an immediate superior harassing her, her assault was intimately tied to the fact of her work. It is unthinkable that a working man would be worried that he may be sexually assaulted if he dares to simply do his job. This, unfortunately, is the reality for a large number of Indian women.

The uproar also coincided with the rising awareness of the pervasive nature of discrimination against women. The judgment by the trial court had been delivered in 1995, the same year that a massive conference had been held in Beijing. The representatives of 189 countries met and hammered out the 'Beijing Declaration and Platform for Action', a document that contained the most progressive charter for women's rights: the Beijing Declaration.[16] The declaration noted that though the status of women across the world had improved over the past decade, they still faced inequalities. A raft of resolutions were passed with a view to ameliorate all forms of discrimination among women, perhaps the most important of which was the recognition that women's rights were human rights.

Drawing the link between the violence meted out to Bhanwari Devi and the menace of harassment, the Court noted[17] that 'the incident reveals the hazards to which a working woman may be exposed and the depravity to which sexual harassment can degenerate and the urgency for safeguards by an alternative mechanism in the absence of legislative measures. In the absence of legislative measures, the need is to find an effective alternative mechanism to fulfil this felt and urgent social need.' This initial statement of the issue also indicated what the Court intended to do. They were not going to be mere bystanders and permit a lethargic Parliament off the hook. The Court had been appointed as the custodian of fundamental rights by the Constitution of India, and it was in no mood to abdicate that role.

The Court accomplished that by traditional legal analysis with an innovative twist. The Court first had to establish that women had a right to a safe working environment. This right was located by the Court in both domestic as well as international law. The Constitution, for its time, was a feminist document, and the Court used its provisions to come to the aid of women. The judgment noted that every instance of harassment was a violation of the right to life and liberty guaranteed under Article 21 of the Constitution, and also a violation of the equality clauses of the Constitution. Interestingly, the Court also noted that the fundamental right to carry on any occupation, trade or profession depends on the availability of a 'safe' working environment. The effect of harassment had a direct impact on a woman's ability to work in a hospitable environment and hence was also a violation of the victim's fundamental right under Article 19 (1) (g). Unusually for the time, the Court also referred to the fundamental duty[18] of every citizen to 'renounce practices derogatory to the dignity of women'.

The Court did not simply use the explicit rights contained in the Constitution in its analysis, but also drew on the principles of international law. This was particularly necessary because while the constitutional provisions did guarantee the right to work with dignity implicitly, there was no specificity about the nature and extent of the right against sexual harassment. Further, since there was no domestic law on the subject, there was no mechanism to ensure that the protections guaranteed by the Constitution were complied with. Faced with such a vacuum, the Court turned to the international treaties and conventions that had been signed and ratified by India.[19]

The most pertinent international treaty on the point was the Convention on the Elimination of All Forms of Discrimination Against Women (CEDAW) to which India was a signatory. More significantly, a resolution had been passed on 25 June 1993, giving effect to the provisions of the CEDAW which India had ratified. The resolution used language that was ultimately adopted by the Court in its guidelines. Specifically, the resolution noted that 'Sexual harassment includes such unwelcome sexually determined behaviour as physical contacts and advances, sexually-coloured remarks, showing pornography and sexual demands, whether by words or actions. Such conduct can be humiliating and may constitute a health and safety problem; it is discriminatory when the woman has reasonable grounds to believe that her objection would disadvantage her in connection with her employment, including recruiting or promotion, or when it creates a hostile working environment. Effective complaints, procedures and remedies, including compensation, should be provided.'

There was therefore a firm basis in domestic law guaranteeing a right against sexual harassment. There was also precedent in international law as to how the right could be modulated and enforced. There was only one thing lacking—an efficacious way to enforce the right in India. The Constitution provided for recourse to the Courts of law only when the harassment (or any other discrimination) was done by the State. An employee could not approach the Courts against a private employer using any constitutional remedy. Such a remedy could only be provided by a legislation, and Parliament had so far not deigned to pass such an enactment.

There was thus a peculiar situation faced by the Court. Having recognized the rights of the employee, there was no remedy to enforce that right. There is a well-known Latin legal maxim—*ubi jus ibi remedium*. The phrase literally means 'where there is a right, there is a remedy.' While lawyers often use Latin to obfuscate, this particular maxim exposes the central concern of any rights-based adjudication. Any right is meaningful only if one can find a way to enforce the right, either by moving the Court or through some other mechanism. To simply declare that an employee had a right without her actually being able to enforce it was an exercise in futility at best and a cruel joke at worst.

The Court noted this dilemma and held that 'the primary responsibility for ensuring such safety and dignity through suitable legislation, and the creation of a mechanism for its enforcement, is of the legislature and the Executive. When, however, instances of sexual harassment resulting in violation of fundamental rights of women workers under Articles 14, 19 and 21 are brought before us for redress under Article 32, an effective redressal requires that some guidelines should be laid down for the protection of these rights to fill the legislative vacuum.'[20]

So, pending the enactment of any legislation on the subject, the Court framed and adopted a set of guidelines on the subject. The guidelines were comprehensive and imposed an obligation on all organizations to take steps to prevent instances of sexual harassment. A specific complaints mechanism was set up under which each organization was mandated to set up a complaints committee that would be headed by a woman and have a majority of women as its members. The guidelines also mandated that an NGO or a third party familiar with the issues of sexual harassment would be involved with the committee.

Importantly, the Court also noted that these guidelines would have the force of law under Article 141 of the Constitution. Thus, the Supreme Court in effect laid down a law attempting to curb sexual harassment. This was beyond the normal role of the Court, which was to interpret legislation and not to actually legislate. However, as the Court noted that in cases of violation of fundamental rights, the Court did not have the luxury of being an impassive bystander while the rights of half the population of the country were being violated with impunity.

The Court had also ruled that these guidelines would apply only till Parliament stepped in and enacted a comprehensive law dealing with sexual harassment. Thus, even if the Court had been guilty of overreach, any criticism would have been short-lived as it was assumed that Parliament would fulfil its responsibility and enact a law. Unfortunately, this pious hope proved to be misplaced.

It took Parliament sixteen long years after the judgment to pass legislation dealing with sexual harassment. The Prevention of Sexual Harassment at Workplace (Prevention, Prohibition and Redressal) Act, 2013, was passed by Parliament and brought into force on 22 April, 2013. An optimist could still look for a silver lining in the drab cloud of delay. Substantial time had passed since the judgment and it was possible that the experience gathered in that time could have been used to improve upon the guidelines suggested by the Court. Unfortunately, this hope was dashed. The act was further evidence of the falling standards of legislative draftsmanship and parliamentary debates. Naina Kapur, one of the main movers and counsels in the *Vishaka* case has validly and trenchantly criticized the act, both for its defective language as well as its substance.[21] Kapur has rightly pointed out that the act contains a section that provides for punishment in case a woman makes a false or malicious complaint. Other than stereotyping women as liars, the section may also have a chilling effect on women who wish to make a complaint, fearing that they would be hounded if for some reason they are unable to establish their claim.

III

The Way Forward

The act has clearly been a disappointment for activists and the victims of sexual harassment. The problem lies not only in the language of the act, but also its implementation. Surveys have shown that the internal complaint committees are not working as well as they should.[22] Two-thirds of the respondents felt that the committees were not functioning fairly and that the provisions of the POSH Act were not being followed. This distrust in the process had an immediate impact on the level of protection sought to be given by the act. Almost 70 per cent of the people surveyed said that they were fearful of making a complaint because of a fear of repercussions and retaliation. This is compounded by the general lack of legal literacy in the country, where citizens are not even aware of their rights and are hence in no position to seek to enforce them.[23]

It is thus apparent that the laws have not been effective in controlling deviant behaviour. Part of the problem is that there has been insufficient focus, at least by the lawmakers, as to what causes workplace harassment, and therefore, what is the best way to cure the problem. As noted above, sexual harassment is a product of an imbalance and abuse of power. Presumably, therefore, attempts must be made to mitigate, if not eliminate, this imbalance. Positive action that deals with both the symptoms as well as the causes of economic disempowerment of women must be undertaken. Specifically in the case of sexual harassment, studies have also indicated that the harassment goes down in organizations that have a robust complaint mechanism.[24]

However, a complaints mechanism requires something more than merely framing a policy on paper. There is a need to create an office environment that permits a victim to be able to enforce her rights without the fear of stigma, economic costs and bureaucratic and legal delays. This would require active participation by the human resource departments of companies to widely prepare, publicize and circulate the anti-harassment policies. The HR department must also liaise with the management to sensitize them to potential acts of harassment happening in the workplace. This is necessary because it has been seen that senior management in the private sector is often in denial about the harassment happening in their organization.[25]

Another potential device can be the imposition of deterrent penalties not only on the person committing the harassment, but also vicariously on the organization. After all, it is the obligation of the employer to ensure a safe working place for the employee. If an employee is to suffer some injury at the workplace due to the negligence or the incompetence of the employer, it is the employer that is expected to pay the compensation other than facing criminal liability. Thus, the liability to pay damages must be upon the employer, and further, these damages must be awarded to a victim expeditiously. The damages paid to the victim will allow her to resume her work, either at the same or a different establishment, without suffering further economic disempowerment.

What is important is that such damages should not merely be compensatory to the victim, but must be penal in nature. The penalties must be high enough so as to capture the 'externalities' of the costs of sexual harassment generally. As has been noted above, acts of harassment have many direct and indirect costs to the employees working there. Some of these costs would not be seen as damages, which would normally be awarded by the Court. This is because the Indian Contract Act only permits the Court to award damages that are direct and clearly caused by an act of harassment. Damages to self-esteem, indirect costs by way of reduction of benefits, as well as the emotional costs of working in an unsafe environment (even when an employee chooses not to complain) are not usually awarded to the victim. These 'external' costs are effectively a benefit to the errant employers since any costs not paid to the victim is money saved by the organization. Most importantly, failing to make an employer pay these costs would encourage them to permit a vicious culture to continue since they would have no incentive to spend money to curb these practices. Such a use of economic quantification is well-known in the law. For instance, in the field of environmental adjudication, the Courts routinely award damages greater than the readily quantifiable loss so as to account for the externalities (i.e., the value of the environmental damage).[26]

Thus, using a calculation of damages that only quantifies a narrow measure of damages specific to the victim should be spurned in favour of a measure that more holistically captures the costs to its victims. Adopting such a measure would have several benefits. First, the factoring in of the externalities would provide a true measure of the losses suffered by the victim than that computed on a more traditional measure. Second, this would give a quantifiable basis, and hence a solid economic underpinning, to the actual costs of sexual harassment. Thirdly, the damages would force the employer to put in place mechanisms that would ensure no sexual harassment takes place by providing a pecuniary disincentive in creating a hostile work environment.

The economic costs to an organization alone should require a greater examination as to the fairness of the labour market to women. When the moral imperative is added to this, the case for change from the status quo becomes irrebuttable. As the International Labor Organization (ILO) has noted, 'Women continue to face many barriers to enter labour market and to access decent work and disproportionately face a range of multiple challenges relating to access to employment, choice of work, working conditions, employment security, wage parity, discrimination, and balancing the competing burdens of work and family responsibilities. In addition, women are heavily represented in the informal economy where their exposure to risk of exploitation is usually greatest and they have the least formal protection.'[27] This statement makes it clear that true economic empowerment of women will not be achieved simply by cracking down on sexual harassment. Much more needs to be done.

Women face systemic disadvantages at the workplace, all of which need to be addressed through a comprehensive piece of legislation. The imbalance of power between men and women will not be cured simply by applying band-aids on gushing wounds. Tinkering with the act to remedy perceived defects is not sufficient any more. If genuine change is required, we need comprehensive legislation guaranteeing every aspect of employment, both in the formal as well as the informal sector. Since Parliament does not seem to be very inclined towards undertaking this exercise, perhaps it is time for the Supreme Court to step in again.

Notes

[1] International Institute for Population Sciences (IIPS) and ICF. 2021. *National Family Health Survey (NFHS-5), 2019–21: India*, Mumbai: IIPS.

[2] 'Number of Women Surpass Men for First Time in India with Sex Ratio 1,020', *India Today*, 21 November 2021.

[3] Sher Veric. 'Women's Labour Force Participation in India: Why Is It So Low?', International Labour Organization (2014).

[4] Amit Kapoor and Manisha Kapoor. 'No Place for Women: What Drives India's Ever-Declining Female Labour Force', *The Economic Times*, 13 June 2021.

[5] Reva B. Siegel. 'A Short History of Sexual Harassment' in *Directions in Sexual Harassment Law*, ed. Catharine A. Mackinnon and Reva B, Siegel (Yale Press, 2003).

[6] (1997) 6 SCC 241.

[7] Deloitte Access Economics. 'The Economic Costs of Sexual Harassment in the Workplace', Final Report (March 2019). The report also offers a rough quantification of these losses in Australia, but the same may not be entirely apposite in the Indian context.

[8] Shiu-Yik Au, Ming Dong and Andreanne Tremblay. 'How Much Does Workplace Sexual Harassment Hurt Firm Value?' 25 January 2022, available at SSRN.

[9] Ariane Hegewisch, Jessica Forden and Eve Mefferd. 'Paying Today and Tomorrow: Charting the Financial Costs of Workplace Sexual Harassment', Report (Washington, DC: Institute for Women's Policy Research, 2021).

[10] S. Gale, I. Mordukhovich, S. Newlan and E. McNeely. 'The Impact of Workplace Harassment on Health in a Working Cohort', *Front Psychol.*, published 24 May 2019.

[11] An interesting hybrid of the moral as well as the economic rationale to prohibit 'obnoxious markets', i.e., trades in services and commodities we

intuitively consider immoral can be found in Ravi Kanbur, 'On Obnoxious Markets', Charles H. Dyson School of Applied Economics and Management, Cornell University (2001).

[12] An interesting discussion about the economic, as opposed to a purely normative analysis, of the costs of sexual harassment can be found in Kaushik Basu, 'Sexual Harassment at the Workplace: An Economic Analysis with Implications for Worker Rights and Labor Standards Policy', Massachusetts Institute of Technology Department of Economics Working Paper Series, Working Paper 02-11 (February 2002). Basu argues that a contract permitting sexual harassment may be economically permissible in a single case, but if permitted to be executed in large numbers, it becomes economically suspect.

[13] Paula M. Popovich and M. Warren. 'The Role of Power in Sexual Harassment as a Counterproductive Behavior in Organizations', *Human Resource Management Review* 20 (2010), pp. 45–53.

[14] The details of the case can be found in Namita Bhandare, 'The Beast in Our Midst', essay in *Sex and the Supreme Court: How the Law Is Upholding the Dignity of the Indian Citizen* (Hachette, 2020), edited by Saurabh Kirpal.

[15] Geeta Pandey. 'Bhanwari Devi: The Rape that Led to India's Sexual Harassment Law', BBC News, 17 March 2017. The judge apparently gave other baffling reasons for the decision, including that men above sixty could not rape or that men of different castes could not indulge in the crime of rape together.

[16] Fourth World Conference on Women, Beijing Declaration, United Nations, September 1995.

[17] Para 2, *Vishaka v. State of Rajasthan.*

[18] The provisions relating to fundamental duties were not part of the original Constitution, having been inserted by the controversial 42nd Amendment during the emergency. They are non-justiciable and hence, create no legal obligations.

[19] The reliance on international law and treaties is well-accepted by the Indian Courts. The general rule is that all domestic law would be interpreted in a manner consistent with international law, unless there is a clear contradiction. See *Gramophone Co. of India Ltd v. Birendra Bahadur Pandey* (1984) 2 SCC 534. Specifically, in Vishaka, the Court held that 'gender equality includes protection from sexual harassment and right to work with dignity, which is a universally recognised basic human right. The common minimum requirement of this right has received global acceptance. The international conventions

and norms are, therefore, of great significance in the formulation of the guidelines to achieve this purpose.'

[20] p. 247, *Vishaka v. UOI.*

[21] Naina Kapur. 'Workplace Sexual Harassment: The Way Things Are', *Economic and Political Weekly*, 15 June 2015, Vol. 48, No. 24, pp. 27–29. She also points out that the bill was passed by the Lok Sabha without any discussion or debate. The discussion in the Rajya Sabha too was perfunctory at best.

[22] Survey conducted by the Indian National Bar Association. See Report 'Sexual Harassment at the Workplace', Indian National Bar Association, Prabhat Books, 2017.

[23] A small study has shown that about 70 per cent of the workforce was not even aware of the Vishaka judgment. See Disha Sangwan and Amit Thakre, 'Sexual Harassment at the Workplace in Public and Private Sectors in India: A Study at National Capital Region of Delhi', *International Journal of Criminal Justice Sciences*, Vol. 13, Issue 1, January—June 2018. The study only had 100 participants and thus has to be viewed with some degree of caution.

[24] Steven H. Lopez, Randy Hodson and Vincent J. Roscigno. 'Power, Status, and Abuse at Work: General and Sexual Harassment Compared', *The Sociological Quarterly*, 50:1 (2009), pp. 3–27.

[25] Anagha Sarpotdar. 'Sexual Harassment of Women: Reflections on the Private Sector', *Economic and Political Weekly*, 5 October 2013, Vol. 48, No. 40., pp. 18–19, 22–23.

[26] This has been through the deployment of the Polluter Pays Principle. See *Indian Council for Enviro-legal Action v. UOI* (1996) 3 SCC 212.

[27] Sher Veric. 'Women's Labour Force Participation in India: Why Is It So Low?'.

Chapter 8

No Business to Be in Business:
The Case for Privatization

There are few other matters of financial importance that generate
as much political heat as the issue of privatization of public sector
undertakings (PSUs). The government of the day usually looks to
privatization as a source of raising funds to shore up the Budget
numbers. This desire to balance books is often disguised by the
accompanying rhetoric of improving efficiency. On the other
hand, the opposition almost invariably raises charges of 'selling
the family silver'. The process of privatization is thus inherently
political; and in India, it is only a matter of time before the political
becomes the legal. The case of the disinvestment of the Bharat
Aluminum Company (BALCO) is just one such example.

BALCO was a profit-making company that was sought to be
excised in a round of privatization initiated by the NDA regime.
Since it was one of the larger PSUs that were privatized, the
disinvestment generated a great amount of controversy. Different
interest groups jockeyed to support or oppose the sale of the
company to a private investor. As expected, the controversies and
issues travelled to the Supreme Court where the employees' union
sought the Court's intervention to set aside the sale.

The Court had traditionally maintained a stance that it
would not enter the thicket of economic policy, leaving the

issues to the political field. At the same time, the Court had been getting increasingly vocal on a host of issues, ranging from the environment[1] to matters relating to corruption and public administration.[2] Thus, the outcome of the case was not certain. There was also a lot of political heat on the government as the decision in the case would have set the course for the future of disinvestment policy in the country.

In the ultimate result, the Court handed a thumping victory to the government in *BALCO Employees Union v. Union of India.*[3] It upheld the sale of BALCO and generally gave its seal of approval to the policy of disinvestment. Armed with the judgment, the government proceeded with further disinvestment, albeit with a few minor hiccups. In the two decades since the BALCO judgment, the policy of disinvestment has become a virtual economic and political orthodoxy. This chapter will trace the history of privatization and the impact that the BALCO judgment has had, not just on the disinvestment policy, but on the financial sector generally.

I

Building and Deconstructing the Public Sector

The large public sector in India was not a gift of the British empire but was part of a Nehruvian economic policy that valued government ownership of vital public enterprises. Shortly after Independence, when the first five-year plan was conceived, there were only five public sector industries. The total governmental investment in these industries was a mere Rs 29 crore[4] and reflected the laissez-faire economic worldview of the British rulers.[5]

Pandit Jawaharlal Nehru had a very different economic vision for India. Educated in Britain and under the influence of the Fabian socialists, he supported a strong public sector. As the president of the first Planning Commission, he stressed on agriculture as the engine for redressing the massive inequities that existed in India. However, by the time of the Second Plan, the focus shifted to industry and the public sector. In 1956, an Industrial Policy Resolution was passed, which favoured a robust public sector. The resolution noted that 'the adoption of the socialist pattern of society as the national objective, as well as the need for planned and rapid development, require that all industries of basic and strategic importance, or in the nature of public utility services, should be in the public sector.'[6] Thus began a series of nationalizations as well as setting up of greenfield PSUs, to the extent that the share of the public sector rose to one-fifth of the GDP by the mid-seventies.

This desire to have an expansive public sector was extended much further during the regime of Indira Gandhi. Whether this was genuinely an ideological choice or whether this was a political lurch to the left for electoral gains has already been discussed in the chapter on bank nationalization. However, the net result was that a large number of industries were brought under government control. By the mid-seventies, the public sector had grown to about 20 per cent of the GDP.[7] Even with the advent of liberalization, the public sector continued to grow and by 2001, it accounted for one quarter of the GDP.

Of course, the attempt to manage the economy through the public sector proved to be an extremely unsuccessful exercise. The PSUs consistently underperformed the private sector and were not producing the desired return on the capital invested. They were inefficient and could not satisfy the needs of the public at large.[8]

There was the added pressure on public finances that finally pushed the government to take the decision to privatize the PSUs. The early nineties saw a difficult time for the economy in India. Years of sclerotic growth, a bloated public sector and a private sector mollycoddled by the licence-raj protectionism, pushed the economy to the brink. India had foreign exchange reserves sufficient to fund only two weeks' worth of imports. Faced with an impending balance of payments crisis, the government was forced to take a loan from the IMF and also to proceed with opening up the economy. However, one immediate concern was to bring down the fiscal deficit. An easy way for the government to raise extra finances was to sell shares held by it in various PSUs. Thus began the first wave of disinvestment in India, born at a time of fiscal emergency.

Even though the government decided to commence the disinvestment process, there was an initial reticence to sell a majority share to private buyers. In the first 10 years of the disinvestment process, only about 19.2 per cent equity in some forty PSUs were sold.[9] The speed of privatization only picked up when the NDA came to power in 1999. Contrary to the protectionist tendencies of the affiliates of the NDA, the government decided to carry out an ambitious project of disinvestment. Finance Minister Yashwant Sinha, in his Budget speech of the year 2000, said that the 'government have recently established a new department of disinvestment and privatization to establish a systematic policy approach to disinvestment and privatization and to give a fresh impetus to this programme, which will emphasize increasingly on strategic sales of identified PSUs'.[10] This department was eventually hived off into a separate Ministry of Disinvestment on 6 September 2001 with Arun Shourie being appointed as the first minister for disinvestment.

Thus began a flurry of privatization. Three hotels owned by the Hotel Corporation of India were sold outright. In a break from the past, majority stakes in various PSUs were sold to strategic partners, handing over managerial control of the companies to private players. In 2001–02, about thirty-two PSUs were sold for a total sum of Rs 11,214 crore.[11]

II

The Disinvestment Process

Of the PSUs identified for strategic sale, BALCO was possibly the most controversial. Prior to the disinvestment, BALCO was a fully owned government company, incorporated in 1965 under the Companies Act, 1956. It had a paid-up share capital of Rs 488.85 crore, was engaged in the manufacture of aluminium, and had plants at Korba in the state of Chhattisgarh and Bidhanbag in the state of West Bengal. The company had integrated an aluminium manufacturing plant for the manufacture and sale of aluminium metal, including wire rods and semi-fabricated products.[12] It was a profit-making entity and accordingly, it was expected that there would be a fair bit of interest in its sale.

The process of disinvestment in BALCO had started much prior to the decision to sell a majority of the shares in the company. In fact, it was in April 1997 that the Disinvestment Commission had recommended the sale of 40 per cent of the shareholding in the company to a strategic investor, with the government retaining only 26 per cent of the shares and selling the rest to other buyers. By 1998, the commission decided to sell 51 per cent of the shares to a private entity.

The government appointed global advisers who invited expressions of interest for the purchase of shares not just in India, but globally. The advertisements were published in leading national and international journals. During this period, the government appointed valuers who submitted their reports on the reserve price of BALCO. After considering a variety of different methodologies for valuation, the government ultimately adopted the discounted cash flow method. The reserve price was set at Rs 514.4 crore for 51 per cent of the total shareholding of the company.

Ultimately, eight companies submitted their expression of interest. There followed a process of attrition where certain companies were held ineligible or dropped out of the race. Ultimately, only three companies, i.e., ALCOA, HINDALCO and Sterlite conducted a due diligence on BALCO between September and December 2000. When it came to bidding, however, ALCOA dropped out of the race and ultimately the government received only two bids. The bids were opened and it was found that Sterlite had bid Rs 551.5 crore, more than double the bid of HINDALCO, which was only Rs 275 crore. In February 2001, the government decided to accept the highest bid and sell 51 per cent of its stake in BALCO to Sterlite.

The decision to privatize BALCO was met with stiff opposition from multiple interest groups. The charge was led by political parties which alleged that the deal had been mired in corruption. The employees of BALCO were also opposed to the privatization and went on an indefinite strike at the company's Chhattisgarh plant. The state government also tacitly supported the striking workers. It was only when the new management intervened, and certain interim orders were passed that the strike was called off after sixty-seven days.

There was also a lot of furore in Parliament. The opposition parties moved a Calling Attention Motion in the Rajya Sabha, which was discussed on 27 February 2001. The matter was also discussed in the Lok Sabha on 1 March 2001. The motion 'that this House disapproves the proposed disinvestment of Bharat Aluminium Company Ltd' was defeated in the Lok Sabha by 239 votes to 119 votes.[13] Thus there was parliamentary approval to the process of disinvestment. The disputes thus moved from the floor of the house to the cloistered confines of the courtroom.

III

The Judgment

The decision of the government to sell its stake in BALCO was challenged in multiple courts. A public interest petition was filed in the Delhi High Court by one B.L. Wadhera, an advocate who used to file multiple petitions in various courts on issues of public interest. The employees of BALCO also moved the Delhi High Court, asserting that they had not been consulted before the decision to disinvest had been taken. The employees claimed that they were vital stakeholders in the company and therefore any decision to privatize should have been taken only after they had been properly and adequately heard. While these petitions were pending in the Delhi High Court, another petition was filed by an individual employee of BALCO before the Chhattisgarh High Court.

As though the legal challenges were not enough, there was another salvo fired by the political opponents of the NDA government. BALCO held its mines in the state of Chhattisgarh, which was, at that time, ruled by Ajit Jogi, a chief minister belonging to the Congress Party. Being opposed to the attempted privatization of BALCO, the state caused multiple notices to be sent to the company alleging violations of the Madhya Pradesh Land Revenue Code, 1959. The notices also claimed that BALCO had encroached on government land. These notices were really in the form of a poison pill, intending to derail the disinvestment process.

Alarmed by the notices, BALCO moved the Supreme Court directly by way of a writ petition. The Court proceeded to transfer all cases relating to the disinvestment to itself. A three-judge bench of the Supreme Court gave its verdict on 10 December 2001, not only upholding the actual disinvestment of BALCO in particular, but also seemingly siding with the government on the issue of disinvestment as a whole. There were several issues raised before the Court, but the three main areas it examined were whether the workers had a say in the disinvestment policy, whether the land in tribal areas was validly allotted to BALCO and whether the process of disinvestment was fair and proper.

The workers claimed that since BALCO was a 'state' under the Constitution, they had certain constitutionally protected rights, i.e., the right to be treated fairly, guaranteed under Articles 14 and 16 of the Constitution. Once BALCO would be privatized, it would cease to be a government company and thus, they would lose the protection of these constitutional rights. This was because these constitutional protections were only available to employees of the state, and not to those of a private company. Relying on this change in their status, the workers argued that they had a right to be heard before any decision that directly impacted them was taken. Their right to natural justice required, at the least, consultation with them before any disinvestment.

The Court rejected this argument of the workers. While noting that any employee would obviously have an interest in the running of a company, it held that the interest could not extend to dictating the policy choices of its employers. As long as the decisions of the employer were taken in good faith and were not illegal, the rules of natural justice would not come into play. The Court held that 'While it is expected of a responsible employer to take all aspects into consideration including welfare of the labour before taking any policy decision that, by itself, will not entitle the employees to demand a right of hearing or consultation prior to the taking of the decision.'[14]

While holding as above, the Court also went on to satisfy itself that the employees would not be worse off by the privatization process. The statement of counsel for BALCO was recorded to the effect employees were not to be retrenched except in the normal course of business, and their pay and pensions were to be protected. A voluntary retirement scheme (VRS) permitting the employees to leave the employment of BALCO was also put into place so as to safeguard the interests of the employees. Of course, now with the wisdom of hindsight, it can be seen that some of these protections were chimerical. However, the Court at that time thought that these were sufficient to meet the interests of the workers.

As regards the claim of the Chhattisgarh government that the land leased to BALCO was tribal land, the Court held that there was no provision of the law that barred such lease. To the extent any approval before such a transfer was required, the relevant state authorities had given the permission. Relying on these facts, the Court went on to hold that the land leased by BALCO was rightly held by it.

The most important part of the judgment concerned itself with the disinvestment process. On the allegation that the assets of the company had been deliberately undervalued, resulting in an artificially low reserve price, the Court pointed out that the reserve price was only made known to the bidders after the bids had been submitted. Thus, there was a chance of the bidders having deflated their bids to take advantage of any undervaluation. In a transparent bidding process, the value of the shares would be reflected by the bids made by those who were in the market. If the highest bid of Rs 551.5 crore, which was higher than the reserve price, was made, then it could not be said that the company had been undervalued. The Court thus held that the privatization process had not suffered from any lack of transparency, holding that 'Transparency does not mean the conducting of the government business while sitting on the crossroads in public. Transparency would require that the manner in which decision is taken is made known.'[15]

Other than upholding the particular disinvestment of BALCO, the Court ruled more generally on the policy of privatization. The government had argued that the PSUs were a drain on public finances while also being extremely inefficient. Attorney General Soli Sorabjee produced figures showing that 'the rate of returns of governmental enterprises had been woefully low, excluding the sectors in which the Government have a monopoly and for which they can, therefore, charge any price. The rate of return on Central enterprises came to minus 4 per cent while the cost at which the Government borrows money is at the rate of 10 to 11 per cent. In the States out of 946 State-level enterprises, about 241 were not working at all, about 551 were making losses and 100 were reported not to be submitting their accounts at all.'[16]

Relying on a series of past precedents, the Court held that it was not competent to rule on the wisdom of the economic policy of the government as it lacked the expertise to determine the correctness of the policy. After noticing that Parliament had given its approval to the disinvestment, the Court ruled that the appropriate place to test the soundness of the policy was Parliament, and not the judiciary.[17] The scope of judicial interference was limited to examining whether there had been any bad faith, extreme arbitrariness or any violation of the law or the Constitution. The Court wanted to give freedom to the government to determine its own economic policy and held that 'it is neither within the domain of the courts nor the scope of the judicial review to embark upon an enquiry as to whether a particular public policy is wise or whether better public policy can be evolved. Nor are our courts inclined to strike down a policy at the behest of a petitioner merely because it has been urged that a different policy would have been fairer or wiser or more scientific or more logical.[18] . . . In matters relating to economic issues, the Government has, while taking a decision, right to "trial and error" as long as both trial and error are bona fide and within limits of authority . . . In a democracy, it is the prerogative of each elected Government to follow its own policy. Often, a change in Government may result in the shift in focus or change in economic policies. Any such change may result in adversely affecting some vested interests. Unless any illegality is committed in the execution of the policy or the same is contrary to law or mala fide, a decision bringing about change cannot *per se* be interfered with by the court.'[19]

This statement of the law came as great relief to the government as it removed the shadow of judicial interference in the disinvestment process. The Courts would henceforth maintain a hands-off approach, leaving the government of the day to battle it out in Parliament.

In a parting shot, the government commented on B.L. Wadhera's petition noticing that he was a habitual public interest petitioner. Somewhat sarcastically, the Court noted that though Wadhera was not an employee of the company nor a bidder, his only concern was that he had been interested in PSUs and thus the 'persistent public interest litigant' did not 'miss an opportunity' to challenge the privatization. The Court went on to reiterate principles in relation to PILs, holding that the purpose of allowing strangers to file petitions was to allow the Court to examine those cases where the impacted persons were too disadvantaged or amorphous to file a petition themselves. Matters of economic policy, the Court ruled, were not amenable to challenge by strangers to the dispute. The Court held that 'The decision to disinvest and the implementation thereof is purely an administrative decision relating to the economic policy of the State and challenge to the same at the instance of a busybody cannot fall within the parameters of public interest litigation.'[20]

The judgment marked a decisive turning point for the Courts in India. No economic policy of India would be judged on its merits. The Courts would take a hands-off approach on issues that were within the sole domain of the Executive or Parliament. Relying on the judgment, the Supreme Court has, with a few notable exceptions,[21] refrained on commenting on matters of policy. The leeway given to the Executive by the judiciary is not only in matters of economic policy but extends to a myriad of other policy areas. The Court has accordingly held that it has no expertise to comment on the need for large dams in the country[22] or whether films must have been approved by the Censor Board before being eligible for participation in the national film awards.[23] However, it is in the area of economic policy where the effect of the BALCO judgment has been felt the most.

The question is whether such reticence is a good thing. In a system of limited government such as that under the Indian Constitution, it is imperative that no action by any governmental authority goes unexamined. The question thus arises as to who has the authority to examine the economic policy in the country. The Court, as seen above, felt that the appropriate authority was the Parliament since it had defeated the resolution whereby the disinvestment process would have been stopped. However, then the question arises as to whether the faith reposed by the Court in the political process has been justified.

IV

The Political and Economic Aftermath

The main political check on any government is through elections. However, elections held every five years and fought on a number of different issues can hardly be an effective check on any individual policy. Thus, any democracy also needs other institutional processes to supervise the functioning and decision-making of the government of the day. Under our Constitution,[24] one of the main mechanisms through which the government is held accountable is through the reports of the Comptroller and Auditor General (CAG).

The BALCO disinvestment was also the subject matter of a CAG report published in 2006.[25] The report noted four major failings in the privatization process. First, the method of valuation ignored certain assets of the company leading to an artificially low reserve price.[26] Secondly, the terms of the shareholders agreements were contrary to the government interest. For instance, the agreements provided for a put option, which allowed the newly privatized management to purchase the shares of the companies at much below the prevailing market price. Thirdly, the contracts provided for the so-called 'post-closing adjustment clause'. This required the government to pay the new owners any depletion in the value of the assets from the date of the last audited balance sheet to the date of the purchase of the shares. Each of the companies with whom such a clause had been agreed with went on to make a claim against the government and demanded vast sums of money. In some instances, the claims under this clause were almost equal to the price paid by the management for acquiring the company.[27] Fourthly, and possibly most importantly, the CAG report found that there was insufficient competition among the bidders. For instance, in the case of three companies sought to be privatized, only one bidder had put in a financial bid and in the case of four more companies, only two bidders had put in a financial bid.

Of course, the CAG report could hardly be taken as gospel. It was quite apparent that the CAG was not as neutral an entity as envisaged by the framers of the Constitution. For instance, there were questions asked at the time as to why the reports were delayed[28] and why only selective audits were conducted by the CAG. Nevertheless, the report did raise issues that deserved greater examination. This was not only to catch any potential wrongdoing in the disinvestment process, but also to provide a guide for how to conduct the process more transparently and efficiently going forward.

Unfortunately, there appears to have been no consequence or redressal after the CAG report. This showed the CAG's limited utility to act as a check on governmental policy. The net result is that under the current state of the law, economic policies often go virtually unexamined. If the Court believes it does not have the competence or the legitimacy to examine decisions in fiscal matters, perhaps they should at least insist on setting up some other formal method through which these policies are subjected to scrutiny.

Further, while the Court may not be competent to go into the merits of economic policy, it might not be out of the jurisdiction of the Court to at least ask the Executive what the policy is. To do so requires one to consider exactly what one means by a 'disinvestment policy'. Such a policy would have many different facets. For instance, there is the question of which PSUs to sell. The mode and manner of disinvestment is also an issue— should the sale be only to induct a strategic partner, or should the majority of shares be sold?[29] How should the business be valued and the reserve price fixed? Perhaps one of the most important questions to be asked is why the disinvestment is taking place. Is it to privatize the inefficient state structure so as to unleash the 'animal spirits' in the economy or is it merely a budgetary exercise? Of course, there is often no consistency on the rationale behind disinvestment across different governments.[30]

What is essential, and something which is generally lacking in Indian fiscal policy, is to determine the aim sought to be achieved by any policy in advance and thereafter to carry out an audit to determine whether the measure was successful for the purpose it was carried out. There is a tendency to judge the same action against multiple, and often changing, parameters. While this may give politicians (or the bureaucrats who frame the policy) reason to tom-tom even a failure as a success, this hardly makes for sound economic policy.

The lasting legacy of the BALCO judgment has been one of liberating the government from the perceived shackles of judicial scrutiny. Every government would like to function with minimum questioning. It is neither in the interest of the politician nor the civil servant to have to explain their decision, particularly when they themselves may not have fully examined the purpose and implications of the policy. It may now be time for the Court to examine the actions of the government with greater scrutiny so as to ensure fuller accountability. While the Courts do suffer from a democratic deficit, judicial review is an important means to ensure that democracy doesn't just mean elections but implies a meaningful and participatory system of checks and balances.

Notes

[1] *MC Mehta v. Union of India* AIR 2002 SC 1696; *TN Godavarman Thirumulpad v. Union of India* (1997) 2 SCC 267.

[2] *Vineet Narain v. Union of India* (1998) 1 SCC 226.

[3] (2002) 2 SCC 233.

[4] Anil Makhija. 'Privatisation in India', *Economic and Political Weekly*, Vol. 41, No. 20 (2006), , pp. 1947–51.

[5] Though this might not have been the case in the UK itself, where the labour movement had made great strides. For instance, the Trade Disputes Act was passed in 1906. This act introduced the concept that trade unions could not be sued for strike action.

[6] Industrial Policy Resolution (30 April 1956).

[7] Anil Makhija. 'Privatisation in India', p. 1947.

[8] Some part of the inefficiency could very well be a result of the poor management and governmental interference. However, this is beyond the scope of this chapter.

[9] Anil Makhija. 'Privatisation in India', p. 1947.

[10] Pradip Baijal. 'Privatization: Compulsions and Options for Economic Reform', *Economic and Political Weekly*, Vol. 37, No. 41 (2002), , pp. 4189–95.

[11] Ibid., p. 4193.

[12] *Balco Employees Union (Regd.) v. Union Of India* 2002 2 SCC 333, paragraph 2.

[13] 'No JPC Probe into Balco Deal', *The Tribune*, 28 February 2001.

[14] Para 47 of the Balco judgement.

[15] Para 67.

[16] Para 30.

[17] Para 93.

[18] Para 46–47.

[19] Para 92.

[20] Para 89.

[21] The policy of disinvestment stuttered a bit after the BALCO judgment. The disinvestment of two oil companies—HPCL and BPCL—were stalled by the Supreme Court on the grounds that the government needed to enact legislation before the two companies could be privatized. See *Centre for Public Interest Litigation v. Union of India* (2003) 7 SCC 532.

[22] *N.D. Jayal v. Union of India* (2004) 9 SCC 362.

[23] *Directorate of Film Festivals v. Gaurav Ashwin Jain* (2007) 4 SCC 737.

[24] Articles 148 and 149 of the Constitution.

[25] Report No. 17 of 2006 for the period ended March 2005, Performance Audit of Disinvestment of Government Shareholding in Selected PSUs during 1999–2003, Comptroller and Auditor General of India.

[26] Non-core assets.

[27] In the case of Paradip Phosphates Ltd, the government realized Rs 151.70 crore through the sale of shares. However, the new owners made a claim of Rs 151.55 crore under this clause. 'Audit Reports in Disinvestment', *Economic and Political Weekly*, Vol. 41, No. 50 (16–22 December 2006).

[28] The concerned ministers had given several assurances in 2002, when the NDA was in power, that the report would be published. Yet the report, which was fairly critical of the government, was published only in 2006, when the UPA government was in power. This has led commentators to question whether the CAG first withheld the report to please its political masters and then released it at a time when it would please the politicians of that time. Report No. 17 of 2006.

[29] A study of partial divestiture, i.e., cases where the government retained management control but sold only part of the shares, indicates that there are limited financial benefits through this form of disinvestment. A better method, if the goal of the policy is to improve the performance of the company sought

to be disinvested, thus appears to be through a sale where the management control also passes on to the buyer. See Sudhir Naib, 'Partial Divestiture and Performance of the Indian Public Sector Enterprises', *Economic and Political Weekly*, Vol. 38, No. 29, pp. 3088–93.

[30] E.A.S. Sarma. 'Disinvestment: What FMs Have Said Since 1991', *Economic and Political Weekly*, Vol. 39, No. 22, pp. 2196–96.

Chapter 9

Whose Gas Is It Anyway?

Sibling rivalries have existed from biblical times with the children of Adam and Eve, the brothers Cain and Abel, going so far as to commit fratricide. In a country like India where a large number of firms are owned by families, it is not unusual to see companies break up and businesses collapse because of disputes within families. However, rarely have these rivalries had the kind of economic impact on a country that the discord between the Ambani brothers had on India. Perhaps that is not surprising, given that they were not just any private individuals but were, at that time, among the richest men in the country[1] Nevertheless, the fight between the brothers resulted in a judgment that not only had a material impact on their own companies (and all the stakeholders), but also on the larger financial landscape of the country.

The case stemmed from a dispute about the implementation of a family settlement between the two Ambani brothers. They had entered into an agreement about the division of family-owned assets after an acrimonious falling out. When the younger brother, Anil, felt that the older brother, Mukesh, was reneging on his side of the bargain, he moved the Courts to seek enforcement of the settlement. At the heart of the dispute was the supply of natural gas by Mukesh's company to Anil's. The family settlement had provided that a specified quantity of gas at a fixed price would be supplied to Anil so as to enable him to set up a power plant that would supply electricity to large tracts of north India. Mukesh denied that he had any such liability while the companies that he controlled claimed that they were independent entities and were not bound by the family settlement.

The parties fiercely contested each other in the Courts, with the matter ultimately reaching the Supreme Court of India. This dispute would have normally resulted in a landmark judgment in matters relating to family settlements and the extent they would bind the companies owned by their promoters. But this judgment ended up deciding far more than mere individual rights under a family settlement. Like the proverbial case of the two monkeys fighting over bread and the cat coming and sneakily stealing it, the Government of India claimed that the natural gas did not belong to either of the brothers and in fact belonged to it. The Supreme Court agreed with the stance of the Union of India and held that all the petroleum resources in the country belonged to the people of India, as represented by the government.[2] The government had the exclusive right to determine the price of the gas and also the final say in its allocation.

Due to the severe under-supply of domestically produced gas, this power of allocation of gas was a very valuable tool for the government and handed it the ability to regulate the entire petroleum sector and all the industries reliant on it. Several commentators have also pointed out that this amounts to a virtual nationalization of the petroleum sector and significantly hampered its growth in the years to come.[3] On a side note, following the decision, Anil never got the gas, the power plants conceived by him were never set up and the path for his group's financial problems were laid.

I

From Rags to Gas: the Reliance Story

Before the brothers could fight over an empire, there was an empire that was required to be built. This happened in the lifetime of the family patriarch, Dhirubhai Ambani. Born in a humble home, Dhirajlal Hirabhai Ambani started a trading company called the Reliance Commercial Corporation in 1957 when he was aged just twenty-five years. He expanded his business from trading in polyester yarn to the manufacture of textiles in a factory situated near Ahmedabad. Through a mixture of business acumen, luck, access to the people in power and several other qualities, Dhirubhai Ambani made Reliance Industries Ltd (RIL) one of India's largest companies. Diversifying from textiles, Reliance Industries became a vertically integrated company manufacturing petrochemicals as well as the end products.[4] By 2002, the Reliance group of companies accounted for 3 per cent of the country's GDP and 10 per cent of the union government's indirect tax revenues. Around that time, the Reliance group also diversified into other promising sectors in the economy, including telecom and electricity generation. Dhirubhai Ambani and his two sons were firmly the new business royalty in India.[5] While Dhirubhai was the undoubted patriarch, the two siblings were also in charge of different facets of the business. But it appears that the joint control of the company was tenuous at best.

When Dhirubhai died of a massive stroke in 2002, it transpired that he had not written any will bequeathing specified shares to any family member. The ownership of the group companies was thus joint between the family members. While the two brothers initially managed the business together, there were murmurs with the media reporting on family disagreements.[6] Mukesh soon confirmed these rumours in an interview with a business channel.[7] The disharmony grew over a period of time, coming to a head in July 2004 when the board of directors of RIL resolved that Mukesh would be the chairman and managing director, with Anil being the vice-chairman who was required to act under the 'overall authority' of Mukesh. This firmly gave control of the businesses to Mukesh and effectively ousted Anil from any independent management.

Faced with these disputes, the matriarch of the family, Kokilaben Ambani, stepped in and brokered a settlement ('the MOU'), which divided the assets of the company. As per a press release issued by her on 18 June 2005, it was announced that the businesses would be split between the brothers.[8] Mukesh would get the cash cow of the group—the petrochemical giant RIL. Anil would get the telecom business, the electricity and certain other businesses. What the letter did not mention was that Anil would get another asset, i.e. natural gas.

Natural gas was an extremely valuable asset of RIL and was essential for its future business development. As part of the drive for vertical integration in the petrochemical sector, RIL had started prospecting for petroleum and natural gas.[9] RIL and its partners had entered into a production sharing contract (PSC) with the Government of India for the right to prospect for gas off the coast of Andhra Pradesh, in the Krishna–Godavari basin. In 2002, the same year as Dhirubhai had passed away, RIL announced a major discovery of gas in the basin, an area called the KG-D6 basin.[10] Vast amounts of gas were said to be in reserve and it was promised that the discovery would go a long way to make India energy self-reliant. It was predicted that the amount of gas produced by the wells in the region would reach almost 80 million cubic metres a day, a feat that would have resulted in doubling India's gas production.[11]

The MOU proposed that a large part of this gas would be sold to Anil at a price of USD 2.34 per mmbtu.[12] This was the same price at which RIL had previously contracted to supply gas to NTPC.[13] Hence it was felt that this was the correct price for the sale of gas as it had been discovered through a market process. Anil would use this gas for the generation of power at a gas-fired power plant to be built at Dadri, Uttar Pradesh. The natural gas was to be sold by RIL to a company that was to be controlled by Anil by way of a contract. The company nominated for this purpose was Reliance Natural Resources Pvt. Ltd (RNRL),[14] which ultimately lent its name to the judgment being discussed in this chapter.

II

The Disputes

The settlement agreement was met with relief in the markets, which had been spooked by the bitter fight between the promoters.[15] Though the exact terms of the MOU were not available in the public domain, its broad terms were known and were duly enforced by all the stakeholders. On the same date that Kokilaben had issued the press statement, RIL called a meeting of its board of directors. At that meeting, the substance (though not the actual document itself) of the MOU was placed before the board. Under the directions of the board, a corporate governance committee was constituted, which was required to operationalize the terms of the MOU in accordance with statutory and regulatory requirements.[16]

One of these requirements was the framing of a 'scheme of demerger'.[17] RIL was the parent company that ran multiple businesses, including petrochemicals. Since RIL was supposed to remain with Mukesh, a mechanism had to be devised through which the businesses falling to Anil's share could be transferred to him. The MOU envisaged a scheme where certain undertakings of RIL would be put into separate companies, which would then be transferred to Anil. This division of the businesses from the parent company into independent companies was called a scheme of demerger. Under this scheme, the telecom, electricity and gas supply businesses were to be hived off RIL and transferred to separate companies, which would be owned and controlled by Anil and would be independent of RIL. These companies were called the 'resulting companies' and included RNRL as the corporate vehicle through which the gas would be transferred to Anil's electricity-generating companies.

The scheme of demerger was prepared by lawyers, accountants and the corporate governance committee of RIL and contained a section in relation to the supply of gas by RIL to RNRL. As required by the law, the scheme of demerger was passed. It was then put to the vote of the shareholders of the concerned companies and was passed overwhelmingly. The scheme was also approved by the Bombay High Court.[18] Thus, it appeared that the MOU was being acted upon by all the concerned parties.

There was, however, a sting in the tail. The shares in the parent company were held through a complex web of holding and subsidiary companies. To transfer the ownership of the resulting companies to Anil, it was necessary to untangle some of this web and transfer the companies to him. This was a process that would take some time. During this interregnum, the companies would be controlled by RIL, i.e. Mukesh. It was in this twilight period that RIL entered into a gas supply agreement with RNRL. The agreement was signed on 12 January 2006 and passed with the consent of two directors of RNRL who were from the Mukesh camp. The sole director from the side of Anil objected but was overruled.[19] RNRL came under the control of Anil shortly thereafter.[20] However, the damage had been done because the gas supply agreement departed significantly from the terms of the MOU. The biggest problem for RNRL was that the agreement required that the gas price of USD 2.34 per mmbtu would have to be approved by the government, which had the power to refuse sale at this price (which it duly refused).[21] This requirement had not allegedly been mentioned in the MOU and the Anil camp alleged that this had been inserted only to scuttle the supply of gas. In the absence of the gas supply agreement, there would be no electricity generation and the very purpose of RNRL would be defeated.

III

The Battle in Court

Not one to take a perceived backstab lying down, Anil proceeded to sue his brother to ensure that the terms of the MOU were complied with in letter and spirit. Towards this end, Anil moved the Bombay High Court by way of a company petition. The scheme of demerger through which the gas supply business had been carved out of RIL and transferred to RNRL had stipulated that the companies would enter into a 'suitable arrangement' for the supply of gas. Before the high court, RNRL argued that the agreement that had been foisted upon it when the company was under the control of Mukesh was not a 'suitable arrangement'. It was argued that if RIL was not directed to supply gas in the manner envisaged under the MOU, the substratum of RNRL would disappear. The company would become a virtual shell with no assets. This, it was alleged, was contrary to the interests of the shareholders and was also against the spirit of the scheme of demerger.

Both the single judge[22] as well as the Division Bench[23] of the high court agreed with RNRL. They decided that RIL was required to supply gas to RNRL strictly as per the terms of the MOU. There was no requirement of seeking any approval from the government. This was particularly important because the government had, as noted before, refused to approve the price of gas agreed to between the parties. Also, during the course of hearing before the Bombay High Court, the government had come out with an alternate pricing formula that valued the gas at a much higher price.[24] Most crucially, the government had also approved a 'gas allocation policy' as per which the gas would be supplied by RIL to the companies and sectors decided by the government.[25] RIL was thus constrained to sell gas to the people selected by the government as per the price determined by the government. This allocation policy, the high court ruled, was beyond the powers of the government, at least to the extent of the gas already agreed to be supplied by RIL to RNRL under the MOU.

The high court judgment dealt a severe financial blow to RIL. As per media reports, RIL's revenues from the gas field would fall by as much as 25 per cent.[26] The price of RIL's shares also plummeted after the judgment. Given the personalities involved as well as the stakes of the matter, it was not a surprise that the matter was carried to the Supreme Court in appeal. Interestingly, even the Union of India filed an appeal against the judgment, asking the Court to uphold its right to determine the price and approve allocations of gas.

The hearing of the case commenced on 20 October and went on for two weeks. During this time, there was the usual parrying between the bench and the bar. Harish Salve, a senior advocate, was appearing for RIL and faced intense questioning during the hearing.[27] However, when the third week of the hearing was about to commence, there were murmurings in the media that there was going to be a development in the matter. In a packed courtroom, Justice R.V. Raveendran, one of the best and brightest judges of the Court who was on the bench hearing the matter, announced that he was recusing himself from hearing the case because his daughter worked for a law firm that was advising RIL. In a statement that he read out in Court he said that 'my conscience is clear and I feel that justice should not only be done but seems to be done. That is the tradition of this court'.[28] There was the usual slew of allegations and counter-allegations about the judge's recusal. However, the chief justice soon constituted a fresh bench to hear the matter, and the hearings commenced afresh. This time the hearings were mercifully devoid of any drama. The hearings went on for twenty-six more days, an extraordinarily long time in what was ostensibly a private dispute between two family members. The judgment was reserved in December and then the wait for the judgment began.[29]

IV

The Judgment

The verdict was delivered just a few days before the chief justice of India, who was heading the bench, was to retire.[30] The website of the Court showed that there were two verdicts—an indication that there could be a split verdict.[31] The day the judgment was to be pronounced by the Supreme Court, the media went into a frenzy. The courtroom was packed with lawyers and reporters. To add to the drama, Anil Ambani personally went to the Court to hear the pronouncement of the verdict.[32]

When the judgments were read out in Court it became clear that there was no substantial disagreement between the judges. The majority decision was authored by Justice Sathasivam and agreed to by Chief Justice Balakrishnan. Justice Sudershan Reddy authored a separate judgment that largely agreed with the majority, but departed significantly when it came to the issue of the binding nature of the MOU. But all three judges unanimously agreed that RIL was not required to supply gas to RNRL strictly as per the terms of the MOU and that the gas really belonged to the Union of India. Anil had decisively lost the battle in the Supreme Court and Mukesh had earned a pyrrhic victory.

While the judgment decided several issues, including the powers of the Court when enforcing a scheme of arrangement, the two areas that most impacted subsequent jurisprudence as well as the economy of the country were the binding nature of the MOU and the ownership of natural gas.

The entire scheme of arrangement and the subsequent events had been based upon the MOU, which was basically a family settlement. In the context of joint families in India, this had seemed an obvious method to divide the family business. After all, many Hindu undivided families (HUF) were aware of the concept of family settlements and regularly used them to partition the properties owned by members of the HUF. The Courts had also accorded the highest sanctity to such settlements, holding that they were an ideal means to end discord within families.[33] Other business families had also used the route of family settlements to divide businesses.[34]

In the popular imagination, the Ambani family 'owned' Reliance. Hence, there was really no issue in the two brothers dividing up the business between themselves. Indeed, even the board of directors of RIL considered themselves bound by the MOU and had even thanked Kokilaben for helping the brothers reach the settlement. The rigour of the law, however, suggested that this was not quite the case. The company was owned not just by the Ambanis, but also by the almost three million other shareholders. The MOU had been signed by just three of the shareholders. Even if they were the promoters of the company, the question was whether they had the power and authority to bind the company.

RIL had argued that the MOU was a mere piece of paper as far as it was concerned. The future and business of a publicly listed company could not be decided by three shareholders sitting behind closed doors. On the other hand, RNRL argued that the Ambanis were the controlling force behind RIL and hence any decision taken by them was, in effect, a decision taken by the company.[35]

The Court took a middle ground. The majority held that the MOU was indeed a private document and was not technically binding on RIL and RNRL. However, that was not the end of the matter. Mukesh, executives of RIL as well as the board of directors had repeatedly referred to the MOU. There was ample correspondence between all parties showing that they considered the MOU was the document on the basis of which the division of assets was occurring. Hence, it was not possible to simply brush aside the MOU and hold that it had no relevance to the dispute. The Court held that in case there was any ambiguity as to the interpretation or meaning of the scheme of demerger, the MOU could be relied upon as a piece of evidence. In the words of the Court, the MoU was 'one of the ways in which the intention of the parties can be made clear with regard to what was considered suitable'.[36] The MOU thus was placed in a no man's land. It wasn't directly enforceable but could be referred to in some instances.

Perhaps the most important finding in the judgment related to the ownership of the gas. The contract entered into between the government and RIL was titled the production sharing contract (PSC). The Court was required to interpret the terms of this PSC as well as the provisions of the Constitution and other laws to answer the question 'Whose gas is it anyway? Whether a contractor becomes the owner of the gas?'[37]

To undertake this exercise, the broad contours of the PSC had to be examined. The PSC recognized that RIL had expended vast sums of money on exploration and operation of the gas fields. Hence, initially, the entire natural gas extracted from the wells would fall to the share of RIL, which would sell the gas to recoup its expenses. This portion of the natural gas was referred to as the 'cost petroleum'.[38] Once the entire expenditure had been recovered, the balance of the gas would effectively represent pure profit (since the expenses had already been paid off). This gas was called the 'profit petroleum'[39] and was to be shared between RIL and the government.

RNRL contended that the entire cost of petroleum as well as RIL's share of the profit petroleum belonged to RIL. Therefore RIL was entirely within its rights to sell the gas to any party it wished to, at any price determined between the parties. On the other hand, the government as well as RIL argued that the gas belonged to the people of India. Even though RIL was entitled to extract and sell the gas, the ownership of the gas remained with the government. It was only once the gas was delivered to the ultimate consumer, at the end of the pipeline carrying the gas, that the title passed from the government. In other words, the government was the owner of the entire natural gas which lay in reserves under the sea bed and therefore had the right to determine its pricing as well as its valuation.

The answer to this question would have had a significant outcome for all parties. For RNRL, the only concern was whether the gas would be made available to it or not. The stakes for the government and RIL were higher. If the gas belonged to RIL, it would have the full freedom to market the natural gas and make substantial profits, particularly in a market over which it had a near monopoly. Even if the government were to step in and regulate the price, RIL would have had the right to use the gas for itself. After all, exploitation of natural gas had been spurred on by its desire for vertical integration. Therefore, RIL could have used the gas for itself rather than supplying it to other entities at the dictates of the government. Finally, for the Union of India, the stakes were nothing less than a return to the licence raj regime. It would have full control over the pricing and distribution of gas. Since gas was in a shortfall, this power would enable the government to be the final arbiter of which sectors it deemed a priority for the supply of natural gas. It would be the government, and not the market, which would determine where resources would flow to. This was probably any bureaucrat's (or politician's) dream.

Ultimately, the Court sided completely with the government's interpretation. In doing so, the Court relied on the wording of Article 297 of the Constitution, which postulates that all lands, minerals and other things of value underlying the ocean within the territorial waters, or the continental shelf, or the exclusive economic zone, of India shall vest in the Union and be held for the purposes of the Union.

As per the Court, the provisions of the Constitution as well as the statutes, the gas belonged to the Union, which was nothing other than the people of India. The government held the gas in a public trust for the people and could only utilize the gas for the larger public good. Even the terms of the PSC were in compliance with government ownership of gas. Thus the government had the full power to regulate and distribute the manner of sale of natural gas in the best interests of the country.[40]

However, the judgment contained some paradoxes. For instance, the Court held that though the PSC gave RIL the freedom to trade, 'but this freedom is exercised by the contractor through a transparent bidding process and non-interference of the Government in the administration of gas supply. As a matter of policy also, the Government must be free to determine the valuation formula as well as the price . . . Thus, the Government has the power to determine valuation as well as price for the purpose of the PSC.'[41] It is difficult to understand how a party can have freedom of trade when someone else dictates both the price as well as the utilization of gas.

Certain parts of the judgment almost read like the communist manifesto. The majority held that though it was commendable that private parties aided the exploration and extraction of natural gas, 'but the nature of the profits gained from such activities can ideally belong to the State which is in a better position to distribute them for the best interests of the people.'[42] The concurring judgment of Justice Reddy held that 'History has repeatedly shown that a culture of uncontained greed along with uncontrolled markets leads to disasters. Human rationality, with respect to pursuit of lucre, is essentially short run.'[43]

These excerpts reveal the barely disguised disdain that the Court had for risk-taking as well as towards the profit motive that made entrepreneurs invest in projects. There was also a touching faith displayed towards the benevolence of governments as the custodian of natural resources.[44]

Conclusion

Even if temporary, the judgment was a massive reprieve for RIL. This was not only because it would not be forced to sell gas at a lower than market price. It was also because all the optimism it had displayed at the time of exploration proved to be unfounded. While RIL had estimated that it had reserves of almost 10 trillion cubic feet (TCF) of gas, fresh estimates revealed that the reserves were 70 per cent lower, i.e., only about 3 TCF. Far from being able to produce 80 MMSCMD of gas every day, production rapidly fell to about 10 MMSCMD by 2018.[45] Clearly, at this rate, RIL would not have been able to supply the contracted amount of 28 MMSCMD of gas to RNRL and would have opened itself up to a substantial claim of damages.

However, this victory came with a significant downside. The government could now control virtually all aspects of marketing the gas. If the government was able to determine price as well as the buyer of the gas, then any entrepreneur would be left with all of the risk and virtually none of the profits. It is true that natural resources often lead to the so-called 'resource curse', where resource-rich countries are victims of a predatory form of capitalism.[46] In such situations, lower-income countries with greater resources often underperform those who do not have such resources. However, the Court, in its eagerness to control the perceived problem, went a bit too far. Rather than effectively nationalizing the petroleum sector, a better course of action would have been to recommend the appointment of a truly independent market regulator. It seems that Indian businesses need to be protected not only from crony capitalism, but also from overreaching State interventions.

Notes

[1] At the time of the dispute, *Forbes Magazine* estimated Mukesh to be the richest man in India with a net worth of USD 27 billion. Brother Anil was not far behind, being the sixth richest Indian with a net worth of USD 13.3 billion. See 'Ambani Brothers Fortune Grows Six-Fold to $40 Bn Since 2004', *The Economic Times*, 4 October 2010.

[2] *Reliance Natural Resources Ltd v. Reliance Industries Ltd* (2010) 7 SCC 1.

[3] 'Backward Intervention', *Open Magazine*, 13 May 2010.

[4] An interesting account of Dhirubhai Ambani's life is to be found in Hamish McDonald, *Ambani and Sons*, Lotus Collection (2010).

[5] By 2002, 'Reliance had 3.5 million individual shareholders, meaning that one in four Indian share investors had a stake in Reliance. They had seen its net profits grow by 29 per cent a year on average during the 1990s. By March 2001, it yielded 30 per cent of the total profits of the Indian private sector and 10 per cent of profits if government-controlled corporations were included. Accounting for about 12 per cent of total Indian share market capitalization, it had weightings of 22 to 25 per cent in the main market indices.' Hamish McDonald, *Ambani & Sons*, Kindle edition, p. 259.

[6] Sucheta Dalal. 'The Ambani Dream and a Mysterious Absence', Rediff.com, 2 January 2003.

[7] 'Mukesh Admits to Differences with Anil', Rediff.com, 18 November 2004.

[8] 'Kokilaben's Settlement Letter', Rediff.com, 18 June 2005.

[9] Vertical integration was a philosophy where RIL wanted to own and produce not only the finished products, but also the raw materials. For instance, in case of polyester fabrics, the company also wished to have control over the petroleum products used to make the fabric. For a critique of this business philosophy, see R. Jannathan, 'Reliance Minus Vimal: Is the Sum of Parts Greater than the Whole', Firstpost, 22 June 2012.

[10] Hemangi Balse. 'Reliance Gas find 40 Times Bigger than Bombay High', Rediff.com, 31 October 2002.

[11] 'Natural Gas Flows from RIL's KG Basin', *The Economic Times*, 2 April 2009.

[12] mmbtu stands for million British thermal units and is a measure of the volume of gas.

[13] NTPC had floated a global tender seeking supply of gas for its thermal power units. RIL had submitted the winning bid where it had undertaken to supply 12 MMCMD (million cubic metres) of gas at the rate of USD 2.34 per mmbtu for a period of seventeen years. Eventually, the parties fell out with RIL claiming that there was no concluded contract between them. NTPC filed a suit in the Bombay High Court against RIL seeking specific performance of the supply agreement in the year 2006. The suit is, at the date of writing this chapter, still pending final adjudication before the high court in spite of a judgment of the Supreme Court directing an expeditious disposal of the case. See *NTPV v. RIL*, Civil Appeal 2395-2396 of 2019.

[14] At the time of the family settlement, the name of RNRL was 'Global Fuel Management Services Ltd'.

[15] 'An Empire Split', *Frontline*, 15 July 2005.

[16] These facts can be found in the judgment of Justice Reddy in the RNRL judgment, particularly paragraphs 160–166.

[17] The scheme was a specie of the 'Schemes of Arrangement' provided under Section 391–394 of the Companies Act, 1956.

[18] Para 167 of the RNRL judgment.

[19] 'RNRL Slams Mukesh Ambani, Oil Ministry in SC', *The New Indian Express*, 26 November 2009.

[20] On 7 February 2006.

[21] RIL applied for approval to the government in April 2006, but the Ministry of Petroleum and Natural Gas rejected this request on 27 July 2006.

[22] *RNRL v. RIL* 2007 Supp Bom CR 925.

[23] *RIL v. RNRL* 2009 Supp Bom CR 1011.

[24] The Empowered Group of Ministers (EGOM) approved a gas price valuation formula on 12 September 2007. The formula used the value of petroleum, which was a freely marketable product, to derive the value of natural gas. As on that date, the value of natural gas was USD 4.2 per mmbtu. 'Press note: EGoM Clears Gas Pricing Formula for KG Block', Press Information Bureau, 12 September 2007.

[25] The EGOM on gas allocation decided that priority sectors like fertilizers and idle power plants would get gas from the KG D6 basin. Given the shortfall of gas, there would be virtually no gas left to be allocated for any new power plants to be set up. 'Press note: Decision Regarding Sale of Natural Gas by

NELP Contractors and Order of Priority to Supply Gas from RIL's KG D6 Gas Basin', Press Information Bureau, 2 June 2008.

[26] 'RNRL to Get Gas at $2.34; RIL May Challenge Decision in SC', *The Economic Times*, 16 June 2009.

[27] 'Judge Recuses Himself from RIL Gas Case on Personal Grounds', *Financial Express*, 5 November 2009. RIL commenced arguments because it had lost the case before the Bombay High Court. The intense questioning had more to do with the practice of judges asking questions to the counsel arguing the matter than the reflection of the strength of the case. Tough questions are usually asked to help judges reach the crux of any matter.

[28] 'Supreme Court Judge Steps out of RIL–RNRL Case', *Business Standard*, 21 January 2013.

[29] 'SC Reserves Verdict on Ambani Gas Row, Govt. Asserts Title', *India Today*, 18 December 2009.

[30] The judgment was pronounced on 7 May 2010 and Chief Justice Balakrishnan was due to retire on 11 May 2010.

[31] 'Judgment Today in Ambanis' Gas War; Split Verdict Possible', *Hindustan Times*, 7 May 2010.

[32] Paranjoy Guha Thakurta, Subir Ghosh and Jyotirmoy Chaudhuri. *Gas Wars: Crony Capitalism and the Ambanis*, Paranjoy Guha Thakurta; 1st edition (1 January 2014), p. 39.

[33] *Kale v. Director of Consolidation* (1976) 3 SCC 119.

[34] One notable instance was the Modi family, which also divided the business in a similar manner. The division of the company also spawned litigation, one limb of which reached the Supreme Court. See *KK Modi v. KN Modi* (1998) 3 SCC 573.

[35] Counsel for RNRL Ram Jethmalani relied upon the doctrine of identification for this purpose. See para 56 of the RNRL judgment.

[36] Para 59 of the RNRL judgment.

[37] Part IV, Justice Reddy's judgment in the RNRL judgment.

[38] Article 1.28 of the PSC.

[39] Article 1.77 of the PSC.

[40] Para 78 of the RNRL judgment.

[41] Para 94 of the RNRL judgment.

[42] Para 118 of the RNRL judgment.

[43] Para 141. The judgment is replete with such references. For instance, in Para 244 the judge ruled that 'India was never meant to be a mere land in which

the desires and the actions of the rich and the mighty take precedence over the needs of the people.'

44 'The court's order, however, opened doors wide for corporate lobbyists to influence government policies. Many saw this as contributing to corruption and crony capitalism in the extraction of minerals (including hydrocarbons) even as ministers swore by the virtues of "economic liberalisation". One interpretation of the Supreme Court judgment was that it set the clock back to the days of the licence-quota raj. Henceforth, only those who were close to politicians and decision-makers would benefit.' *Gas Wars: Crony Capitalism and the Ambanis*, p. 43.

45 'The Curious Case of Reliance's KG D6', DNAindia.com, 19 March 2018.

46 'Making Natural Resources into a Blessing Rather than a Curse', from *Covering Oil: A Reporter's Guide to Energy and Development*, Svetlana Tsalik and Anya Schiffrin, eds., The Open Society Institute: New York, 2005, pp. 13–20.

Chapter 10

The Only Certainties in Life: Death and Taxes

Tax law, as most legal practitioners would agree, is one of the drier areas of law. The Indian Income Tax Act, 1961, has been amended so often and is so complex that it requires a dedicated and devoted specialist to understand even its basic nuances. In this backdrop, the Vodafone case[1] is an exception. It is rare that a case relating to the arcane principles of tax can be gripping, but the Vodafone case reads more like a thriller than a legal battle. The case involved not only the determination of tax liability in a particular case, but also shook international investor confidence in the Indian economy. The use of the contentious bilateral investment treaties by foreign companies also invited charges of economic imperialism.

The heart of the dispute, shorn of other details, concerned the relationship between the taxpayer and the tax collector. The relationship between the Indian taxpayer and the income tax department has always been fraught. Taxpayers seem to resent paying tax, even if it is a reasonable and genuine demand. On the other hand, the department often views every assessee through the lens of suspicion and often considers that the sole purpose of business is to generate revenue for itself. To that extent, the department is often a law unto itself. Armed with the coercive power of the State and the ear of the finance minister, the department often flexes its muscles to extract dues that it considers itself entitled to.

The Vodafone case was just one such instance. After having lost a tax dispute, the department seemed like a sore loser and then asked for the law itself to be amended. The finance minister duly obliged and recommended to Parliament to pass a piece of legislation that was to take effect retrospectively. The stated intention was to undo the judgment of the Court so as to enable the taxman to levy a huge tax. However, it seems that the department had overplayed its hand. Retrospective taxation led to an outcry, both domestically and internationally. At the date of writing this chapter, it seems that the disputes are finally drawing to a close.[2] However, the case should be read as a cautionary tale on how the government ought not to behave in matters relating to taxation.

I

Death and Taxes[3]

Possibly one of the most eagerly anticipated parts of the annual Budget speech is the one about taxes. The entire spectrum of the taxpaying public, from the salaried classes to the CEOs of large corporations, must plan their finances depending on how generous (or indeed, rapacious) the finance minister has been in any particular year. Most of the policy decisions laid down in a Budget are operationalized through incorporation in the Income Tax Act. Inevitably, this has caused the Income Tax Act to become increasingly complex.

In spite of the complexity of the minutiae, historically, the principles of taxation of a domestic concern were relatively simple. The canons of taxation had been posited by Adam Smith in his seminal work, *The Wealth of Nations*. In the case of residents (corporate or individual), all income accrued in India from any source is deemed to be income.[4] Subject to statutorily deductible exemptions, tax was liable to be paid on the entire income. Determining the total income could give rise to some interesting questions of law, but the scope of inquiry was usually limited.

This system of corporate taxation had been designed for companies that existed in individual countries. With increasing globalization and with companies operating in multiple tax jurisdictions, there was bound to be some change to this model. Initially, an international consensus on taxation developed, which has been described as a 'flawed miracle'.[5] A miracle because a consensus was reached, a rare phenomenon in the world of competing national economic interests. However, the system was fundamentally flawed as it was based on the format of independent, single-state companies conducting business internationally, through branches or through agreements with unrelated foreign enterprises.[6] This simplistic form of international business transaction was quite removed from commercial reality. Increasingly, companies were owned by a web of holding companies spread across multiple jurisdictions. Some of these companies were resident in so-called tax havens—countries that either had a very low regime of taxation or offered substantial banking secrecy. This regime allowed companies to be based in jurisdictions which would be the most tax-efficient. There could also be operational reasons as to why a multinational company would like to have subsidiaries in different jurisdictions. The larger multinationals used this structure to operate in many of the countries they did business in. One such case was of an Indian telecom enterprise owned by the Hong Kong-based telecom giant, Hutchison Whampoa (Hutchison).

II

The Deal

In the nineties, the telecom industry had witnessed a virtual revolution. The monopoly of State-owned companies, MTNL and BSNL, had been done away with. The doors had been opened to private players offering both fixed and mobile telecommunications services. With the shift from a licence-fees regime to a revenue-sharing regime, the entire sector started growing exponentially.

In 1992, Hutchison decided to enter the Indian telecom market. To that end, it acquired interest in a company that came to be known as Hutchison Essar Ltd (HEL). HEL initially held the licence for just one telecom circle—Delhi. However, with the growing consolidation and expansion that was taking place in India, HEL grew to acquire a pan-India presence. Each of these licences was owned and operated by a fully-owned subsidiary of HEL.

The structure of the holding companies, as could be expected, was extremely complex and also constantly changing with time. However, at the time of the Vodafone acquisition, the structure was roughly as follows: Hutchison had a fully-owned subsidiary in the Cayman Islands, CGP Investments (Holdings) Ltd (CGI). This Cayman Islands company in turn held shares in certain other companies incorporated in Mauritius. It was these Mauritius-based companies that owned 52 per cent of the shareholding in HEL and a further 15 per cent options in HEL. CGI and the Mauritius companies, and thus indirectly Hutchison, effectively controlled 67 per cent of the shareholding of HEL.

In 2006, Hutchison decided to exit the Indian market and invited offers for purchase of the Indian telecom business internationally. After a fair bit of wrangling, Vodafone PLC, a company incorporated and listed in London, made a bid for

HEL. A deal was struck for some USD 18.5 billion, under which Vodafone would take over the running of Hutchison's Indian telecom business. Rather than acquiring HEL directly, Vodafone purchased Hutchison's entire shareholding in HEL's parent company, i.e., in CGI, the Cayman Islands company. A subsidiary of Vodafone PLC, i.e., Vodafone International Holdings BV (VIH, a company resident for tax purposes in the Netherlands) was the chosen vehicle for the acquisition of shares.

Since Hutchison was selling the shares it indirectly held in HEL at a profit, a question arose as to whether capital gains tax was payable in India. The underlying assets of HEL were the licences and the telecom businesses, which were all located in India. However, what was being sold at a profit was not the business of HEL or even the shares of HEL. What was being sold were the shares held by Hutchison in CGI, which was located outside India. Under the Income Tax Act, a capital gains tax is payable on the profit made upon the sale of any asset located in India. Section 9[7] of the Income Tax Act contains a deeming provision, i.e., any income is deemed to accrue in India if, among other things, the income is earned 'through the transfer of a capital asset situated in India.' Therefore, there would have been no tax liability in India if the transaction was seen solely of the sale of shares, and not a capital asset. If, however, the asset being sold was seen as something other than merely the shares of CGI and was relatable to any 'capital asset' in India, tax would be payable.

In the case of Vodafone, it was VIH, a Dutch company, which purchased the shares of CGI, a Cayman Islands company from Hutchison, a Hong Kong-based company. No part of the sale and purchase of shares happened in India, even though the assets of HEL were based entirely in India. Vodafone obtained a legal opinion which said that since no part of the transaction had happened in India and no asset in India had been directly transferred, the Indian tax department did not have any jurisdiction to levy tax. This belief was bolstered by the fact that even in the past, Hutchison had purchased shares in offshore companies that had assets in India and had never been subjected to any tax demand.[8] This belief in the benign nature of the tax department was soon shown to be misplaced.

Calling the Vodafone takeover a 'test case', thereby acknowledging its failure to levy tax in similar transactions in the past, the department sent notices to Vodafone demanding payment of the withholding tax. Notices were not sent to Hutchison even though they were the actual beneficiaries of the transaction. This was because the Income Tax Act provided that whenever a purchaser paid any money to a non-resident, it had to withhold the amount of tax due from the payment made by it to the seller. This was akin to the tax deducted at source (TDS) that has been provided for under the Income Tax Act. While this was a legally possible argument, it is quite likely that the department went after Vodafone as it had a business presence in India, unlike Hutchison, which had by that time exited India.

III

The Supreme Court Judgment

The dispute was initially decided by the Bombay High Court, which ruled in favour of the tax department and held that Vodafone was liable to pay the withholding tax. Vodafone immediately appealed to the Supreme Court urging that the Court quash the tax demands of the department. Vodafone essentially argued that the entire share purchase agreement had taken place outside the territory of India. The entire payment had been made outside India and no capital asset located in India had been transferred. Since the income tax department did not exercise its jurisdiction beyond the territory of India, it could not tax any transaction that had taken place abroad.

The government put forward a number of arguments as to why the high court judgment was right and why they should be able to levy the withholding tax on Vodafone. Primarily, the department asked the Court to 'look through' the transaction and see what the real asset being sold was. In the eyes of the government, the ultimate asset being sold was not the shares of Hutchison in CGI located in the Cayman Islands, but the assets of HEL located in India. In fact, the government argued that the whole structure of the sale was a sham. The very purpose that CGI had been included in the corporate set-up was allegedly to formulate a scheme so that no tax would be payable in India. Since the purchase of CGI shares would ostensibly be outside India and thus out of the jurisdiction of the Indian tax department, the parties had deliberately structured their deal so as to avoid payment of tax in India. At the heart of this argument was the assertion that tax avoidance was not a permissible exercise for a taxpayer under any circumstance.

This conflated two well-recognized and distinct principles in tax law—tax evasion and tax avoidance. It was clear that tax evasion, i.e., a wilful violation of the laws and a failure to pay tax otherwise due, was an illegality. Tax avoidance, on the other hand, was the structuring of a deal to take advantage of any loopholes in the law so as to avoid paying a tax that would otherwise have been payable. In such a case, the assessee would be strictly within the four corners of the law but would escape some portion of the tax liability. Historically, this had been considered to be permissible under the law. However, the government, relying on an earlier judgment of the Supreme Court, contended that even tax avoidance was an illegality.[9] The government argued that sale of shares of the Cayman Island company was merely a tax avoidance deal, and the Court could proceed to ignore it and tax the transaction as though it had happened in India. In effect, the government argued that the splitting of the corporate structure between a parent company and its subsidiaries should be ignored, and the true nature of the transaction should be seen—a sale of the assets held by an Indian company to another entity.

This argument was soundly rejected by the Court. The Court held that tax avoidance was a permissible activity, as long as the transaction had not been structured *solely* with a view to avoid payment of tax. In the words of the Court, 'when it comes to taxation of a holding structure, at the threshold, the burden is on the Revenue to allege and establish abuse, . . . To give an example, . . . a case where the Revenue finds that, in a holding structure, an entity which has no commercial/business substance has been interposed *only to avoid tax* then in such cases applying the test of fiscal nullity it would be open to the Revenue to discard such interpositioning of that entity.'

In effect, the Court held that a heavy onus lay on the revenue department to show that the entire structure of holding companies and subsidiaries had been planned with the sole aim of avoiding payment of tax. If, however, there were any business reasons for creating such a structure, the Court could not pierce the corporate veil even if tax was being avoided.

The essence of this finding was that the Court had to 'look at' the transactional documents and take what it said at face value. The revenue department was not supposed to 'look through' the transaction, dissecting different clauses of the documentation so as to determine some ostensible purpose. Thus, if one 'side effect' of a deal, which otherwise had a commercial purpose, was the avoidance of tax, the tax man had to accept the deal. In other words, the judgment held that only when the corporate organizational structure was fraud or subterfuge could it be ignored. On the facts, the Court found that the purchase of shares by Vodafone was not a 'colourable device', i.e., not a strategy designed with the sole aim and objective of avoiding tax.

Another argument put forward by the income tax department was that the sale purchase agreement (SPA) effectively handed over the management rights over HEL, the Indian asset, to Vodafone. This right of control and management of a company was a property right and was located in India. Hence, argued the government, the sale amounted to a transfer of a capital asset located in India and would attract a capital gains tax. This argument had been accepted by the Bombay High Court, but was rejected by the Supreme Court. The Court held that when examining the SPA, the revenue department was supposed to 'look at the entire transaction holistically and not to adopt a dissecting approach'.[10] The revenue department was also required to determine whether it was a 'pre-ordained transaction', i.e., a transaction created solely for tax avoidance purposes, or whether it was one done for the purposes of 'investment to participate'. There were many factors to be taken into account when making such a determination— 'duration of time during which the holding structure existed, the period of business operations in India, generation of taxable revenue in India during the period of business operations in India, the timing of the exit, the continuity of business on such exit.'[11] Examining the facts of the case, the Court held that the structure of Hutchison's ownership had been in place from 1994 until 2007 and was thus not created solely for the purpose of avoiding tax. The Court also noted the huge amount of taxes, amounting to thousands of crores in direct taxes, paid during that time. It thus concluded that the transaction was one of 'investment to participate' and not a sham transaction.

More conceptually, the Court relied on one of the most fundamental principles of corporate law—the principle of independent corporate personality. This was the principle that a company was a distinct juristic entity and could not be equated to its shareholders. Thus, parent companies and their subsidiaries were distinct entities with independent tax liabilities. The Court acknowledged the business reality that a parent company may lay down policies which would have to be followed by its subsidiaries, but ruled that this would not be enough by itself to show that the parent and the holding companies were to be treated as one for the purpose of payment of tax.

The Court found that in the case of multinational parent companies, their subsidiaries typically enjoyed a great deal of autonomy. While the parent company may have had some control over the subsidiary through the powers it exercised as a shareholder, the subsidiary nevertheless operated by its own Articles of Association. The directors may have been appointed by the parent company, but once appointed, they owed their duties to the subsidiary and not the parent. The Court did envisage certain situations where the subsidiary was merely an alter ego of the parent, for instance where the parent exerted such an overwhelming control over the subsidiary that it had virtually no independent existence. The test, as per the Court, was 'whether the parent company's management has such steering interference with the subsidiary's core activities that the subsidiary can no longer be regarded to perform those activities on the authority of its own executive directors.' In the case of Vodafone, the Court found that there was no such overwhelming control, and it thus rejected the contention of the government.

In probably one of the most important parts of the judgment, the Court gave its understanding of why multinationals adopted this particular organizational structure. 'A typical large business corporation consists of sub-incorporates. . . . On top is a parent or a holding company. The parent is the public face of the business. The parent is the only group member that normally discloses financial results. Below the parent company are the subsidiaries which hold operational assets of the business, and which often have their own subordinate entities that can extend layers. . . . Subsidiaries reduce the amount of information that creditors need to gather. Subsidiaries also promote the benefits of specialisation. Subsidiaries permit creditors to lend against only specified divisions of the firm. These are the efficiencies inbuilt in a holding structure. Subsidiaries are often created for tax or regulatory reasons. They at times come into existence from mergers and acquisitions. . . . The courts have evolved doctrines like piercing the corporate veil, substance over form, etc. enabling taxation of underlying assets in cases of fraud, sham, tax avoidance, etc. However, genuine strategic tax planning is not ruled out.'

The judgment had recognized, and accepted, the paradigm of multinational companies that operated with a web of subsidiaries. The Court, unlike the tax department, did not view these structures with suspicion but simply as a commercial reality. The Court thus decided that the Indian income tax department had no jurisdiction to issue any tax demands since the transaction was a genuine transaction, not undertaken simply to avoid payment of taxes otherwise due. In doing so, the Court showed a greater sensitivity to business and specifically held that in case the country wished to attract more foreign direct investment, it would be required to have a stable and predictable tax regime rather than the capricious and avaricious view that the income tax department was so keen on taking.

Vodafone no doubt reacted to the judgment with some relief. The pink papers also welcomed the judgment as a 'big boost for cross border mergers and acquisitions'.[12] The judgment was also subject to trenchant criticism, with various commentators going so far as to say that the judgment legitimized tax avoidance even in cases where the transaction was merely subterfuge, designed solely to avoid paying taxes.[13] It appears that the government and the tax department were equally miffed at this unfavourable ruling.

In the very next Budget after the judgment, the finance minister proposed to amend the Income Tax Act with retrospective effect. The aim of the proposed amendments was to undo the basis of the Supreme Court judgment. Certain definitions were amended, and two explanations were added to Section 9 of the act. One insertion in the act made the intention of the draftsman quite clear. The explanation inserted in the act provided that 'an asset or a capital asset being any share or interest in a company or entity registered or incorporated outside India shall be deemed to be and shall always be deemed to have been situated in India, if the share or interest derives, directly or indirectly, its value substantially from the assets located in India.' This amendment effectively stated that the corporate structure of any entity could be ignored and all that had to be examined was whether the underlying assets of the company were located in India.

The amendment was a wolf in sheep's clothing. The language of the amendment, though couched as a clarification or an amendment, was clearly in the nature of a substantive change. In other words, the department could now pursue its claims against Vodafone with retrospective effect and without being bound by the judgment of the Supreme Court. The amendment caused dismay in business circles. It appeared that in a battle with the Indian tax department, one could not win. Even if the highest court in the land ruled in your favour, the government would simply change the rules of the game. Further, no business could plan its affairs with any certainty if this form of retrospective transactions were to be permitted.

Businesses, both domestic and international, hoped that the government would understand their concerns and roll back the legislation. Their hopes were unfounded. Even though India saw a change of government in 2014, the incumbent political party did not restore the position before the amendment.

It appeared that the only recourse would once again be through the courts of law.

IV

The Aftermath

Once the retrospective amendment was passed, Vodafone could potentially have challenged it, arguing that the act was a clear attempt to overrule a judgment of the Supreme Court, something that is prohibited under the Constitution. However, the chances of success were probably not very high. The government would have argued that its attempt was not to overrule the judgment, but merely to change the law with retrospective effect. This was a tool the government had employed often in the past, to a great degree of success.[14] The modus operandi was something like this—typically in any judgment, the Court would have given its interpretation on a particular provision of law based on the language of the section. To undo the effect of the judgment, the government would not attempt to undo that interpretation, since that was constitutionally prohibited. Instead, the legislature would amend the words of the section itself with retrospective effect, thereby removing the underlying basis of the judgment. In effect, the judgment of the Court would stand; however, the section that the Court had interpreted would no longer be in existence! Such actions had been upheld by the Courts in the past, holding that this was a legitimate exercise of power by the sovereign legislature and did not amount to usurpation of the judicial function.

It is possible that the government expected Vodafone to challenge the section. Certainly, the counsel for Vodafone thought that this was what the government expected.[15] However, Vodafone did not do so and proceeded to file a claim under the Bilateral Investment Treaty (BIT), entered into between India and the Netherlands (the country where VIH was domiciled).

The BIT was part of several such agreements entered into by India with other countries whose purpose was to give assurance to the investors of those countries that they would be treated fairly. This was considered necessary by the Government of India as it created a positive business environment where large multinationals would consider it safe to invest in India. This was largely through the provision of an independent dispute resolution mechanism. Clause 9 of the BIT provided that in the case of any claim by a company against India, it could seek a reference of that dispute to the Permanent Court of International Arbitration, which was a neutral body and could thus be presumed not to be beholden to the Government of India.

Vodafone invoked the arbitration clause under the BIT saying that India had breached its obligations under the BIT, i.e., had violated its promise that companies operating in India would be 'accorded fair and equitable treatment and shall enjoy full protection and security in the territory of the other'. A tribunal of three arbitrators was constituted, which heard the case while sitting in Singapore. The Government of India argued that the tribunal had no jurisdiction to decide the matter and that in any case the imposition of the retrospective tax was not contrary to the treaty obligations.[16]

The tribunal was not impressed with the arguments of the Indian government and held that it was in breach of its obligations under the BIT. Specifically, the tribunal ruled that the government's 'conduct in respect of the imposition of the Claimant of an asserted liability to tax notwithstanding the Supreme Court Judgement is in breach of the guarantee of fair and equitable treatment laid down in Article 4(1) of the Agreement, as is the imposition of interest on the sums in question and the imposition of penalties for non-payment of the sums in question.' The tribunal thus restrained India from pursuing its claim against Vodafone for recovery of tax.[17] Further, a sum of almost USD 6 million was awarded to

Vodafone in relation to the costs incurred by it in the arbitration. Thus, not only did the government lose, it also ended up having to pay Vodafone for the arbitration.

The initial response of the government was combative. The award was challenged before the Courts in Singapore even though the scope of challenge to such awards was extremely limited and the government was not likely to win any appeal in the Court.[18] This was in line with the government's hostile approach to BITs. The general perception in the corridors of power was that the BITs were skewed against developing countries such as India. Since 2016, some seventy-nine of the eighty-seven BITs have been terminated.[19]

Ultimately, however, better sense prevailed in the government. Faced with adverse international press as well as arbitral awards, it decided to repeal the retrospective amendments and give up its claim against Vodafone.[20] This repeal, however, was not merely for Vodafone. Ever since the misadventure in the case of retrospective amendments, the government had sought to collect Rs 1.1 lakh crore as back taxes from seventeen entities. Perhaps the fact that, of this amount, the government had managed to raise only Rs 8100 crore[21] showed the futility of such retrospective taxation.

The government has now notified the rules that operationalize the settlement procedures.[22] The rules require that any person wishing to avail the benefit must furnish an undertaking that they will not pursue any claim against the government or seek to enforce any arbitral award or judgment that they may have obtained. If Vodafone does give such an undertaking, the sordid chapter of the tax department's overreach might finally come to an end.

Conclusion

Of all the matters relating to finance and economics, matters of taxation generate the most heat. This is because tax has a direct, and, most importantly, visible impact on the wallets of the taxpayers. Matters of fiscal policy might generally affect the bottom line of people and companies, but direct taxes have an immediacy that evokes a particularly visceral reaction. On the other hand, governments also rely on tax for the generation of revenues to fund themselves. The government must walk a tightrope between charging enough tax to fund its expenses and not charging so much as to act as an economic dampener or to evoke a hostile political reaction.

It has been said that the art of taxation consists of plucking the goose so as to obtain the largest possible amount of feathers with the least possible amount of hissing. However, in the case of the Indian tax department, it appears that there is also the feeling that the goose is one that lays golden eggs, whose feathers need to be plucked and the eggs need to be confiscated. This belief causes the department to overextend their jurisdiction and seek to procure taxes even at the cost of the economic well-being of the companies they tax, as well as of the larger economy. As the Vodafone case demonstrated, even the orders of the highest Court in the land were not sufficient to stop the demands of the tax department. In doing so, lasting damage may have been done to the reputation of India as an attractive business hub in the international economic sphere. In the end, it appears that economic considerations for the wider economy caused the government to rein in the tax department. It remains to be seen whether this act is a false start or the beginning of a sustained push against the so-called tax terrorism of the department.

Notes

[1] *Vodafone International Holdings BV v. Union of India*, (2012) 6 SCC 613.

[2] 'Vodafone Confirms Filing for Retro Tax Dispute Settlement with India', *The Economic Times*, 4 December 2021.

[3] Attributed to Daniel Defoe's *The Political History of the Devil*, published 1726.

[4] Section 4 and 5 of Income Tax Act, 1961.

[5] G.T. Loomer. 'The Vodafone Essar Dispute: Inadequate Tax Principles Create Difficult Choices for India', *National Law School of India Review, 21*(1) (2009)., pp. 89–116.

[6] Ibid.

[7] Section 9. Income deemed to accrue or arise in India. (I) The following incomes shall be deemed to accrue or arise in India: (i) all income accruing or arising, whether directly or indirectly, through or from any business connection in India, or through or from any property in India, or through or from any asset or source of income in India, or through the transfer of a capital asset situated in India.

[8] H. Salve. 'Retrospective Taxation—the Indian Experience', *British Institute of International and Comparative Law*, 2015.

[9] *McDowell & Co. v. The Commercial Tax Officer* (1985) 3 SCC 230. This is what is referred to as a 'judicial anti-avoidance' measure, i.e., a principle of law developed by the judges to catch certain forms of tax avoidance in the tax net. The other method is known as the legislative anti-avoidance measure. This would cover cases where Parliament enacts rules to cover cases of tax avoidance. Once such legislative device is the General Anti Avoidance Rules, or the GAAR. See 'Anti-Avoidance Measures', Ostwal and Vijayaraghavan, *National Law School of India Review*, Vol. 22 (2010), pp. 59–103.

[10] Vodafone International Holdings BV, para 96.

[11] Para 81.

[12] 'Vodafone Wins $2 bn Tax Case in Supreme Court', *Business Standard*, 20 January 2013.

[13] P. Bhushan. 'Legitimising Tax Avoidance', *Economic & Political Weekly*, Vol. 47, No. 9 (2012), and 'Curious Conclusion', *Frontline*, 23 March 2012.

[14] Such a technique was used to validate imposition of property taxes in Gujarat and was upheld by the Supreme Court in *Shri Prithvi Cotton Mills Ltd v. Broach Borough Municipality* (1969) 2 SCC 283. The law in this regard has been extensively discussed in *Cheviti Venkanna Yadav v. State of Telangana* (2017) 1 SCC 283.

[15] H. Salve. 'Retrospective Taxation—the Indian Experience'.

[16] The Government of India had also moved the Delhi High Court seeking a stay of the arbitration. The high court initially granted a stay in August 2017, but ultimately vacated it in May 2018, whereafter the arbitration commenced.

[17] PCA Case No. 2016-35: *Vodafone International Holdings BV (The Netherlands) v. India Award* (p. 121).

18 'Vodafone Case: Singapore Court to Hear India's Appeal against Arbitration Order in September', *The Economic Times*, 27 November 2021.

19 Website of the Department of Economic Affairs, Bilateral International Treaties.

20 'Union Govt Introduces Bill to Repeal Retrospective Tax, Cairn & Vodafone to Benefit', *The NewsMinute*, 6 August 2021.

21 Of which about INR 7900 crore were from Cairn Energy. This amount was also liable to be returned by the government as it had lost an arbitration under a BIT against Cairn Energy.

22 The Income Tax (31st Amendment) Rules, 2021, notified on 1st October 2021.

Chapter 11

The Telecom Counter-Revolution

The image of justice in the popular imagination is that of a woman who is blindfolded with a weighing scale in her hand. The blindfold represents the idea of impartiality, i.e., the belief that the judge has to be completely neutral and decide the matter before her without being influenced by any consideration other than the merits of the case. The scale is supposed to reflect the ideal process of adjudication. The Court is supposed to examine the evidence produced by each party and reach a decision solely on the basis of the strength of each side's case. This belief in neutrality and objectivity is also reflected in the constitutional oath of office of the judges. At their swearing-in, judges of the higher judiciary promise to uphold the Constitution and dispense justice 'without fear or favour, affection or ill will'. The intention of the framers of the Constitution was that the judges would decide cases uninfluenced by the pulls and pushes of public opinion and would be guided solely by the words of the Constitution and the laws.

Whether this ideal of objectivity is factually true or not, the assertion that the Courts are meant to be neutral does give some comfort to most people. If the Court is simply supposed to take the pieces of evidence placed before it and apply the law to those facts, the result of any case would appear to be fair, consistent and just. In a society governed by the rule of law, it would seem evident that this method of judicial decision-making would be a goal worth striving for. Such a conception of justice would also imply that the outcome of a decision would not be influenced by any extraneous factors, including the personal views of the judge. The decision-making process would be almost robotic—once the facts as determined by the Court are applied to the applicable law, the judgment would follow as a matter of practical reasoning. The judges would render their judgments regardless of who the parties before the Court are or what their ultimate interest in the final decision is.

However, does neutrality imply that the Court should be completely oblivious to the outcome of their decisions? There may be cases where the conclusion of the Court might require it to strike down Executive decisions or pass judgments that have a very grave impact on the economy. In such circumstances, should the Court take the economic considerations of its possible verdict into account before giving its final judgment?

The position becomes even more compelling when the person whose actions are being judged is the government. After all, the government is supposed to be the custodian of the public interest and it is the duty of the Court to keep a check on the power exercised by the Executive. At least in theory it is the judicial branch of the State that is supposed to uphold the Constitution and strike down arbitrary or whimsical action on the part of the government. There are then two separate interests before the Court—the need to contain any illegalities that the Executive may have committed will have to be weighed against the financial impact that any potential judgment will have on the larger economy.

The famous 2G spectrum case was an instance where the Court was confronted with a situation where the Executive had acted in a constitutionally impermissible manner.[1] In the judgment of the Court, it was held that the telecom licensees had been given spectrum,[2] which was a scarce public resource, arbitrarily. There were also allegations of criminality and corruption in the entire process leading the Comptroller and Auditor General (CAG) of India to come out with a report claiming that a loss of Rs 1.76 lakh crore had been caused to the public exchequer. Unfortunately, while holding that the actions of the government were illegal, the Court simply proceeded to cancel the grant of spectrum. The judgment was absolutely silent on the effect that it would have on the economy of the country. It was as though the Court was completely oblivious to this very vital impact. The decision of the Court was no doubt a victory for transparency, but it had a devastating impact on the growth of the telecom industry, the results of which are being felt even to this date. Many entities who were set to enter the Indian telecom market found that their licences were cancelled. This led to a sharp reduction in the number of players in the telecom market and also sent out negative signals to international investors about India being a safe place to invest.

I

The Telecom Revolution

The use of mobile phones today has become ubiquitous. While the problem of Internet addiction may not be as acute in India as it is in certain other parts of the world, there has been an explosive growth in Internet usage at least in urban areas.[3] Most people access the Net through their mobile phones. Given this level of use of mobile telephony in the general public, it is easy to forget that this was not the norm till relatively recently. Of course, most people of a certain vintage would remember the time when one had to book a 'trunk call' much in advance before making a call to any city in India or abroad. At the time of Independence, there were only about 150,000[4] exchange lines which grew to about 2.15 million in the early eighties.[5]

Though there was a push towards increasing access to telephone services in the mid-eighties, there was no major improvement in enhanced tele-density till the late nineties. It was at that point that mobile telephony was developing as technology and competing with the traditional fixed line services. In 1994, the government came out with a National Telecom Policy for the liberalization of the sector. Tenders were invited for commencement of fixed as well as mobile services with the licensees paying the government a set license fee every year. However, the policy was not a great success as the bidders were unable to pay the high licence fees that they had quoted. To remedy the problem, the government then came out with a new telecom policy in 1999. The policy did away with the system of fixed licence fees and required the telecom operators to pay the government a share of the total revenue generated by them.

This decision revolutionized the telecom industry in the country. The four-year period from the date of the policy (1999–2003) saw the addition of 12 million subscribers as opposed to the mere 1 million subscribers that had been added prior to the policy (1995–99). Further decisions by the government, including the reduction of the so-called access deficit charges, spurred the growth in the sector.[6] The effect was that in the early years of the twenty-first century, the rate of growth of subscribers was nearly 33 per cent per year.[7] Most of the growth in the sector was through the use of mobile telephones, which in turn saw fixed lines becoming far less common.[8]

The growth in mobile use was dependent on a very important, but scarce natural resource—spectrum. Fixed line networks required cables to be laid before two users could speak to each other. This was a costly and often difficult exercise to undertake. The newly developing technologies permitted a bypassing of the laying of these lines through the use of the radio spectrum where information is exchanged between mobile devices and cellular towers through radio waves. The radio spectrum is nothing other than part of the electromagnetic spectrum that constitutes everything from X-rays to the light visible to the human eye. Because of its comparatively lower frequency, the radio spectrum lends itself to being used more efficiently in mobile technologies. However, the spectrum is a finite resource and cannot be used limitlessly. Further, in India, the spectrum is owned by the government, which has the power to license and allocate its use to different parties.[9]

Any growth in the mobile sector was thus crucially dependent on the efficient allocation of spectrum. Perhaps equally importantly, spectrum was seen as a national resource whose licensing to any private party would generate revenue for the country. It was with these considerations in mind that the government came out with the National Telecom Policy, 1999. That policy, while focusing on the need to increase telecom services, also emphasized the need for a transparent mechanism for the allocation of spectrum.[10] Detailed discussions commenced among various governmental agencies as to how any additional spectrum was to be allocated.

The question as to what policy to adopt and how to deal with the applications seem to have sparked off a turf war between different branches of the government.[11] The law ministry and the regulators preferred to have a transparent method of allocation of spectrum, possibly through auction. However, this seems to have miffed the minister of telecom who felt that the correct policy was a first-come-first-served one, i.e., the spectrum should be allotted to the person who had applied for it first at that point of time. The disagreement even led to an exchange of letters between the prime minister and the minister of telecom. When the prime minister gently suggested that fairness and transparency ought to be maintained in the process of spectrum allocation, the minister responded by saying that any auction would be 'unfair, discriminatory, arbitrary and capricious'. The minister reasoned that requiring new entrants to bid for spectrum in an auction, which would require them to pay large sums of money, would give an unfair advantage to the existing players. As per the minister, the fair thing to do would have been to process the applications received on a first-come-first-served basis after payment of the spectrum usage charge.[12] The justification given by the telecom ministry and the regulatory agencies was that any greater charge would distort the level playing field for newcomers.

Market players must have been aware that the methodology for allotment of spectrum was about to be finalized because, when the government announced on 24 September 2007 that no fresh applications would be accepted after 1 October 2007 (i.e., about a week after the announcement), over 300 people filed their applications. This was far greater than the total of four applications that had been made from 2004 to 2007. However, even this goalpost was also soon changed and on 10 January 2008, a fresh press release was issued by the department of telecommunications. As per the latest press release, only applications that had been received until 25 September 2007 (and not until 1 October 2007 as had been provided for earlier) were to be considered for the grant of a telecom licence.

No ostensible reason was given for the change of this date, which would have the effect of severely limiting the total number of applications. All in all, the entire process smacked of arbitrariness and ad hocism. What made the situation even more grave was the fact that the successful applicants sold their equity shortly after the grant of the licences at a very large profit. For instance, Unitech, which had obtained the licence for Rs 1651 crore transferred its stake of 60 per cent equity in favour of Telenor Asia Pte Ltd, a part of Telenor Group (Norway), for Rs 6120 crore between March 2009 and February 2010. These windfall profits would obviously have come at the cost of the public exchequer.[13]

It was not surprising that there were murmurs in the press about the manner in which the spectrum had been arbitrarily allotted. The scandal also captured the public imagination as it fitted into the narrative that the government was mired in a series of scams. There was a growing anti-corruption movement and the 'spectrum scam' was almost the rallying call for civil society to express its anguish against the culture of corruption. In no time, the matter also assumed political dimensions with the Opposition taking not only the telecom minister but also the prime minister to task over the report.[14]

As if the pressure exerted upon the government was not enough, the CAG of India came out with a scathing report[15] virtually indicting the government of squandering public assets. In a recognition of the controversy surrounding the transaction and justifying why it had conducted the audit, the report said that 'this department had been receiving innumerable references from members of Parliament and other sources repeatedly, questioning the allocation process and the price fixed for such allocation.'[16] The reason for providing this justification was that the traditional role of the CAG had been merely to conduct an audit of the government's finances and not to comment on policy issues,[17] no matter how out of the pale they might have seemed, since that was a matter for politics and not accountants. However, that did not stop the CAG from commenting adversely on various policy decisions of the Court and coming to the dramatic conclusion that a failure to allot the spectrum by auction had caused a loss of Rs 1.76 lakh crore rupees to the public exchequer.[18]

II

The Judgment

As expected, the decision to allot the spectrum through the 'first-come-first-served' method did not go unchallenged. An advocate, Prashant Bhushan, representing the Centre for Public Interest Litigation, filed a writ petition before the Supreme Court seeking the cancellation of the licences. He was joined in this endeavour by a galaxy of esteemed persons, including former chief vigilance commissioners, a governor, a chief of naval staff and several retired chief election commissioners. It was as though the entire crème-de-la-crème of the civil society had had enough of the perceived arbitrary actions of the minister and decided to take matters to the Court.

The Court, in its judgment, referred to the CAG report but refrained from commenting on its correctness as at that point in time the Public Accounts Committee (PAC) of Parliament was examining it. This did not stop the Court from conducting its own review over the decision to award the licenses on a first-come-first-served basis. At the heart of the determination of the Court was the question as to whether 'the Government has the right to alienate, transfer or distribute natural resources/national assets otherwise than by following a fair and transparent method consistent with the fundamentals of the equality clause enshrined in the Constitution?'[19]

The Court held that the spectrum was a scarce, finite and renewable natural resource that was susceptible to degradation in case of inefficient utilization.[20] Having held that spectrum was a natural resource, the Court considered the question of the ownership of such resources and came to the conclusion that the resources belonged to the people of the country, but that the government was the custodian of the resources and held them legally on behalf of the people. The State was, in a sense, the trustee on behalf of the people and was thus cast with the same duties as would be cast on any trustee—the obligation to act in the utmost good faith in matters relating to disposing of the resources. The Court relied on the doctrine of public trust when it held that "the State is empowered to distribute natural resources. However, as they constitute public property/national asset, while distributing natural resources the State is bound to act in consonance with the principles of equality and public trust and ensure that no action is taken which may be detrimental to public interest. . . . As natural resources are public goods, the doctrine of equality, which emerges from the concepts of justice and fairness, must guide the State in determining the actual mechanism for distribution of natural resources."[21]

Once the Court held that the government was obliged to dispose of the spectrum in consonance with the principles of equality and the larger public good, the next question that naturally arose was whether the procedure adopted in the case met the constitutional standard. In other words, was the principle of first-come-first-served a constitutionally permissible method for the award of the licences? The Court answered the query with an emphatic no, holding that the policy, rather than being fair and transparent, involved pure chance and accident.

More dangerously, the policy was liable to be abused by those who had 'access to the power corridor at the highest or the lowest level may be able to obtain information from the government files or the files of the agency/instrumentality of the State that a particular public property or asset is likely to be disposed of or a contract is likely to be awarded or a licence or permission is likely to be given'. This would be a situation akin to insider trading where powerful vested interests could use their special knowledge and hurriedly make applications for the disposal of any natural resource. They would thus place themselves at the head of any queue to the detriment of those who may not have had the same access to the levers of power. Although it was not stated, it was clear that the Court intended that a system that advantaged the first movers could easily be corrupted, especially given the opacity that normally surrounded any decision-making process in the government.

So, the Court had held that the first-come-first-served method was constitutionally impermissible, but how did the Court believe that the spectrum ought to have been distributed? Here again, the Court was completely clear that the only permissible method was by way of auction. The Court perhaps made an overbroad statement when it held that "while transferring or alienating the natural resources, the State is duty-bound to adopt the method of auction by giving wide publicity so that all eligible persons can participate in the process'.[22] In the opinion of the Court, it was a constitutional mandate that the government had no option but to try to seek the highest price for any natural resource without consideration for any other policy considerations.

Having held the policy was arbitrary and that the government ought to have conducted an auction for the allocation of spectrum, the Court went further and proceeded to cancel the licences that had already been allotted. There was no discussion of the economic outcome of the decision or the fact that some licences had since been bought by innocent third parties. The Court simply seemed to jump from holding the actions to be illegal to going and quashing the licenses. In this regard, the judgment was rather abrupt. It was not as though the issues of the economic fallout of licence cancellation had not been argued;[23] however, the Court seems to have simply ignored this aspect.

Curiously, the Court did not cancel the few telecom licences that had been granted from 2001 to 2007, even though those licences had also been awarded without conducting an auction. This was ostensibly on the grounds that they were not parties to the petition. However, once the Court had found that the action of the government in not conducting an auction was unconstitutional, one can only wonder why the Court did not use its power to issue a show-cause notice to the licence-holders for the cancellation of their licence. It appears that in the entire judgment, there was the looming presence of the allegations of criminality. The same judge who authored the judgment was also heading the bench that was looking into the issues relating to the charges of bribery against the telecom minister. It would have been no surprise therefore, if the judgment was coloured by these allegations.[24]

III

The Economic Fallout and Criticism

The decision had an immediate and grave impact in many areas. Politically, the judgment was a shot in the arm for the Opposition, which had alleged corruption against the government.[25] Legally, there were now doubts raised about all statutes that provided for a mechanism of allocation of natural resources without following the auction process; for instance, the allocation of coal mines.[26] Finally, and needless to say, there was also a massive economic fallout.

The effect of the judgment was felt not only by those companies that had allegedly abused and corrupted the system, whose licences were cancelled. Many foreign companies had invested in the successful allottees of spectrum at a time well before the Supreme Court cancelled the licences.[27] This resulted in a complete loss of their investments, prompting fears that India would not be viewed as an investor-friendly destination. After the cancellation of the licences, the competition in the sector got drastically reduced, leading to almost an oligopolistic position in the market.

In fact, the judgment has been a looming omnipresence over the sector even to date with the government fearful of reducing the auction price of spectrum to avoid accusations of another scam.[28] To add to the misery, the fear psychosis created by the judgment caused the government to make bidders auction for the spectrum they already possessed, driving up the indebtedness of the industry.[29]

The judgment was also criticized by economists who questioned whether the aim of seeking the highest possible revenue through the sale of natural resources was correct. For instance, there may be instances where the government wishes to dispose of natural resources at a low cost so as to foster competition. For instance, if the highest value was to be sought for any resource, the bidder would surely factor in the price in the end product sold by it to the consumer. This could result in services becoming unaffordable for the general population, particularly in sectors where the government thought it expedient to increase market penetration. Equally importantly, most auctions also have eligibility requirements that are set and assessed by governmental committees, a process that introduces arbitrariness into the auction process. Further, firms (especially those already entrenched in the market) can act in concert and indulge in closet cartelization, leading to inadequate revenue realization.

These economic considerations are not merely esoteric writings found in journals, but are real issues that weigh in the minds of Courts too. The Supreme Court has held that it is 'the bounden duty of the Court to have the economic analysis and economic impact of its decisions'. In the same decision, the Court went on to hold that 'the Court needs to avoid that particular outcome which has a potential to create an adverse effect on employment, growth of infrastructure or economy or the revenue of the State. It is in this context that economic analysis of the impact of the decision becomes imperative.'[30]

There was not only criticism of the judgment from economists but also from within the legal fraternity. Both senior members of the bar[31] as well as retired judges[32] of the Supreme Court questioned whether the judgment was correct. Indeed, some went so far as to pin the subsequent economic slowdown on the doors of the Supreme Court. [33] Finally, the Supreme Court had to step in and restrict the scope of the judgment. A Constitution bench of the Court held that an auction, though a preferable means of disposal of natural resources, was not a 'constitutional requirement or a limitation for alienation of all natural resources' and hence 'every method other than auction cannot be struck down as ultra vires the constitutional mandate'.[34]

Ultimately, there was even doubt on the issue of criminality as well as the calculations of the actual loss caused to the exchequer. As regards the criminality, the politicians and the businessmen accused of wrongdoing were acquitted by the trial court in a mammoth judgment, holding that it had 'absolutely no hesitation in holding that the prosecution has miserably failed to prove any charge against any of the accused, made in its well-choreographed charge sheet.'[35]

Equally, there have been grave doubts about the methodology as well as the calculation of the presumptive loss of Rs 1.76 lakh crore. Indeed, even at the time that the report was prepared, the director general of audit (post and telegraph) had offered a more conservative figure of Rs 2645 crore but had been overruled by the then CAG.[36]

Conclusion

Thus, in some ways, the entire underlying basis of the judgment was wiped out, if not in letter but certainly in its spirit.[37] However, since the licences had already been cancelled by this point in time, the position could not be reversed. The scrambled telecom business egg could not be unscrambled and the damage caused to the Indian economy as well as the reputation of Indian business could not be undone. These considerations also lead one to question whether it is always the wisest move to quash actions that the Court considers inappropriate. Certainly, this is not always the course of action that the Court takes. The dilemma faced often by the Court in the present case was neither new nor novel. The Courts are often faced with situations where the verdict may have such a negative impact that they refrain from passing orders. The Court in such cases performs an exercise called 'moulding the relief'. This is a legal device whereby the Court can issue directions which, in its view, does substantial justice between parties and also accounts for public interest.[38] The law does not compel the Courts to issue judgments without regard to that great virtue—mercy.

Just as the government is supposed to be the custodian of the public interest, the Court too cannot be oblivious of the impact its judgments have on the economy. Of course, in matters where the illegality is writ large and the statute itself provides for a certain consequence, the Court would be duty bound to follow the mandate of the law. However, where the prohibition is determined only through a process of constitutional interpretation after the occurrence of the action, the Court ought to have at the very least considered the impact its decision would have on innocent third parties.

Unfortunately, it is not clear as to why the Court felt compelled in this particular case to quash the licences, especially since the Court did not give any reasons as to why some other relief had not been considered. Since the judgment of the Supreme Court cannot be appealed, those reasons will forever remain shrouded in mystery. The effect that the judgment had on the Indian economy is less of a mystery.

Notes

[1] *Centre for Public Interest Litigation v. UOI* (2012) 3 SCC 1.

[2] Spectrum, in the context of telecommunication, means the radio frequency part of the electromagnetic spectrum. This part of the spectrum is a low frequency electromagnetic wave which is used to communicate between devices.

[3] Pragya Lodha. 'Internet Addiction, Depression, Anxiety and Stress among Indian Youth', *Indian Journal of Mental Health* (2018), pp. 2394–4579.

[4] Amba Kak, Mayank Mishra, Dhiraj Muttreja and Smriti Parsheera. 'A Twenty Year Odyssey (1997–2017)', Report commissioned by the Telecom Regulatory Authority of India (TRAI), April 2017.

[5] Pre-liberalization statistics—Telecommunications in India, wikipedia.com.

[6] 'A Twenty Year Odyssey', p. 7.

[7] Market Study on the Telecom Sector in India, Competition Commission of India, 2021.

[8] In 2016, the share of fixed line networks had become only about 2 per cent of the total market. 'A Twenty Year Odyssey', p. 8.

[9] Section 4 of the Indian Telegraph Act, 1885.

[10] The NTP 1999 noted that it was 'essential that the spectrum is utilised efficiently, economically, rationally and optimally'.

[11] Para 24 of the CPIL judgment.

[12] This charge was fixed at Rs 1658 crore per licence and was calculated on the basis of the price that had been allegedly discovered in 2001.

[13] Para 45 of the CPIL judgment.

[14] 'Is Prime Minister Manmohan Singh Culpable in the 2G Spectrum Scam?', *Business Today*, 23 January 2011.

[15] Report No. 19 of 2010, 'Performance Audit of Issue of Licences and Allocation of 2G Spectrum of Union Government', Ministry of Communications and Information Technology, 16 November 2010, Comptroller and Auditor General of India.

[16] p. iii of the CAG report.

[17] The CAG is appointed as per the provisions of Article 148 of the Constitution. The reports of the CAG are submitted to the Parliament under Article 151 of the Constitution. As per procedure, they are first examined by the PAC whose chairman is, by convention, a member of the opposition. After that, the report of the Joint Parliamentary Committee (JPC) as well as the PAC is placed before the House.

[18] The JPC rejected the CAG report and further exonerated both the finance minister and the prime minister of the time. The Lok Sabha also adopted the JPC report in December 2013. More recently, Mr Rai, the CAG at the time the report was released, has made an apology to Mr Nirupam for falsely alleging that he had pressurized Mr Rai to keep the then Prime Minister Manmohan Singh's name out of the CAG report. See Vikas Pathak, '2G Spectrum Back in News with ex-CAG Vinod Rai's Apology', *Outlook India*, 29 October 2021.

[19] Para 1 of the CPIL judgment.

[20] Para 77 of the CPIL judgment.

[21] Para 75 and 88 of the CPIL judgment.

[22] Para 96 of the CPIL judgment.

[23] Para 62 and 63 of the CPIL judgment.

[24] This focus on the criminality was apparent from the imposition of costs only on those applicants who had been awarded the spectrum after the policy was announced. Costs were not imposed on those applicants who had applied earlier but had been awarded the spectrum under the new policy, even though both had benefited under the unconstitutional policy. See Para 102 (v) of the CPIL judgment.

[25] Even though the JPC set up to examine the CAG report rejected its findings, it was widely believed that the report and the allegations of corruption contributed to electoral losses for both the DMK as well as the UPA government at the Centre. See, for instance, the editorial in *The Times of India*, 'System in Shambles: The 2G Spectrum Scandal's Impact was Felt in the Economy, Governance and Politics', 21 December 2017.

[26] This uncertainty prompted the government to seek an opinion from the Supreme Court as to whether auction was mandatory by way of a presidential reference. See '2G Case: Presidential Reference in SC on Issues Arising from 2G Verdict', *The Economic Times*, 12 April 2012.

[27] Norwegian telecom company Telenor invested Rs 6100 crore. It finally exited India in 2017 after accruing accumulated losses of USD 2.87 billion. See 'Telenor Exits India as Airtel Acquires Local Arm to Fight Reliance Jio', *Hindustan Times*, 23 February 2017.

[28] Surjeet Dasgupta. 'How 2G Case Impacts Telecom Sector to This Day', Rediff.com, 23 December 2017.

[29] 'How 2G Case Impacts Telecom Sector to This Day', *Mint*, 22 December 2017.

[30] *Shivashakti Sugars Ltd v. Shree Renuka Sugar Ltd* (2017) 7 SCC 729.

[31] 'Supreme Court "Lost Its Way" while Cancelling Coal Block, 2G Licences: Mukul Rohatgi', NDTV, 16 May 2020.

[32] Ashmit Kumar. 'Retired SC Judge Faults 2G, Coal Verdict for Not Considering Eco Impact, Adv Hingorani Claims PILs Now Hijacked by Middle Class Interests', CNBCTV.com, 27 May 2020.

[33] Apoorva Mandhani. 'Supreme Court Squarely to Blame for Economic Slowdown, Says Senior Advocate Harish Salve', *The Print*, 16 September 2019.

[34] *In re Natural Resources Allocation, Presidential Reference No. 1 of 2012*, (2012) 10 SCC 1, Para 148.

[35] Paragraph 1818 of *CBI v. A. Raja and others* CC No: 01/11.

[36] Akshaya Mishra. '2G: Loss Numbers Don't Matter Much, But Crime Is Key', firstpost.com, 3 October 2011.

[37] Mihir Sharma. 'Who Sold Us the 2G "scam"?', *Business Standard*, 22 December 2017.

[38] This is a power vested in all constitutional courts (and even in the lower courts in certain matters pertaining to civil law). In the case of the Supreme Court, Article 142 of the Constitution empowers it to pass 'such decree or make such order as is necessary for doing complete justice in any cause or matter pending before it'.

Chapter 12

Man versus Wild: Industry and the Environment

Judgments are usually the product of adversarial litigation. Two sides, represented by their lawyers, argue their case before a judge who delivers a verdict. The judge is supposed to decide the case neutrally, without being personally interested in any one side of the argument. In some cases, however, these disputes take on deeply ideological overtones which may even transcend the actual issue facing the Court. Often these deeper questions are not apparent at first sight, but have to be teased out by reference to the context of the case and the reasoning of the Court. Also, in these cases, the Court cannot afford to be neutral and is required to take a view on one or the other sides of an ideological debate. This chapter is concerned with just such a case where the concerns of the environment in cases of mining were ostensibly pitted against the interests of economic growth.

In a case titled the *Goa Foundation v. Sesa Sterlite,*[1] the Supreme Court was called upon to decide a very narrow issue, i.e., whether the mining leases of the Goan mine owners were valid. The mine owners asserted that they had a right to mine iron ore under leases granted to them by the Portuguese. On the other hand, petitioners who had filed the petition as a public interest litigation claimed that the leases had expired a long time ago. The Supreme Court came to the conclusion that the leases had expired and that all the mining done by the owners after the expiry was illegal.

As is often the case, the true nature of the dispute that the Court was to consider was not immediately obvious. Though the judgment was primarily concerned with the matter of the validity of mining leases, the Court was clearly concerned about the environmental impact that mining had had in the state of Goa. The directions as well as the reasoning offered by the Court in reaching its decision show that the judges were concerned not merely with narrow legal interpretations, but with the broader interests of protecting the environment. There lay the subtext of the judgment—the dispute between environmental concerns and economic growth.

The immediate outcome of the judgment was to put a stop to all mining activity in Goa. While the effective stoppage of mining was a respite to the rapidly degrading environment, the unanswered question is the impact that the stoppage of mining had on the economy of Goa as well as of the country at large. The Court is often faced with the situation where the demands of the environment clash with the needs of economic development. In such circumstances, the Court has usually said that the two competing interests can be reconciled and seeks to do a balancing exercise, weighing environmental concerns against the economic interests involved. However, given the complexity of the problems and the vast number of stakeholders involved, not all of whom can be heard by the Court, the question arises as to whether it is the judiciary or the legislature that is best suited to make these determinations. This conundrum is compounded by the lack of adequate data on the impact a judgment has on the economy or the environment. In the absence of data, it is difficult to assess whether the Court's interventions in areas relating to the environment have been successful or even desirable.

However, even with this uncertainty, the answer cannot be stasis. Given the bias that the government has towards economic growth at the cost of the environment, it is clear that these decisions cannot be left to the government alone. Further, the government also seems to be unable or unwilling to take a comprehensive view on these issues, with ministries and departments often at loggerheads with each other.[2] Thus, even if the judiciary may not be the best arena to make the required value judgments for balancing economic interests against those of the environment, the truth is that the courtrooms will continue to be the battlegrounds where these fights are fought. Given this practical reality, it is important to understand how the Courts view issues relating to the environment. This chapter is one such attempt at an analysis.

I

Mining and the Portuguese Connection

Goa immediately conjures up a vision of sandy beaches and a relaxed lifestyle. To most tourists, Goa feels like an idyll which is different from their travels elsewhere in the country. Goans also pride themselves on their unique heritage, one that is attributable to its history as a Portuguese colony rather than a British one.[3] This distinction did not result merely in a difference in the culture of Goa but had a profound effect on the legal regimes applicable to it. For instance, the personal laws in matters relating to inheritance in Goa are completely different from the rest of the country. This legacy of the Portuguese thus continues to be on the statute books, with Goa being the only state in the country that has a uniform civil code.

There were significant variations in the laws applicable in Goa vis-à-vis the rest of the country even in other areas, one such being the law relating to the grant and operation of mining leases. In the case of mining, the law was extremely lax and was in the nature of largesse granted by the colonial rulers. In fact, the applicable Portuguese law did not contemplate the grant of any mining leases. Instead, any person who discovered any mineral made an application for the grant of a mining manifest. Upon examination of the claim of the applicant, she was granted a mining concession that was 'unlimited in duration as long as the concessionaire complied with the conditions which the law and title of concession imposed on him'.[4] In effect, the mining concession was a permission to mine for mineral ore in perpetuity, and that too without payment of royalties. This was a virtual carte blanche for the miners to carry on excavating the land without any check whatsoever.

In the meanwhile, the law of mining in the rest of India had developed quite differently. Shortly after Independence, the law of mining in India had been consolidated through the enactment of the Mines and Mineral (Regulation and Development) Act, 1957(MMRD Act). Prior to the MMRD Act, the regulation of mining had been within the realm of control by the states. However, the MMRD Act gave virtually the entire power in matters of allotment of mines to the Central government.[5] The debates in Parliament indicated that the intention of Parliament was to bring mining under the control of the public sector, as this was part of the socialist ethos of the time.

After the integration of Goa in the Indian Union, the MMRD Act was extended to Goa.[6] Even though the act was now applicable to the territory, the mine owners held to the position that their mining concessions were not covered by the act and that they were not liable to pay any dues to the government. In fact, when the Controller of Mines asked the mine owners to pay royalties, they moved the Bombay High Court against the demand. The high court gave a verdict in favour of the owners and held that the concessions were not mining leases and therefore the government was not entitled to collect any royalty.[7] In effect, the Court held that the law applicable in the rest of India was not applicable to Goa.

After this verdict, it was clear that such a dual regime in respect of mining leases could not be allowed to continue. To undo the judgment of the high court, Parliament passed the Goa, Daman and Diu Mining Concessions (Abolition and Declaration as Mining Leases) Act, 1987 ('the Abolition Act') which received the assent of the President on 23 May 1987. The Abolition Act abolished the mining concessions and declared that every mining concession was deemed to be a mining lease granted under the MMDR Act.[8]

It was at this point that the going started to become a bit tough for the Goan mine owners. So far, they had rested secure in the knowledge that their concessions were of unlimited duration. The Abolition Act curtailed this right and required the owners to follow the same laws as were prevalent across the rest of the country. If the owners wanted to carry on mining, they had to secure renewals of their mining leases from the government. The mine owners had no choice but to apply to the government for renewals of their mining leases under the provisions of the MMDR Act.

II

The Shah Commission

Even though the mine owners had applied for renewals of their mining leases, the government, with its customary bureaucratic lethargy, sat over the applications and did not decide them one way or the other. Interpreting the inaction of the government as a deemed permission to mine, the miners kept on extracting iron ore and exporting it to China.[9] This position would probably have carried on unabated, had there not been another event that put a spoke in the wheel of the miners, and this was the establishment of a commission of inquiry headed by a retired judge of the Supreme Court, Justice M.B. Shah.

Around 2010, there was a growing concern about the scale of illegal mining happening in various states around the country, in particular in Karnataka[10] and Goa.[11] Faced with the outrage being expressed in the media, the government decided to order a comprehensive inquiry into these allegations and appointed Justice M.B. Shah to conduct an investigation into these allegations. The scope of the investigation was to determine the extent of the illegal mining and the losses that it had caused. The commission was also charged with determining the extent of 'destruction of forest wealth, damage to the environment, prejudice to the livelihood and other rights of tribal people, [and] forest dwellers'. The commission immediately got to work and visited Goa to fulfil the terms of its appointment. After extensive consultations with the public authorities as well as the mining leaseholders, a report was submitted to the government and was eventually placed before Parliament.[12]

The report of the Shah Commission was damning. Justice Shah, in his report, stated that the leases of the mine owners had expired and that they had carried on mining illegally after encroaching on land. The report was also scathing when it noted that no adequate environmental clearances had been obtained by the mine owners and that these irregularities were with the abetment of powerful figures, including bureaucrats and politicians. On a rough and ready estimate, Justice Shah calculated that the loss to the exchequer as a result of the illegal mining was almost Rs 35,000 crore.[13]

The release of the Shah Commission report was shortly after Goa had witnessed a change in government. The BJP government had come to power in March 2012 partly on the promise to eradicate corruption in the mining sector.[14] The report was thus a vindication of sorts for the newly elected government's charge against the previous regime. Seizing upon the report, the Goa government banned mining and issued show-cause notices to all the mining lessees. Not to be outdone, the central government also directed that all environmental clearances granted to mines in the state of Goa be kept in abeyance.

However, it was not only the government which was apparently incensed by the finding of the Shah Commission. A local NGO, the Goa Foundation, filed a writ petition before the Supreme Court seeking cancellation of the mining leases as well as prosecution of 'all those who have committed offences under the different laws and are involved in the pilferage of State revenue through illegal mining activities in the State of Goa including the public servants who have aided and abetted the offences.'[15] The Goa Foundation also relied upon the report of the Shah Commission to allege that all the mining leases which had been extended by virtue of the Abolition Act had since come to an end and that hence all the mining done on the basis of the expired leases was illegal.

By the time the Supreme Court heard the matter, the attitude of the Goa government towards the miners had become distinctly friendlier.[16] In oral hearings before the Court, the government (and the lessees) argued that, on a proper reading of the MMDR Act, the leases were valid and that the Shah Commission had got it wrong. The Supreme Court accepted this argument, but only partially. The Court held that the leases of the miners were indeed valid for a period of twenty years after the Abolition Act, i.e., till 2007. Any mining thereafter was held to be invalid as the Court held that the mining was done without the authority of law.

Though the judgment was not fully in favour of the miners, there was a lifeline kept open for them. As regards mining in the future, the Court held that it was for 'the State Government to decide as a matter of policy in what manner mining leases are to be granted in future but the constitutionality or legality of the decision of the State Government can be examined by the Court in exercise of its power of judicial review.'[17] Crucially, there was a gap in the judgment in relation to the issue of the environmental concerns raised in the Shah Commission as well as by the Goa Foundation.[18] The Court failed to consider the report of an expert committee that had pointed out various irregularities in relation to the procurement of environmental clearances.[19]

The judgment was thus inchoate and incomplete. Neither did it finally decide the issue of the validity of leases, nor the issue of environmental clearances. This position was clearly untenable, and it was only a matter of time before the Court would have to step in again. The miners had so far escaped closure of their mining operations either due to administrative laxity or judicial diffidence. The second Goa judgment would close both these avenues and finally bring the unrestrained mining in Goa to a stop.

III

The Judgment

Seeking to use the ambiguity in the judgment to their own advantage, the mine owners began to argue that the effect of the Supreme Court order was to permit them another renewal of their mining lease. They applied to the Government of Goa for fresh renewals of the leases under the provisions of the MMRD Act. When the government did not comply with these requests, the miners moved the Bombay High Court asking it to direct the government to direct the grant of the renewal. The high court examined the judgment of the Supreme Court and held that the miners were indeed entitled to a fresh renewal of twenty years, i.e., leases that would last until 2027, and directed the government to execute the leases.[20]

After the directions of the Bombay High Court, the state government formulated the Goa Grant of Mining Leases Policy, 2014 ('the mining policy'). Unfortunately, the mining policy, rather than seeking to maximize the revenue for the state or display any concern for the environment, read more like a manifesto on behalf of the mine owners. Using the judgment of the high court as an excuse, the mining policy said that it was impossible for the government to consider the grant of lease through competitive bidding. The mining policy noted that the 'High Court virtually leaves no choice to the State Government, thereby to completely abandon the process of competitive bidding for earning the best revenue to the State Government.' The government was thus conscious of the fact that the renewal of leases would amount to a revenue loss but pleaded helplessness in light of the order of the high court. It appears that the government, for reasons best known to it, was willing to accept the order of the high court, which had significantly curtailed its executive discretion rather than challenging it before the Supreme Court.

The situation became curiouser and curiouser when examined in the context of the timeline of the issuance of this policy and the renewal of the leases. The general elections had been held in May 2014 and the new NDA government had come to power. One of the election promises of the new government was to amend the MMDR Act so as to avoid the scams that had plagued the previous grants of mining leases. In November 2014, a draft Mines and Minerals (Development and Regulation) Act, 2014 ('the new MMDR Act') was prepared and uploaded on the ministry's website for comments. The draft bill provided for a mandatory auction process for any mining leases. The mine owners now had a narrow window of time. If the new MMDR Act was brought into operation before their leases were renewed, they would be bound by the new law and would be forced to participate in the auction process. In other words, they would lose their perceived rights to renewal. Thus began an unholy race to obtain the renewals of the leases so as to avoid falling under the new legal regime of auctions. If any renewals happened after the MMDR Act was brought into force, the Courts would surely have held them to be illegal. There was therefore a grave urgency as far as the mine owners were concerned.

The renewals happened at a speed uncharacteristic of the usual bureaucratic lethargy of government departments. The mining policy was uploaded on the website of the Government of Goa on 4 November 2014. The state government started granting a second renewal of the mining leases from the very next day, with the last of the leases being renewed on 12 January 2015. Interestingly, this was the date on which the ordinance promulgating the new MMDR Act had been issued. As the judgment of the Court noted, 'The approval of the Ordinance by the Cabinet of the Government of India became public knowledge on 5-1-2015 and it is within a week from that date that the Government of Goa granted a second renewal to 25 mining leases, and to make matters worse, a second renewal was granted to 31 mining leases on 12-1-2015, the day the Ordinance came into force making a total of 56 renewals of mining leases.' It was thus apparent to the Court that the rush to renew the leases was to defeat the stricter provisions of the new MMDR Act. The effect of the government's speed was to deprive itself of additional revenue.

Even though the state government had thrown up its hands after the judgment of the Bombay High Court, the Goa Foundation challenged the judgement before the Supreme Court. The Goa Foundation was a local NGO that had been founded in the eighties to fight for the conservation of Goa's natural environment. Over the decades, the Goa Foundation had become a force to reckon with, after having filed and won many environmental matters before the Courts. In this time the foundation became the bête noir of the miners as it had consistently waged a battle against what it perceived to be the pillage of the natural resources of the state by the wanton and unrestrained mining in the state.

Though the focus of the judgment of the Court was ostensibly the permissibility of a second renewal of the mining leases, the very first paragraph of the judgment showed that the Court was primarily concerned by the effects of mining. The Court ruled that the 'rapacious and rampant exploitation of our natural resources is the hallmark of our iron ore mining sector coupled with a total lack of concern for the environment and the health and well-being of the denizens in the vicinity of the mines. The sole motive of mining leaseholders seems to be to make profits (no matter how) and the attitude seems to be that if the rule of law is required to be put on the backburner, so be it. Unfortunately, the State is unable to firmly stop violations of the law and other illegalities, perhaps with a view to maximise revenue, but without appreciating the long-term impact of this indifference. Another excuse generally put forth by the State is that of development, conveniently forgetting that development must be sustainable and equitable development and not otherwise.'

The Court analysed its earlier judgment in the *Goa Foundation* case and held that mining leases could not be renewed for a further period as sought for by the mine owners. Instead, a fresh allocation of the leases, whether by way of auction or otherwise, was required to be done. Commenting adversely on the speed with which the Goa government had granted the renewals of mining leases, the Court held that rather than the concerns of development of mining, the government had 'non-statutory interests' in mind. Driving a dagger further into the heart of the government, the Court used rather strong language and declared that the 'urgency suddenly exhibited by the State therefore seems to be make-believe and motivated rather than genuine.'

Having said that, the Court could simply have disposed of the cases. However, the Court had flagged its concerns at the environmental impact of mining at the very outset of its judgment. Therefore, it was only to be expected that the Court turn its attention to this issue. The judgment was scathing in its indictment of the miners in matters relating to the environment. The Court noted that there was 'not a single environment related or mining-related law or legal requirement that was not violated by one or the other mining leaseholder.'[21] Further, no approval was taken from the Central Groundwater Board for extraction of water for mining purposes. The Court also castigated the Central government for taking the position that certain mine owners were not required to take fresh environmental clearances when their leases were renewed.

Ultimately, the Court directed that all the mining leases were to be applied for and granted afresh. The successful lessees were required to apply for environmental clearances afresh. The erstwhile mine owners were not let off easily either. The government was directed to expeditiously determine the amounts payable by them for the extraction of ore in excess of the environmental clearance granted to them.

IV

The Aftermath

The immediate impact of the judgment was to stop all the mining activity in Goa. This was no doubt welcome for the villagers in the interiors of Goa, where most of the uncontrolled mining had occurred. Mining had devastated the pristine eco-sensitive forests in areas away from the eye of the beach-going public and had a disastrous effect on the health of the people.[22] The direction of the Court to stop mining was part of its long tradition of stepping in whenever it felt that the environment was being adversely impacted. In fact, it was the Supreme Court that had directed the effective implementation of the Forest Conservation Act, 1980, and had banned all non-forest activities in forested areas.[23] That case had led to not only halting the increasing deforestation in India, but also led to a positive increase in the forest cover.[24]

There was, however, also a flip side to the judgment of the Court. Stopping mining had a direct economic impact not only on the mine owners but also on many of the other stakeholders. Clearly for the mine owners, the stoppage of mining meant that they could not generate any revenue, which also had a cascading effect on their inability to pay royalties, cesses and taxes to the government. Further, almost all of the ore mined in Goa had very low iron content and was thus not used domestically, but was exported.[25] The net result was that the stoppage of mining resulted in a stoppage in exports with an attendant loss of foreign exchange earnings. Various other persons associated in the mining infrastructure also bore the brunt of the closure— from barge operators and truck owners who mined the ore to the employees who worked in the mines. One study has suggested that the stoppage of mining has led not only to a loss of revenue for the state, but also a reduction in the income of the residents of Goa varying from 30 per cent to almost 50 per cent in some districts.[26] The economic impact of the judgment has thus proved to be quite severe and was not something that the Court had taken (or possibly could have taken) into account.

Conclusion

There is thus a dilemma. The judgments of the Court lean in favour of environmental protection because a failure to intervene can result in devastating and irreversible damage to the environment and the health of the people. At the same time, the economic impact is felt not only by the large industrialists but also the common employee or the small tradesman who is part of the supply chain. In any economy, both these interests have to be accommodated. The question is simply this—who is better suited to do the balancing, the Court or the Executive? One way to resolve the issue is to examine which authority has been better able, thus far, to perform such an exercise.

One could suggest that the legislature has the expertise and the wherewithal to perform this balancing act. In the last several decades, a large number of laws and judgments have been passed, ostensibly for the purpose of protecting the environment. However, they have rarely been successful in stopping the wanton destruction of the environment by rapacious businessmen.[27] In fact, it was only once the Executive had proved itself unwilling or unable to address environmental concerns that the Court had stepped in to pass judgments directing the Executive to implement the very rules and regulations framed by it.

Another reason for advocating a robust role for the Courts in protecting the environment is the inability, or the unwillingness, of the government to account for the externalities of environmental damage. Damage caused by pollution to natural resources, such as air and water, has an actual economic cost. These resources are not the property of any single individual but of the community as a whole. Hence, any accounting done to measure the economic impact of a project that causes pollution should also properly have to factor in the loss that would be suffered by the public at large, even though the financial costs are often not tangible or apparent. Unfortunately, the major concern of governments is to ensure enhanced economic growth, and in doing so, they usually ignore the environmental costs of pollution. Thus, the Courts are needed to ensure these external costs are properly accounted for. These costs would include not only the externalities mentioned above, but also other non-tangible interests, such as inter-generational equity and balanced regional development.[28]

However, in the ultimate analysis, leaving the ultimate control over environmental management to the Courts is a deeply dissatisfactory solution. This is in part because of the limits of the kind of orders the Court can provide for infractions of the law. The Court can enforce the law through the rather blunt instrument of prohibitions and bans. While such measures do have a place in the enforcement mechanism relating to environmental protection, a more holistic and nuanced approach is needed in matters where the concerns of the environment are balanced against developmental needs. One possible solution could be to set up a truly independent environmental regulator, which would be free of the pulls and pushes of any particular lobby.[29] In any event, it can only be hoped that the judgments of the Courts are a wake-up call for the government to finally do justice to both equally.[30]

Notes

[1] Goa Foundation II.

[2] This discordance was particularly prevalent in early 2010, the same period when the Goa mining case first arose. See for instance 'Hit by Short Supply, "Black Diamond" Fails to Dazzle Coal Sector in 2011', *The Economic Times*, 29 December 2011 and Subash Narayan, 'Chhattisgarh UMPP Likely to be Scrapped', *The Financial Times*, 11 May 2011.

[3] Goa was conquered by the Portuguese in 1510 when Alfonso de Albuquerque defeated the forces of Yusuf Adil Shah, the founder of the Adil Shahi dynasty of Bijnaur. A nominal local ruler by the name of Timoji was installed as the governor, but in practice the actual control over the territory was exercised by the Portuguese. Thus, unlike the rest of India, which was under British dominion, Goa's legal system developed differently, being heavily influenced by the civil law system of the European continent.

[4] This history is recorded in the judgment of the Supreme Court in the case of *Vinod Kumar Shantilal Gosalia v. Gangadhar Narsindas Agarwal* 1982 (1) SCR 392.

[5] Rajeev Dhavan. 'Mining Policy In India: Patronage or Control?', *Journal of the Indian Law Institute*, Vol. 34, No. 2, 1992, pp. 218–46.

[6] Goa was liberated from Portuguese rule on 19 December 1961 and the MMRD Act was extended to Goa on 1 October 1963.

[7] *Vasudeva Madeva Salgaocar v. UOI* (1985) 1 Bom CR 36.

[8] The Abolition Act was challenged before the Bombay High Court, but was ultimately upheld. *Shri Qucxova Sinal Cundo v. Union Of India* (1998) 2 Bom CR 87.

[9] See the report of the expert committee set up pursuant to the order of the Supreme Court dated 18 November 2013. Goa Foundation I, para 69.

[10] Jim Yardley. 'Despite Scandals, Indian Mining Bosses Thrive', *New York Times*, 18 August 2010.

[11] See a discussion in 'Out of Control: Mining, Regulatory Failure and Human Rights in India', *Human Rights Watch*, June 2012.

[12] Para 5 Goa Foundation.

[13] 'Goa Mining Scam Worth Rs 34,935 crore: Justice Shah Commission' | Latest News India', *Hindustan Times*, 7 September 2012.

[14] 'Goa Elections 2012: BJP Promises to Appoint Lokayukta in 100 Days and a Cut in Petrol Prices', *The Economic Times*, 20 February 2012.

[15] Goa Foundation I. (2014) 6 SCC 590, para 7.

[16] 'Goa CM Parrikar Flip-Flops on Key Promises about Mines, Casinos, Drugs and Corruption', Scroll.in, 20 September 2014.

[17] Para 87.5 of Goa Foundation I.

[18] It is not as though the Court was completely oblivious to environmental concerns. The Court did lay down that it had the power to ban mining, even if there was a subsisting valid mining lease, if the mining adversely impacted the environment. Using this power, the Court banned mining within 1 kilometre of the boundary of any national park in the state of Goa. However, as regards the determination of eco-sensitive zones where no mining was permitted, the Court did not pass any directions restricting mining. Instead, the Court left it to the government to take a call on the matter and merely directed the government to complete the process of identifying the eco-sensitive zones within a period of six months.

[19] As highlighted in the Goa Foundation II, para 15.

[20] *Lithoferro v. State of Goa* 2014 SCC OnLine Bom 997.

[21] Para 88 Goa Foundation II.

[22] C. Alvares and R. Saha, 'Goa, Sweet Land of Mine,' 2008.

[23] *TN Godavarman Thirumulpad v. Union of India* (1997) 2 SCC 267.

[24] The judgment also had its fair share of critics. For instance, see Armin Rosencranz and Sharachchandra Lele, 'Supreme Court and India's Forests', *Economic and Political Weekly*, Vol 43, Issue 2 (2008).

[25] Para 12 Goa Foundation II.

26 'Study on Impacts of Stoppage of Mining in Goa on Socio-Economics', Department of Environmental Science and Engineering, IIT (Indian School of Mines), Dhanbad.

27 'How Effective are Environmental Regulations to Address Impacts of Industrial and Infrastructure Projects in India', Centre for Policy Research (CPR)—Namati Environmental Justice Programme (2016).

28 For an interesting analysis of how the Courts have stepped in to correct these externalities, see U. Sankar, 'Laws and Institutions Relating to Environmental Protection in India', presented at the conference on 'The Role of Law and Legal Institutions in Asian Economic Development', held at the Erasmus University, Rotterdam, November 1998.

29 Such a regulator was proposed in 2011; however, not much came of the proposal. Shibani Ghosh. 'The National Environment Assessment and Monitoring Agency: A Step Forward?', *Economic and Political Weekly*, Vol. 46, No. 38 (2011), pp. 12–16.

30 Unfortunately, the experience during the Covid pandemic has been that the government appears to favour industrial growth at the cost of the environment. See, for instance, Meenakshi Kapoor and Krithika A. Dinesh, 'Throughout the Pandemic, Environmental Clearance Law Has Been Under the Chopping Block', *The Wire*, 23 May 2021.

Chapter 13

The Price of Privacy: the Aadhaar Case

It has been said that there is no such thing as a free lunch. Whenever a person gets any benefit, there is always a cost that may be explicit or hidden. In economics, this idea is captured as the concept of 'opportunity cost', or the idea that often a financial decision involves a trade-off where one goal may have to be sacrificed to secure a competing goal.[1] A rational person is supposed to balance these contradictory claims and arrive at the most logical and efficient outcome. This spectre of mutually inconsistent and competing interests is often found in the field not only of economics but also in the adjudicatory process.

Just such a dispute arose in the case of the Aadhaar scheme where the interests of efficient utilization of State resources were pitted against the privacy interests of the individual. In the case of the Aadhaar scheme, the alleged clash between competing interests was particularly stark, and the differences further magnified, by the emotional and political nature of the debate around the issues.

The Aadhaar project was envisaged as a means to enable an efficient distribution of State largesse. The country had a leaky system of subsidies, where a large amount of subsidy money never reached the intended beneficiaries. To counter this, a system of transferring benefits directly to a person was proposed, whereby the intended beneficiaries would be paid the subsidy amount in cash rather than through the sale of subsidized goods.[2] An important limb through which this system of direct transfers was to be operationalized was the issuance of a unique identification number to each resident of the country. To ensure that there was no duplication of beneficiaries, the system required that certain biometric parameters unique to the individual would be linked to the ID.

The benefits of the scheme included the promise of helping those citizens who truly needed government aid. This would, in the eyes of the proponents of the scheme, be a win-win situation. The poor would get money equivalent to the subsidies intended for them and the country would stand to gain through the elimination of waste and corruption that was endemic in the system. The costs, at least to the opponents of the scheme, included the potential loss of privacy of a person who was to be compulsorily enrolled into the database. Coupled with this was the fear that the database could be hacked and put to misuse by State as well as non-State actors.

The argument seemed to crystallize into the question whether it was worthwhile to give up part of your privacy so as to ensure that government subsidies were efficiently distributed. The debate polarized activists and economists often on the grounds of their ideological convictions rather than on the issues raised. It was in this background that the Supreme Court of India was called upon to rule on the legality of the Aadhaar (Targeted Delivery of Financial and Other Subsidies, Benefits and Services) Act, 2016 ('Aadhaar Act').[3] A retired judge of the Karnataka High Court petitioned the Supreme Court by way of a petition challenging the scheme. In its final judgment titled *KS Puttuswamy v. Union of India*[4] ('the Aadhaar judgment'), the Court upheld substantial portions of the act and substantially saved its heart and soul, while striking down certain provisions that had the possibility of abuse. The Court sought to undertake a balancing act that would protect the most fundamental aspects of a person's privacy while permitting the use of the Aadhaar scheme for the welfare of the general population.

The jury is out on the question as to whether the system of direct benefits through the Aadhaar scheme will revolutionize India's fiscal environment. However, the validity of the Aadhaar Act was not the only issue decided by the Court. During the course of the long litigation, the Court also ruled on the very right of privacy that had been taken for granted by the citizens of the country. Perhaps the abiding legacy of the judgment will be this right to privacy rather than the actual issue about the validity of the Aadhaar scheme as decided by the Court.

I

The Need for Aadhaar

After Independence, the country set about adopting a socialist economic system. One of the aims of the so-called welfare state was the grant of subsidies to the poor, either in the form of food through the public distribution system (PDS) or through other subsidies in goods such as fertilizers for farmers or kerosene for consumers. The expenditure on subsidies soared over the years.[5] Unfortunately, the intended beneficiaries did not end up receiving the actual benefits, which were lost through a leaky and corrupt distribution system.[6] Even after economic liberalization, the situation did not improve substantially.[7]

The system was clearly broken and had to be fixed.[8] The only question was how. One suggestion involved transferring the cash equivalent of the subsidies directly to the beneficiaries, a direct benefit transfer (DBT) scheme. The belief was that such a system would exclude the corrupt bureaucratic interface as well as the middlemen in the system. Such a scheme required the government to have a database of all the persons who were entitled to benefits. The integrity of such a database was crucial for any DBT scheme to avoid excluding those who were entitled to such a benefit while eliminating duplication of beneficiaries. Though there were several databases in existence, such as voter ID cards and ration cards, the data contained in them was thought to be flawed and unreliable.[9]

It was with this need of creating a reliable database that the Government of India authorized the creation of the Unique Identification Authority of India (UIDAI).[10] The mission for the UIDAI was clear—it had to create a database whose primary task would be to validate the identity of any person. In other words, was a person who was claiming to be Ms X indeed Ms X? For this purpose, the idea was to record biometric data that was unique to all individuals, i.e., fingerprints and iris scans.[11] This information would be stored in a central database. Every time the identity of any person was to be verified, their fingerprints and/or iris scans would be taken and transmitted to the central database where they would be matched with the records on file. If the records matched, the database would send a message saying that the person was indeed Ms X (or not, in case the records did not match). The only information that would be received would be a simple yes/no, i.e., whether the person was or was not who they were claiming to be.

This system had several ostensible advantages. Other than facilitating the easy transfer of subsidies, another purported rationale of the Aadhaar scheme was the fact that it would provide identity documents to a large number of residents who did not have them. This was particularly necessary for a country where identity documents were asked for in virtually any interaction with the government. These documents were often unavailable to those citizens who needed government assistance the most. For instance, the large migrant population was heavily dependent on government subsidies but was unlikely to have the identity papers that demanded proof of residence.[12] Aadhaar was supposed to be an identity document that would permit such migrants to receive subsidies regardless of where they moved to in the country.[13]

II

The Privacy Detour

Despite the purported benefits of the Aadhaar scheme, there was one glaring problem and that related to the concerns about the privacy of the individual. Opponents of Aadhaar were worried not so much about giving biometric information as about how the scheme had been structured. The Aadhaar scheme required the collection of biometric information, its storage on a central database and its usage by State as well as private entities. There were concerns about each of these three stages.

The collection of these details was outsourced to private parties and hence there was a concern as to the safety of the data during the process of collection. Once the data was collected, it would be stored on central servers and there was always the fear of hackers accessing the biometric information of a huge number of people. However, it was the fear of how the data could be misused once it had been gathered that was the greatest concern.

The Aadhaar scheme envisaged that every time an individual's identity was to be authenticated, her biometrics would be scanned and transmitted to the central database where they would be matched with the records stored on it. The server would then transmit the information about whether the identity had been verified back to the requesting authority. It was feared that there could be a leakage of information during this process. There was also a very grave fear that the use of such a database would enable the State to create a profile of its citizens in relation to the services availed by them. Over a period of time, the State would get to know the behaviour of the citizens, which data could be used to suppress dissent and to influence the political interactions of the citizen with the government. Collation of the immense amount of information about an individual would permit the creation of a 'surveillance state' where Big Brother would always know what a citizen was doing.

The act also provided that non-State parties, including private individuals and companies could use the Aadhaar ecosystem for the purpose of verification of an individual's identity.[14] Even a private company could demand that a user of its goods/services use the Aadhaar ID to verify their identity. Thus Aadhaar could be required for opening a bank account or getting a telephone line from a private telecom company. This expansion meant that the government could now track an individual's activities not only in her interactions with the government but also in a range of her private acts. Every time a private company required Aadhaar identification, it would enable the government to add information as to her habits, preferences and other choices to a dossier that it maintained.

Perhaps most fundamentally, it was feared that the Aadhaar scheme would fundamentally alter the relationship between the citizen and the State. The Court noted the argument of the petitioners that 'at its core, Aadhaar alters the relationship between the citizen and the State. It diminishes the status of the citizen. Rights freely exercised, liberties freely enjoyed, entitlements granted by the Constitution and laws are all made conditional, on a compulsory barter. The barter compels the citizen to give up her biometrics "voluntarily", allow her biometrics and demographic information to be stored by the State and private operators and then used for a process termed "authentication".'[15]

These concerns in relation to privacy were compounded by the creeping mandate of the Aadhaar scheme. Initially envisaged for the efficient distribution of subsidies, the government started expanding its scope and usage in other areas as well. For instance, the government made it mandatory to link the Aadhaar number to the PAN card for the purposes of payment of income tax.[16] The government also came out with a gazette notification making it mandatory for schoolchildren to have an Aadhaar card before they were supposed to receive a midday meal.[17]

Faced with the arguments relating to privacy, the government adopted a somewhat extreme position. Rather than claiming that the scheme did not seriously impinge on the right to privacy of a citizen, the government claimed that the Constitution of India did not recognize any right to privacy at all. In doing so, the government relied on a decision of the Supreme Court rendered in the fifties by a bench of eight judges, which had held that there was no constitutional right to privacy.[18] This was in spite of the fact that the jurisprudence of the Court after that judgment had moved on substantially.

When the attorney general argued this proposition on behalf of the Union of India, the Court felt it necessary to refer the matter to a bench of nine judges.[19] After an extensive hearing, the Court ruled unanimously in favour of the right to privacy, holding that the Constitution indeed recognized privacy as a fundamental right.[20] The basis of the right was to be found in the right to live a life of freedom and dignity and its constitutional foundation was to be found 'across the spectrum of protected freedoms'.[21] The right to privacy afforded each individual a space where she could make an autonomous life choice. It was the responsibility of the State to enable the person to make those choices, rather than making those choices for her. Repelling the argument that the right to privacy was an elitist construct, the Court held that 'civil and political rights and socioeconomic rights do not exist in a state of antagonism. The conditions necessary for realizing or fulfilling socioeconomic rights do not postulate the subversion of political freedom'.[22]

While holding that each individual was entitled to a right to privacy, the Court did not hold that the right was absolute. Like all fundamental rights, the right to privacy of the individual would have to be balanced against the legitimate interests of the State. However, while protecting these interests, the State was required to follow three fundamental principles. First, privacy could be curtailed only by an enacted law and not by Executive diktat. Second, the interest that the State claimed to have was required to be reasonable and legitimate. The final requirement was that the infringement of the right to privacy was proportionate to the legitimate State interest. In other words, this restriction required that the 'means which are adopted by the legislature are proportional to the object and needs sought to be fulfilled by the law'.[23]

Thus the Court found that the Constitution of India not only recognized a right to privacy, but that the right was one of its most cherished values. Having laid down the contours of the right to privacy, the Court proceeded to hear the substantive challenge to the Aadhaar Act. A bench of five judges assembled to hear the matter over a period of thirty-eight days, the second longest hearing of any matter before the Court till that time.[24] The judgment was reserved shortly before the long summer recess of the Court and was finally delivered in September 2018. Unlike the privacy judgment in the same matter, this time the verdict was not unanimous but fractured. Three of the five judges, Chief Justice Dipak Misra, Justice A.K. Sikri and Justice A.M. Khanwilkar, upheld the majority of the act, but struck down those portions of the act that they felt unfairly impinged on the privacy of an individual. On the other hand, Justice D.Y. Chandrachud voted to strike down the entire act while Justice Ashok Bhushan held that the act as a whole was valid and there was no occasion to strike down parts of it. The decision of the majority was authored by Justice A.K. Sikri in a judgment that ruled on many areas other than just the legality of the Aadhaar Act.[25]

The majority judgment repelled the argument that the Aadhaar judgment created a surveillance state. The petitioners had argued that the Aadhaar card was akin to an electronic leash with which an individual was tethered to a central database that contained information about all aspects of her living. The Court held that data was secure and that there were sufficient safeguards securing the sanctity of the data both when it was collected, stored and also when it was transmitted for the purpose of authentication.[26] In coming to this conclusion, the Court relied heavily on a PowerPoint presentation that had been made to it by Ajay Bhushan Pandey, who was the CEO of the UIDAI.[27] This led the Court to conclude that the scheme made it 'very difficult to create profile of a person simply on the basis of biometric and demographic information stored in CIDR (Central Identities Data Repository)'.[28]

The Court noted that there was a barter involved in most uses of data. While new technologies greatly empowered citizens, they often necessitated parting with personal information with a concomitant loss of privacy. For instance, the simple task of searching the Internet on a search engine meant that cookies that could track your movements across various sites would be installed on your computer. In drawing that balance, it was necessary for the Court to examine whether the loss of privacy, if any, was proportionate to the corresponding interest or concern of the State. To do so, the Court would need to examine two issues—first, how much of the personal and private information a resident was being asked to surrender and secondly, what the corresponding State interest was. Once these parameters were determined, the Court would proceed to determine the constitutionality of the scheme.

While examining the extent of the loss of privacy, the Court ruled that the amount of data that was collected and stored was minimal. In fact, the act specifically excluded storage of any data that was not required for the purpose of authentication.[29] Similarly, even at the stage of authentication, no data as to the purpose for which authentication was being sought was ever recorded or stored by the requesting entity or the CIDR. Thus, there was no real possibility of profiling citizens with the trivial amount of data that was collected and stored. Further, this data was secure from tampering and hacking because of the multiple layers of security. Therefore, the invasion of the privacy of any individual whose biometric data was being collected was minimal.

In so far as the legitimate interest was concerned, the Court held that there were at least two justifiable bases for the Aadhaar scheme. First, the Aadhaar would supply identity documents to the hitherto uncounted. These identity documents would be unique to the individual since they would be based on the biometric information of that person. Hence, there would be no possibility of any duplication of identity documents.[30] The second interest of the State was that the scheme would enable efficient distribution of subsidies to the marginalized. The Court ruled that the welfare state required that its most impoverished citizens be fed, clothed and given the basic necessities of life so that they may live a life of dignity. The Aadhaar scheme was a tool that empowered the marginalized and enabled the fulfilment of the constitutional promise to secure to all citizens justice, liberty, equality and fraternity.[31]

Having determined these parameters, the Court proceeded to conduct a proportionality analysis, i.e., a legal examination as to whether the infringement of the privacy interests of an individual was disproportionate to the corresponding promotion of the underlying rationale of the Aadhaar scheme. The Court laid down four criteria, all of which had to be met if the scheme was to pass constitutional muster. These criteria were as under:[32]

1. A measure restricting a right must have a legitimate goal (legitimate goal stage).
2. It must be a suitable means of furthering this goal (suitability or rational connection stage).
3. There must not be any less restrictive but equally effective alternative (necessity stage).
4. The measure must not have a disproportionate impact on the right holder (balancing stage).

The Court examined these criteria and held that the Aadhaar scheme met each of them. The benefit to the citizens in securing identification papers and subsidies was a legitimate goal which was furthered by the Aadhaar scheme. The scheme was, in the opinion of the Court, the least possible restrictive measure that could further the interests of the State. Finally, the Court ruled that the loss of privacy was not disproportionate to the benefits a citizen received. In the words of the Court 'the Aadhaar Act has struck a fair balance between the right to privacy of the individual with right to life of the same individual as a beneficiary. In the face of the all-pervading prescript for accomplished socioeconomic rights, that need to be given to the deprived and marginalised section of the society, as the constitutional imperative embodied in these provisions of the Act, it is entitled to receive judicial imprimatur.'[33] For these reasons, the Aadhaar scheme was upheld by the Court. However, the Court ruled that Aadhaar could be made mandatory only for those services that were akin to subsidies.

Finally, the Court upheld the mode and manner in which the Aadhaar Act had been passed by Parliament, i.e., as a 'money bill'. Under the Constitution, if a bill is classified as a money bill, it needs to be introduced in the Lok Sabha and once it is passed there, it is sent to the Rajya Sabha.[34] The Rajya Sabha does not have the power to amend the bill, but can at best make recommendations and return the bill to the Lok Sabha. Thus, the power of the Rajya Sabha is considerably diluted in the case of a money bill. This was the route that had been adopted while passing the Aadhaar Act. The petitioners contended that certifying the act as a money bill was incorrect and was a mere subterfuge to avoid the normal democratic process. The Court rejected this argument and held that since the Aadhaar scheme largely related to the payment of subsidies, which would be paid for from the consolidated fund of India,[35] the act was rightly passed as a money bill.[36]

However, while the Court upheld the Aadhaar scheme, its endorsement was not absolute. Several of the provisions of the act did not meet with constitutional scrutiny and were struck down. For instance, the Court was informed that under the act and the regulations the data collected was to be stored for a period of seven years. The Court thought that this time frame was unnecessarily long and bore no connection with the object of the act. The provision was therefore struck down with the Court holding that the data could at best be stored for six months.[37] The Court also struck down other provisions of the act, including the provision that enabled private entities to use the Aadhaar scheme and the provision that permitted officers of the rank of joint secretary to release biometric data in case of a threat to national security.[38]

III

The Jury is out

All in all, the judgment was a victory as well as a relief for the government. As noted earlier, Justice Chandrachud had ruled to strike down the entire act, holding it to be unconstitutional. Had the other judges agreed with him, the entire investment of the government—both political and financial—would have been wasted. In the end, the position of the government was largely upheld by the Court. However, the jury is still out on the question as to whether the Aadhaar scheme has paid the financial dividends that the government had promised.

The main rationale for starting the Aadhaar scheme, as well as the justification for upholding it, was the presumed efficiency in the distribution of subsidies. The government had sought to use technology for improving the system of distribution of subsidies. To improve financial inclusiveness, every adult was to have a bank account, the Jan Dhan account.[39] This account would be linked to their mobile phones and their Aadhaar cards, under the so-called JAM (Jan Dhan-Aadhaar-Mobile) scheme.

Shortly after the judgment, there was a sense in government that the legal victory handed by the Supreme Court was also beginning to yield financial benefits. Writing shortly after the pronouncement of the judgment, the then finance minister pronounced the scheme a success. He wrote that 'The Government estimates that Rs. 90,000 crore have been saved in the last few years till March, 2018 by the use of the Aadhaar. Several duplicate beneficiaries, non-existent beneficiaries and fake beneficiaries have been eliminated. The Digital Dividend Report prepared by the World Bank estimates that India can save Rs. 77,000 crore every year by the use of Aadhaar. The savings through Aadhaar can fund three schemes of the size of Ayushman Bharat.'[40]

On the other hand, there has been a fair bit of analysis which suggests that the case for Aadhaar has been overpitched. For instance, one paper suggests that the decline in corruption predated Aadhaar and that the purported savings by the government are more illusory than real.[41] There are still a large number of problems in relation to getting an Aadhaar number and linking it to one's phone or using the technology to authenticate transactions.[42] Further anecdotal evidence suggests that the scheme has not been particularly useful in rural areas given the problems of network connectivity.[43]

Thus, the critics of Aadhaar state that the scheme has not worked as it was envisaged and therefore, the loss of privacy can in no way be justified since there is no corresponding gain.[44] A particular concern is that in the attempt to weed out fake beneficiaries, a large number of genuine beneficiaries had also been excluded from the welfare system.[45] The media reported the story of a widow who had lost her Aadhaar card. Since the scheme was based on biometrics, she should have easily been able to get a replacement card once she verified her identity with her fingerprints. In practice, however, it proved extremely difficult to get a replacement. The process took weeks and weeks, and that too with the assistance of activists. In the meanwhile, she was unable to access the benefits of the various schemes floated for the benefit of destitute women such as herself.[46]

There is thus a need for a dispassionate analysis of how the Aadhaar scheme has worked. The problem of exclusion of intended beneficiaries appears to be real and clearly needs to be addressed on an urgent basis. On the other hand, the scheme has had very positive economic benefits, with one report stating that digital payments (backed through the JAM scheme) could save India USD 22 billion per annum.[47] Unfortunately, the discussion about the success and failure of Aadhaar scheme, at least in political circles, seems to be fractured along party political lines.[48] These divisions often end up hardening the positions of the opinion makers, with little dispassionate analysis of the merits of the scheme. Consequently, while the legal verdict on the Aadhaar scheme is clear, the verdict on its financial efficacy is still awaited.

Notes

[1] N. Gregory Mannkiw. *Principles of Macroeconomics*, 6th Edition, Cengage, p. 4.
[2] The DBT scheme was officially launched by the Government of India on 1 January 2013. However, the discussions in relation to the scheme began much earlier. See Rajesh Sharma, 'Direct Benefit Transfer Scheme, India', in

'Digitalization of Public Service Delivery in Asia', Jinho Choi and John Xavier (eds.), Asian Productivity Organization, 2021.

[3] At its inception, the Aadhaar Scheme was commenced through an Executive notification. However, the Aadhaar scheme was ultimately given a statutory basis through the enactment of the Aadhaar Act.

[4] *KS Puttaswamy v. Union of India* (2019) 1 SCC 1.

[5] Food subsidies soared from Rs 2000 crore in 1986 to Rs 27,000 crore in 2004. Fuel subsidies rose from Rs 6200 crore in 2004 to Rs 76,000 crore in 2009. See Shankkar Aiyar, *Aadhaar: A Biometric History of India's 12-Digit Revolution*, Westland, 2017. p. 18.

[6] At the time the UIDAI was set up, the chairperson of the Planning Commission pointed out that only 16 paise out of every rupee spent was reaching the targeted poor. See 'Rajiv Was Right: Montek Says Only 16p of Re Reaches Poor', *The Times of India*, 14 October 2009.

[7] *Aadhaar: A Biometric History of India's 12-Digit Revolution.*

[8] Several government studies labelled the systems in India as inefficient, wasteful and unduly large. See the Discussion Paper of 1997 issued by the union finance ministry or the follow-up paper published by D.K. Srivastava, C. Bhujanga Rao, Pinaki Chakraborty and T.S. Rangamannar titled 'Budgetary Subsidies in India: Subsidising Social and Economic Services', National Institute of Public Finance and Policy, March 2003.

[9] In fact, some states in India had more ration cards than households. See *Aadhaar: A Biometric History of India's 12-Digit Revolution.*

[10] Initially part of the Planning Commission, the UIDAI grew in its scope and ambition. In 2009, Nandan Nilekani, the co-chairperson of one of India's largest corporates, Infosys, was made the chairperson of the UIDAI.

[11] The idea was to ensure a sufficient amount of biometric information to be able to recognize all individuals. For instance, manual labourers often had worn-out fingerprints, which were hence not available for the purpose of identification. In such a situation, the iris scan would provide a backup. *Aadhaar: A Biometric History of India's 12-Digit Revolution*, p. 38.

[12] As regards the merits of the Aadhaar project as a proof of identity, there is some academic work which suggests that the scheme is faulty. See Reetika Khera. 'Impact of Aadhaar in Welfare Programmes', 29 September 2017. As Khera notes 'having rejected existing IDs as error-ridden, UIDAI used those very flawed IDs to enrol for Aadhaar. This circularity has gone largely unnoticed. It has serious implications for the reliability of the Aadhaar database'.

[13] Of course, an insistence on the Aadhaar card in times of unusual crises like the Covid lockdown will inevitably exclude those who have not been registered with the scheme, further compounding their misery. See Sangeeta Yadav and Kumar Ravi Priya, 'Migrant Workers and COVID-19: Listening to the Unheard Voices of Invisible India', *Journal of the Anthropological Survey of India*, December 2020. On the contrary, there is material to support the view that the Aadhaar scheme benefited migrant workers during the Covid crisis. See Dipankar Sengupta, 'Direct Benefit Transfer: A Blessing during the Time of Pandemic', National Informatics Centre.

[14] Section 57 of the Aadhaar Act.

[15] Para 50 of the Aadhaar judgment.

[16] The constitutionality of this compulsory linkage was initially upheld by the Court in the case of *Binoy Viswam v. Union of India* (2017) 7 SCC 59. However, a challenge under Article 21 is pending before a Constitution Bench in *Binoy Viswam v. Reserve Bank of India* WP(C) No. 1038/2020.

[17] 'Govt Makes Aadhaar a Must for Mid-Day Meal at Schools', *Mint*, 4 March 2017.

[18] *MP Sharma v. Satish Chandra* 1954 SCR 1077 as well as *Kharak Singh v. State of UP* (1964) 1 SCR 332.

[19] See reference orders in WP(C) No. 494 of 2012 dated 18 July 2017.

[20] *K.S. Puttaswamy v. Union of India* (2017) 10 SCC 1 (Privacy judgment). There was one judgment delivered by Justice D.Y. Chandrachud on his own behalf and on behalf of three other judges. There were separate concurring judgments by Justices Chelameshwar, Bobde, Nariman, Sapre and Kaul.

[21] Para 298 of the Privacy judgment.

[22] Para 267 of the Privacy judgment.

[23] Para 310 of the Privacy judgment.

[24] 'Aadhaar Hearing: Highlights from 38 Days of Supreme Court's 2nd Longest Hearing in History', Firstpost, 25 September 2018.

[25] The judgment has a lengthy discussion on the philosophical and legal basis of the concept of human dignity. For further reading on this topic, see the essay by Justice Sikri in *Sex and the Supreme Court: How the Law Is Upholding the Dignity of the Indian Citizen* (Hachette, 2020), edited by Saurabh Kirpal.

[26] Para 184 of the Aadhaar judgment. Interestingly, the Court noted that the data would also be protected through the legislative enactment of the Personal Data Protection Bill (Para 261). However, this hope eventually did not materialize because till the writing of this chapter, Parliament has not enacted such a bill into law.

[27] This manner of adjudication where the affidavit of a party to the litigation has been accepted without (allegedly) having expertise has been criticized by some commentators. See Amber Sinha, 'Questions of Fact: India's Aadhaar Matter and the Limits of the Supreme Court', *Asie. Visions*, No. 101, Institut Français des Relations Internationales, October 2018.

[28] Para 186 of the Aadhaar judgment.

[29] Section 32 (3) of the Aadhaar Act.

[30] Para 508.7 of the Aadhaar judgment.

[31] Para 511.3 of the Aadhaar judgment.

[32] Para 319 of the Aadhaar judgment.

[33] Para 368 of the Aadhaar judgment.

[34] Article 110.

[35] Article 266 of the Constitution provides for a Consolidated Fund of India into which all revenues, loans and other incomes are collected.

[36] Paragraph 472. Interestingly, this position was dissented from in the judgment of Justice Chandrachud who held that the bill had been wrongly classified as a money bill. In a later judgment, the correctness of the Aadhaar judgment on the issue of classification of a bill as a money bill has been doubted, and the matter has been referred to a larger bench which is yet to be constituted. See *Rojer Mathew v. South Indian Bank Ltd* (2020) 6 SCC 1.

[37] Para 510.4.1 of the Aadhaar judgment.

[38] Section 57 and 33 (2) respectively of the Aadhaar Act. See Para 510.4.5 of the Aadhaar judgment.

[39] Over 40 crore bank accounts were opened under the scheme. See 'Jan Dhan Yojana: 41.75 Cr Accounts Opened under the Scheme', Rural Marketing. com, 9 February 2021.

[40] 'Benefits of the Aadhaar—Where It Stands Today', arunjaitley.com, 6 January 2019.

[41] Reetika Khera. 'Impact of Aadhaar in Welfare Programmes'.

[42] Reetika Khera. 'Aadhaar Failures: A Tragedy of Errors', *Economic and Political Weekly*, Vol. 54, Issue No. 14, 6 April 2019.

[43] Aayush Ailawadi and Alex Mathew. 'Has Aadhaar Worked for Rural India?', *Bloomberg*, 27 January 2018.

[44] Studies also seem to indicate that while there has been some gain in lessening corruption in the system, that gain is overshadowed by the number of genuine beneficiaries of the PDS scheme who have been excluded due to poor implementation of the scheme, particularly in the transition phase. See Karthik Muralidharan, Paul Niehaus and Sandip Sukhtankar, 'Identity Verification

Standards in Welfare Programs: Experimental Evidence from Working Paper 26744', National Bureau of Economic Research, February 2020.

[45] Vidhi Doshi. 'India's Biometric ID Program Was Supposed to End Welfare Corruption. But the Neediest May Be Hit Hardest', *Washington Post*, 25 March 2018.

[46] Vyom Anil and Jean Dreze. 'Without Aadhaar, Without Identity', *Indian Express*, 5 July 2021.

[47] The World Bank Report titled 'World Development Report: Digital Dividends', 2016.

[48] 'Aadhaar Verdict Reaction: The Judgment Will Promote Dignity, Not Surveillance, Says BJP', *Indian Express*, 26 September 2018.

Chapter 14

Insolvency and Bankruptcy

One of the fundamental principles of corporate law is that a company is a distinct juristic entity and has a corporate personality that is separate from that of its shareholders. However, that is not where the anthropomorphic analogy ends. Many eastern philosophies believe in the karmic cycle of birth and rebirth. One can draw a similar analogy in the case of companies, which also have a cycle of birth, innovation, growth and eventually, death. This chapter is concerned with the stage of a company when it undergoes severe financial stress and must be revived or wound up, i.e., face legal death.

The mortality of a company has a significant impact not only upon the company itself but also on several stakeholders, often with competing interests. The management of a company may be interested in ensuring its viability as a going concern, while workers almost certainly would also like the revival of a company. The position of its creditors may be more nuanced. While they may also be supportive of its continuation in business, much would depend on its ability to service its debt. There would come a point where the creditors would rather have the company wound up and its assets sold so that they may recover whatever they can. The law is then required to balance these competing interests.

For the longest period, the focus of the law was to ensure the continuance of industrial companies through the infusion of funds by its shareholders and promoters. However, this proved to be unsuccessful as the promoters were unable, or unwilling, to revive the companies. They defaulted on their loans as well as payments to their suppliers, leading to a domino effect on defaults across sectors of the economy.

Faced with increasing loan defaults and non-performing assets, Parliament passed an innovative piece of legislation called the Insolvency and Bankruptcy Code of India (IBC). The aim of the law was a revival of the stressed company rather than its winding up. What was novel about this piece of legislation was that the revival of the company was sought to be accomplished by bringing about a change in management of the company. This was something the mollycoddled promoters were not willing to accept. They, and other stakeholders, challenged the law before the Supreme Court on multiple grounds. However, the Court rejected this challenge in its judgment in the case of *Swiss Ribbons v. Union of India*.[1] This chapter will examine how the IBC came to be enacted and what the judgment of the Supreme Court decided.

I

Non-Performing Assets and the Role of the Promoters

Though the IBC was passed into law in 2016, the seeds for its enactment can be traced back much further, to the time of a regulatory regime that empowered the promoters of a company at the expense of the creditors.

The company, it has been said, represents a contract between equity and debt.[2] As long as the shareholders of a company can service the debt, they have complete control over the company and the freedom to run it how they think fit. However, corporate governance demands that in the event the shareholders are unable to service the debts, thereby jeopardizing the interests of the creditors, they lose the right to run the company. This is especially important in highly leveraged companies where the promoter shareholders have only a small percentage of the shareholding. In such a case, the promoter has little personal interest in the successful running of the business since it is largely most of the creditors that are at risk.

However, contrary to this principle of the contract between equity and debt, the law in India prior to the enactment of the IBC was heavily skewed in favour of the promoter shareholders. The socialistic economic worldview prevailing prior to liberalization prioritized the preservation of the company over the interests of its shareholders. This policy was largely enforced through the provisions of the Sick Industrial Companies Act, 1985. The act sought to identify companies that were 'sick', i.e., had a negative net worth. These companies were referred to a specialized body called the Board for Industrial and Financial Reconstruction (BIFR), which would frame a scheme so as to attempt to salvage the company as a going concern. The act was meant to secure 'the timely detection of sick and potentially sick companies' with the intention that the BIFR would suggest remedial measures, with 'speedy determination' and ensure their 'expeditious enforcement'.[3]

Even though the act used language that screamed urgency, in practice, companies that were referred to the BIFR were hardly ever revived. The BIFR, when it was functional, took years to frame any scheme. During this period, the act provided for a moratorium during which period the creditors could not pursue their claims against the companies.[4] There was no upper time limit for the moratorium. Effectively, the promoters of the company stayed in control while the creditors could only wait and watch. The system was heavily skewed against the creditors. In the nineties, the legislature did attempt to rectify this imbalance and enacted legislation that was meant to enable a speedy recovery of loans.[5] However, given the glacial pace of the legal system, these enactments had a limited impact.[6]

As a result of this loose regulatory control, companies were unable (or unwilling) to pay their creditors. The loans went into default and were classified as non-performing assets (NPAs). By 1999, almost 15 per cent of the total amount lent by banks to its customers were classified as NPAs,[7] a problem which only became more acute as the years passed.

This NPA problem was exacerbated by the events that transpired in the mid-2000s. At that time there was an unbridled mood of optimism in Indian industry with the GDP growing between 9–10 per cent per annum.[8] Growth expectations soared and companies borrowed large sums of money to ensure that they did not miss out on the Indian growth story. Banks were also only too keen to lend the money, often giving large sums without doing adequate due diligence. Investment, fueled by bank borrowings rather than equity participation boomed.[9] Banks aggressively lent money based on growth projections of companies, ensuring a huge amount of liquidity in the financial sector.

The party, however, ended up like most with an excess of the good stuff do, i.e., with a hangover. By 2008, the financial crisis hit the world as well as India. Economic growth slowed and companies' profits fell. Corporates that had taken large loans found it difficult to make repayments. The problem was compounded by the increasing interest rates—the RBI lending rate went from 4.75 per cent in September 2009 to 8.5 per cent in December 2011.[10] Companies that had borrowed money had to pay larger sums on account of this rising rate of interest. On the other hand, even the banks, which were the lenders, came under severe financial stress. This led to what is commonly referred to as the 'twin balance sheet problem,' a situation where both the creditors as well as the debtors were under severe financial strain.

II

The Build-up and the Legislation

By 2016, almost 40 per cent of the companies to which the loans had been given earned enough only to pay the interest on the same, leaving no room for profits or other expenses.[11] Faced with this situation, banks often resorted to the process of evergreening. This was a case where banks gave new loans to companies that were on the verge of defaulting. The companies could use the fresh loans to repay the interest and remain, in the books of the bank at least, as standard accounts. This had often worked in other countries where the downturn in economic growth was only temporary, permitting them to ride over the crisis.

In India's case, the outcome was not quite so rosy. In 2014–15, banks restructured almost 6.4 per cent[12] of the outstanding loans on their books. They also infused fresh funding into corporates hoping that the problems would blow over. Unfortunately, matters did not improve in that way. There was a lengthy period of economic stress, and evergreening only served to kick the can down the road. The problem was so acute that the Economic Survey of India in 2016–17[13] noted that almost one-fifth of all loans given by public sector banks were bad loans.

The same economic survey candidly admitted that expecting that the corporate world could grow its way out of financial stress was a false hope. Too many sectors—particularly the infrastructure companies and power producers—faced may uphill economic challenges. Most disturbingly, the survey noted that 'There is yet another reason why the economy may not be able to grow out of its debts: the problem itself is beginning to take a toll on growth.' It pointed out that the levels of investment were in free fall 'as stressed companies reduce their new investments to conserve cash flow, while stressed banks are unable to assume new lending risks'.

In sum, there were several reasons that created the NPA crisis in India. According to Raghuram Rajan, the governor of RBI at the relevant time, these causes included over-optimism, slow growth, malfeasance and fraud.[14] However, one of the most worrying reasons was 'loss of promoter and banker interest'. As mentioned earlier in this chapter, many promoter companies owned only a small portion of the shares in their companies. This was coupled with a legal regime that made it difficult to throw out an incompetent (or dishonest) management. Rajan noted that 'Once projects got delayed enough that the promoter had little equity left in the project, he lost interest. Ideally, projects should be restructured at such times, with banks writing down bank debt that is uncollectable, and promoters bringing in more equity, under the threat that they would otherwise lose their project. . . . bankers had little ability to threaten promoters, even incompetent or unscrupulous ones, with loss of their project. Writing down the debt was then simply a gift to promoters, and no banker wanted to take the risk of doing so and inviting the attention of the investigative agencies. Stalled projects continued as "zombie" projects, neither dead nor alive ("zombie" is a technical term used in the banking literature).'

In other words, one of the biggest reasons in creating the NPA crisis was the lack of a legal framework to remove errant managements. Simply waiting out a rough economic patch was not the answer. Equally, writing down of loans was fraught with moral hazards. The various schemes floated by RBI for restructuring of the loans had also failed to provide a solution to the problems. Clearly, Executive tinkering was not helping, and some bold economic reform was needed to solve the NPA crisis that was threatening the financial stability of the country.

It was in this background that a dramatic new piece of legislation was envisaged. A committee on bankruptcy law reforms was constituted under the chairmanship of Dr T.K.

Viswanathan, a former secretary-general of the Lok Sabha.[15] The committee submitted its report in November 2015, giving the draft proposal of a new Insolvency and Bankruptcy Code. The report[16] contained a draft Insolvency Code as an annexure that was intended to replace all the existing patchwork of laws into a single comprehensive code. The report of the committee was accepted by the government, the draft Code was passed into law and was christened the Insolvency and Bankruptcy Code, 2016 (the IBC).

The code contained an elaborate set of procedures that were meant to address the underlying causes of the insolvency on an expeditious basis. The process under the IBC would be triggered when a company defaulted on its debt. Once that happened, the creditor of a company was required to send it a legal notice demanding that the creditor be paid its dues. If the company failed to make the payment even after the receipt of the notice, the creditor would move the National Company Law Tribunal (NCLT). The NCLT would examine the claim of the creditor, and if it was found to be genuine and due as per the IBC, a commercial insolvency resolution process (CIRP) would commence.

In the earlier law, if a similar action was initiated by the creditor, the court would order a winding up of the company if it was adjudged to be unable to pay its debts. The IBC had a markedly different philosophy as compared to the legislation as it existed at that time. The aim of the code was the rehabilitation of the company rather than its liquidation. This was because, as the committee had noted, liquidation wasted the organizational capital of the firm. Liquidation of companies would also imply a loss of jobs as well as the (admittedly remote) chance that the creditors could recover more money than was possible simply by the sales of the assets of the company.

With this philosophy in mind, instead of liquidation as the first option, the new law provided that an attempt would be made to sell the company as a going concern to some investors. This would require the identification of fresh buyers who would submit proposals to rehabilitate the company—the so-called Resolution Plans.

However, during the period when the hunt for a new buyer of a company was going on, the owners of the company would not be allowed to remain in management to ensure that they did not indulge in asset stripping. Also, it was presumably easier to find buyers for a company if the management was not in the hands of the intransigent owners but lay with some independent agency. The IBC provided that as soon as the CIRP process commenced, the management of the company would be transferred to an interim resolution professional (IRP). It was the responsibility of the IRP to run the company as a going concern while the next steps under the CIRP were undertaken. The erstwhile owners were effectively excluded from the management. Further, to enable a successful sale of the company, the law provided for a 'calm period' or a moratorium where the creditors of a company would not be able to sue it.

Perhaps the most controversial feature of the law was the priority given to the financial creditors. The IBC created two separate classes of creditors. Financial creditors were those who were owed money pursuant to a purely financial transaction such as loans, debentures, etc. The other class of creditors were the operational creditors, i.e., creditors who were owed money for the goods or services they had supplied to the company in the past. Thus, raw material suppliers, unpaid employees and service providers were operational creditors in the company.

The IBC provided that the main decision-making body in the company undergoing the CIRP process would be a Committee of Creditors (COC) that comprised the financial creditors of the debtor company. During the pendency of the CIRP process, it would be the COC which would manage the company and take all the major decisions for the debtor company.[17] The COC could undertake the activities of the management,[18] the board of directors[19] and the shareholders of the corporate debtor[20] and hence wield power greater than any other stakeholder in the company.

One of the most important decisions to be taken by the COC would be to approve a restructuring plan that would be proposed by the prospective buyer. The resolution plan would not only contain details about the revival of the company, but also how the various creditors would be paid off, i.e., the quantum and priority of payments would be exclusively in the hands of the financial creditors. Operational creditors would not have any say in determining how the payments would be made to them. Nevertheless, the resolution plan would be binding upon *all* creditors and stakeholders. In effect, financial creditors could determine the mode, manner and quantum of recoveries of debts to the operational creditors through a mechanism in which they would have no voting rights.[21]

The IBC came into force from 28 May 2016. However, almost immediately, one loophole was discovered. When a corporate debtor was sought to be put up for sale, its erstwhile management also made a bid to purchase it, often at a steep discount. In effect, the promoters of a company tried to buy the company they had brought to the brink of ruin after making its creditors take a massive cut in their dues. This was a moral hazard that the government could not countenance. To rectify this, a new provision was inserted in the IBC that barred the promoters (or their related parties), or persons whose accounts were NPAs from making a bid for the company.[22] The statement of objects and reasons of the act noted that 'Concerns have been raised that persons who, with their misconduct contributed to defaults of companies or are otherwise undesirable, may misuse this situation due to lack of prohibition or restrictions to participate in the resolution or liquidation process, and gain or regain control of the corporate debtor.'

<h1 style="text-align:center">III</h1>

<h2 style="text-align:center">The Judgment</h2>

As has now become the norm, the provisions of the IBC were immediately challenged before the Supreme Court of India. While the Court granted a stay of CIRP proceedings initially, the final judgment was a ringing endorsement of the act.

The opening part of the judgment contained the judicial philosophy that underpinned the entire decision, and that was the principle of judicial restraint in matters relating to economic policy. The Court quoted an earlier decision of the Supreme Court, where it had been held that 'Every legislation, particularly in economic matters is essentially empiric and it is based on experimentation or what one may call trial and error method and therefore it cannot provide for all possible situations or anticipate all possible abuses. There may be crudities and inequities in complicated experimental economic legislation but on that account alone it cannot be struck down as invalid . . . The Court must defer to legislative judgment in matters relating to social and economic policies and must not interfere, unless the exercise of legislative judgment appears to be palpably arbitrary.'[23] Thus, the Court seemed to be willing to give the Parliament a long rope when it came to framing legislation.

However, this was not merely a case of the Court keeping a hands-off approach in matters of legislation. The Court also seemed to actively approve of the underlying economic basis of the IBC. The IBC, the Court noted, was meant to provide for a speedy insolvency process of the corporate debtor. A drawn-out resolution process[24] would result in the depletion of the assets and that would be to the detriment of all the stakeholders of the company—from the creditors to the employees. The ultimate aim of the IBC was not distributing the assets of a company after its liquidation, but lay in reviving the company so as to improve the credit markets. As the Court held, the 'timely resolution of a corporate debtor who is in the red, by an effective legal framework, would go a long way to support the development of credit markets. Since more investment can be made with funds that have come back into the economy, business then eases up, which leads, overall, to higher economic growth and development of the Indian economy.' Given this benevolent view of the credit market, it is perhaps not surprising that the Court ultimately upheld the provisions of the IBC that accorded primacy to the financial creditors in *Swiss Ribbons*.

One of the main challenges to the act was the creation of two classes of creditors. The petitioners had argued that all creditors were essentially in the same boat, i.e., that they were owed money by the company in default. By giving substantial control to the financial creditors, the operational creditors had been deliberately put at a disadvantage. This, it was argued, was a case of hostile discrimination and 'manifestly arbitrary'. In essence, the petitioners argued that this was a violation of the equality clause in the Constitution because identically placed people (operational and financial creditors) had been treated differently.

The Court brushed aside this argument of discrimination, noting that the Constitution only prohibited treating equally placed persons unequally. The test under Article 14 of the Constitution would be satisfied if it could be shown that the classification of the two categories of creditors was based on real (and not fanciful or imagined) differences between the two. Further, it was also required to be shown that the basis of differentiation had some rational connection with the object sought to be achieved by the act. If the two groups of creditors were fundamentally different in nature, dealing with them in a distinct manner was not a case of discrimination. In other words, the fundamental premise of the petitioners that the two groups of creditors were identically placed was fundamentally flawed.

The Court accepted the argument of the government that the classification was based on valid grounds. Operational creditors were, as noted above, suppliers of goods and services. They would, typically, be a larger number than the financial creditors who were usually banks and other financial institutions. The debts owed to operational creditors could be easily disputed—for instance it could be said that a supplier supplied sub-standard goods or that the service provider gave negligent or erroneous advice. This dispute would not normally arise in the case of financial creditors since the factum of the loan was a matter of financial records maintained by the company itself. Some other differences were also noted by the Court. Financial creditors would typically be fewer in number and would also be secured creditors, i.e., have some form of security for the money that they had lent to the company. On the other hand, operational creditors would usually be much larger in number and would also be unsecured. After all, a goods supplier would not usually ask the company for some asset as security before any goods were sold to the company.

However, the greatest distinction in the mind of the Court was the nature and competence of financial creditors. This class of creditors would be involved in assessing the viability of the debtor at the time of extension of the loan. In times of financial stress, they would also approve any restructuring of the debts or reorganization of the company's business. This was a task that was not to be undertaken by the operational creditor since they would be interested in payment to themselves rather than the larger interest or ability of the company to pay up the debts. Since the aim of the IBC was the reorganization and sale of the business of the debtor, financial creditors were a distinct class that had a rational nexus with the object sought to be achieved by the legislation.

The Court held 'since the financial creditors are in the business of money lending, banks and financial institutions are best equipped to assess viability and feasibility of the business of the corporate debtor. Even at the time of granting loans, these banks and financial institutions undertake a detailed market study which includes a techno-economic valuation report, evaluation of business, financial projection, etc. Since this detailed study has already been undertaken before sanctioning a loan, and since financial creditors have trained employees to assess viability and feasibility, they are in a good position to evaluate the contents of a resolution plan. On the other hand, operational creditors, who provide goods and services, are involved only in recovering amounts that are paid for such goods and services, and are typically unable to assess viability and feasibility of business.'[25]

While holding that the classification was reasonable, the Court also noted that the interests of the operational creditors were safeguarded since any resolution plan was required to give them a mandatory minimum of the liquidation value of the debts.[26] Further, any plan would also have to be approved by the NCLT, which agency was expected to weed out any plans that were grossly unfair to the operational creditors. Thus, the Supreme Court held that the power vested in the financial creditors of the company to take all major decisions during the CIRP process, to the exclusion of the operational creditors, was not unconstitutional.

The Court then trained its guns on the other controversial provision in the act—the newly inserted Section 29A by which the former owners of an enterprise had been made ineligible to bid for the company. After examining the purpose for the enactment of the provision, the Court held that no erstwhile management had any vested right[27] in making an application for the consideration of its resolution plan. The main grounds for the challenging of this provision was that it treated unequals as equals. The provision excluded all managers whose accounts were NPAs, regardless of whether they were guilty of any wrongdoing. Thus, an erstwhile manager who was a good manager but merely suffered a difficult business scenario, would be excluded from management. It was argued that such persons could not be equated with managements who had siphoned off money and deliberately mismanaged the company. The Court rejected this argument as well saying that the intention of the act was not to exclude only cases of malfeasance, but to exclude all those who, for whatsoever reason, had led the company to the doorstep of dissolution and default.

Another grounds of challenge raised by the petitioners was the time period before the classification of an account as an NPA and the commencement of the CIRP process. The act provided that a period of at least one year ought to have passed from the date of classification of the account as an NPA and the initiation of the CIRP process. It was argued that this was an arbitrary period. This argument was also rejected by the Court, which pointed out that the one-year period was in the nature of a 'grace period' available to the management to make good on the debts to the creditors. Rather than simply writing off the debtors at the time of the default, the act gave them an opportunity to make the payment to the creditors. However, in case they were unable to make such payment, there was no rational reason to allow them to make a bid for the company. In the eloquent words of the Court, 'a person who cannot service a debt for the aforesaid period is obviously a person who is ailing itself. The saying of Jesus comes to mind—"If the blind lead the blind, both shall fall into the ditch." The legislative policy, therefore, is that a person who is unable to service its own debt beyond the grace period referred to above, is unfit to be eligible to become a resolution applicant.'

The judgment was a comprehensive one, running into 150 pages, in which the Court considered challenges to various other provisions of the act. A comprehensive discussion of the judgment would perhaps be more apposite for a law journal or an academic treatise than this book. However, what needs to be pointed out is that the Court ultimately dismissed all challenges to the constitutionality of the act and upheld the IBC in its entirety. In its epilogue, the Court noted with some satisfaction that 'in the working of the Code, the flow of financial resources to the commercial sector in India has increased exponentially as a result of financial debts being repaid.' After noting the huge amounts of money that had been recovered under the newly enacted IBC, the Court said that the 'figures show that the experiment conducted in enacting the Code is proving to be largely successful. The defaulter's paradise is lost. In its place, the economy's rightful position has been regained.'

Conclusion

Whether the optimism expressed by the Court is justified probably requires more analysis than the preliminary figures released by RBI. Certainly, some part of the hope expressed in the judgment, that the financial creditors and the NCLT would ensure an equitable treatment of the operational creditors, does not seem to have come true. Independent evidence suggests that, at the very least, there is a perception that the vesting of near absolute power with the COC has resulted in operational creditors being treated unfairly.[28] Further, the research also shows that the resolution professional usually acts in a manner that was aligned to the interests of the financial creditors and that the resolution process is often marred by 'procedural unfairness'. Part of the problem in deciding these issues is the lack of empirical evidence—some of which has been inexplicably kept out of the public domain.[29]

Thus, on the question whether the IBC has contributed in reducing the NPA crisis, the jury is still out. Of course, this is generally a problem in India where the audit of the impact of a law, or a legislative impact assessment, is rare. However, the concern is that the IBC may fail in achieving its purpose not because of some internal flaws, but because of extraneous reasons. This could be a soft-pedalling approach on the part of the government[30] or making the IBC a less attractive proposition through legislative or policy changes.[31] While there may be frustration in some quarters as to the slow pace of NPA reduction, surely the answer cannot be to replace a relatively new piece of legislation with some other alternative. While experimentation in the field of economic policy is something which the Courts keep their hands off, it would be good to remember that markets like stability. That stability includes not only fiscal or monetary stability, but also legislative stability. It would be prudent to give the IBC time to work itself out. The IBC was a flagship piece of legislation with ambitious goals, which may take time to work out. The Court has expressed its faith in the act. It is hoped that all the policy-makers will give it a chance to succeed too.

Notes

[1] (2019) 4 SCC 14.

[2] The Report of the Bankruptcy Law Reforms Committee, Vol. I, (2015), p. 9,

[3] The long title to the Sick Industrial Companies (Special Provisions) Act, 1985, states that it is 'An Act to make, in the public interest, special provisions with a view to securing the timely detection of sick and potentially sick companies owning industrial undertakings, the speedy determination by a Board of experts of the preventive, ameliorative, remedial and other measures which need to be taken with respect to such companies and the expeditious enforcement of the measures so determined and for matters connected therewith or incidental thereto'.

[4] Section 22 SICA.

[5] Recovery of Debts and Bankruptcy Act (RDB Act), 1993 and Securitization and Reconstruction of Financial Assets and Enforcement of Security Interests Act (SARFAESI Act), 2002.

[6] In the committee report for the Insolvency and Bankruptcy Code, 2016, it was stated that 'The existing framework for insolvency and bankruptcy is inadequate, ineffective and results in undue delays in resolution.' See Report of the Joint Committee on the Insolvency and Bankruptcy Code, 2015, Sixteenth Lok Sabha, presented to Lok Sabha on 28 April 2016, p. 7.

[7] Handbook of Statistics on Indian Economy, 15 September 2009, p. 120.

[8] Yogendra Singh. 'The NPA Crisis (3 of 4)', *The Economic Times*, 28 November 2017.

[9] Ahita Paul. 'Examining the Rise of Non-Performing Assets in India', prsindia. com, 13 September 2018.

[10] Yogendra Singh. 'The NPA crisis (3 of 4)'.

[11] Economic Survey of India 2016–17, Ministry of Finance, January 2017.

[12] Economic Survey of India 2016–17, 'The Festering Twin Balance Sheet Problem', Chapter 4, p. 82.

[13] Economic Survey of India 2016–17, Ministry of Finance, January 2017.

[14] 'Raghuram Rajan Explains the Origins of India's NPA Crisis', *The Wire*, 12 September 2018.

[15] Prior to his appointment as secretary-general, Viswanathan was the secretary to the union law ministry. He has headed several committees on various law reform proposals, including on hate speech and fair market conduct in the securities market.

[16] The Report of the Bankruptcy Law Reforms Committee, Vol. I: Rationale and Design, November 2015.

[17] Section 28 IBC.

[18] For instance, alter the terms of appointment of personnel, Section 28 (1) (l).

[19] Make any change in the management of the corporate debtor or its subsidiary, Section 28 (1) (j).

[20] For instance, alter the constitutional documents of the corporate debtor, Section 28 (1) (j).

[21] Though the operational creditors could be represented on the COC, they do not have any voting rights.

[22] Section 29A of the IBC was introduced through the Insolvency and Bankruptcy Code (Amendment) Ordinance, 2017, which amended the Insolvency and Bankruptcy Code on 23 November 2017.

[23] *RK Garg v. UOI* (1981) 4 SCC 675.

[24] The Court had noted in the case of *Innoventive Industries Ltd v. ICICI Bank* (2018) 1 SCC 407 that 'per the data available with the World Bank in 2016, insolvency resolution in India took 4.3 years on an average, which was much higher when compared with the United Kingdom (1 year), USA (1.5 years) and South Africa (2 years)'.

[25] Paragraph 75 *Swiss Ribbons v. UOI.*

[26] Section 30 (2) (b) read with Section 31.

[27] In *Bibi Sayeeda v. State of Bihar*, (1996) 9 SCC 516, 527, the Court held that 'Rights are "vested" when right to enjoyment, present or prospective, has

become property of some particular person or persons as present interest; mere expectancy of future benefits, or contingent interest in property founded on anticipated continuance of existing laws, does not constitute vested rights.' Such rights can only be taken away by specific words or by necessary implication in the statute.

[28] C. Scott Pryor and Risham Garg. 'Differential Treatment amongst Creditors under India's Insolvency and Bankruptcy Code, 2016: Issues and Solutions', *American Bankruptcy Law Journal 123*, Vol. 94.

[29] For instance, the regulations require that the net liquidation value has to remain confidential. The Insolvency and Bankruptcy Board of India (Insolvency Resolution Process for Corporate Persons) (Third Amendment) Regulations, 2018, *Gazette of India*, Pt. III, Sec. 4, 4 July 2018, ('The resolution professional and registered valuers shall maintain confidentiality of the fair value and the liquidation value.').

[30] Urjit Patel. *Saving the Indian Saver*, Harper India (24 July 2020).

[31] Devender Mehta. 'View: Is IBC Being Relegated as an NPA Resolution Option of Last Resort?', *The Economic Times*, 14 December 2021.

Chapter 15

Bit by Bitcoin

In a book related to finance, it is perhaps apparent that the subject of greatest discussion would be money. But what is 'money'? For most people, it is the currency notes in their wallets or their savings in the bank or even the assets held by them in the stock market. However, in a world witnessing rapid technological advancement, it is not surprising that this traditional conception of money would also be challenged. Over the last decade, the world has seen a boom in bitcoin and other cryptocurrencies, all of which make some claim to being money, or at least something akin to it.

When technology and finance meet, regulation can be found not far behind. The reasons for this are not hard to find. Cryptocurrencies have the potential to upend the standard role of the central banks in their countries. Central banks are usually the only authority entitled to issue currency in a country and hence enjoy a monopoly over regulating the money supply. Cryptocurrencies also have a potentially subversive role due to their anonymity, which means that they can be used for potentially nefarious activities. For these reasons, it is but natural that government will seek to regulate these currencies and it is indeed what many countries around the world have done.

The Indian central bank, i.e., the Reserve Bank of India (RBI) also sought to regulate the cryptocurrency world. However, rather than framing regulations and then following up with the tougher job of ensuring their implementation, RBI adopted the nuclear option. As so often happens in India, the knee-jerk reaction of the authorities was to effectively ban cryptocurrencies rather than regulate them.[1].

Faced with this ban, an industry body of companies representing the interests of the online and digital services industry approached the Supreme Court seeking to have the ban set aside. Since the technology was a relatively young one, it was not surprising that a fair number of young tech entrepreneurs also moved the Supreme Court, challenging the ban. The Court, in the judgment titled *Internet and Mobile Association of India v. Reserve Bank of India*,[2] held the ban to be unconstitutional and struck it down.

Significantly, the Court did not strike down the ban on the grounds that cryptocurrencies were not money or that RBI did not have the power to regulate them. On the contrary, the Court found that several of the attributes of cryptocurrencies were the same as that of money as understood by a lay person. The Court also held that RBI was entitled to regulate cryptocurrencies since they could potentially affect the macroeconomic stability of the country. The rationale of the Court was that the reasons given by RBI to justify the ban were not sufficient to justify the extreme act of banning cryptocurrencies. In other words, the Court used the well-entrenched legal test of proportionality to determine the constitutionality of a relatively emergent concept. This also showed how the Constitution and its text were flexible enough to deal with questions that could not even have been envisaged at the time of its framing.

I

What is Money?

Money in some form or the other has existed since the Stone Age.[3] Originally, it was conceived of as a method that would permit two strangers to exchange goods or services at an agreed value. A pre-monetary society relied largely on barter or debt. While a barter permitted an immediate exchange, debt permitted commerce by allowing a seller to sell her goods and receive other goods or services at a future point in time. However, maintaining an account of who owed what to whom must have been no easy task. There was also the risk in trading on a system of IOUs or debt when the two parties to a transaction were strangers. Debt required a degree of trust, i.e., a belief that the obligations would be honoured, which was not always possible if the parties did not know each other well enough (or trust each other) to be sure of repayment.[4]

Money evolved as a concept that allowed people to carry on trade easily, without having to rely on a complicated system of accounting or a mechanism that would require a seller to enforce debts against unknown third parties. The earliest solution to these complicated transactional problems was a form of money called 'commodity money'. The item used as the medium of exchange used as money had a certain intrinsic value. For instance, items such as a fixed unit of grain, cowries or even precious metals like gold and silver were used as commodity money. However, this required the money to itself be valuable and hence made high-value transactions more difficult.[5]

Therefore, another form of money was evolved, what is called 'representative money'. Here, the actual medium of exchange was not valuable in itself, but represented a claim on something of equivalent value. For instance, an issuer of the money who printed a piece of paper claiming it to be worth Rs 5000 would have to have an asset worth exactly that amount in reserve. The money would no longer be 'commodity money', but more accurately 'commodity-backed money'. However, this form of money also posed a problem since it required that persons accepting the 'representative money' trust that the issuer actually had the corresponding assets in reserve. This need, coupled with the growth in the power and authority of nation states, eventually caused the evolution of sovereign-backed currencies. In this system, the central bank of a country would issue money and would be required to maintain a corresponding store of value as an asset.[6] The most common form of this money was the so-called 'gold standard', where central banks would issue currency while maintaining an equivalent amount of gold in its reserves.

The Great Depression in the 1930s caused the banks to move away from the gold standard since that system limited the amount of money a bank could print.[7] The central banks adopted the concept of 'fiat money'. This was money that was issued by the bank and was not linked to any underlying asset. The reason why the money had any worth was because of the legislation in the country, which declared that the money was worth a certain value. For instance, it is common to see 'I promise to pay the bearer a sum of Rs X', duly signed by the governor of RBI, printed on bank notes. There is no underlying commodity, merely a promise by the bank that the money is worth what it says on the note. Most of the money in circulation in the modern era is this form of fiat money and is dependent on the trust that users have in the central bank and the sovereign guarantees that it promises.

While there are different forms of money, they all share at least three broad characteristics. Money has to be a medium of exchange, a measure of value and a store of value.[8] A medium of exchange implies that money can be used to buy and sell goods without having to engage in barter. A measure of value is also called a unit of value and simply permits items to be denominated in terms of money so as to facilitate their purchase. As a store of value, money is a way to transfer purchasing power from the present to the future. In other words, money has a certain worth, which could be intrinsic or representative, and would be a means to hold that. A ten-rupee note put in a wallet would ensure that the note is still worth ten rupees whenever it is used in the future.

This discussion of money is not only fascinating in itself, but is imperative because one of the main claims of the petitioner was that cryptocurrencies were not money at all and hence RBI had no authority to regulate them. This argument also requires us to investigate what the essential nature of cryptocurrencies is, so as to determine whether they would fall within the rubric of the term money and in particular, whether they fulfilled the three characteristics of money.

II

Blockchain Technologies and Cryptocurrencies

If teasing out the core functions of money is a surprisingly complicated task, understanding the true nature of cryptocurrencies is even more difficult given how novel they are and how unfamiliar with technology economists and lawyers often are. Nevertheless, it is necessary to try to have some basic nature of cryptocurrency as well as its functions to determine whether it would qualify as 'money'.

If one were to look for a definition of cryptocurrencies, one could turn to one of the earliest definitions of the term. The Financial Action Task Force (FATF) issued a report that defined a 'cryptocurrency' to mean 'a math-based, decentralized convertible virtual currency protected by cryptography by relying on public and private keys to transfer value from one person to another and signed cryptographically each time it is transferred.'[9]

Unfortunately, the definition does not clarify the nature of cryptocurrencies to most laypeople. A better course may be to explain exactly how it functions and how it can potentially act as a substitute for currency. Cryptocurrencies work with blockchain technology. A blockchain is basically an electronic ledger where every transaction ever made with the currency is recorded in a database. Every time a fresh transaction is made, it is appended as a fresh entry to the blockchain. To ensure the authenticity of transactions, the blockchains are verified against the database maintained by a decentralized network of computers, each of which is called a node. The privacy of a transaction is secured through the use of a cryptographic key. A user of the cryptocurrency chooses a private key, which is kept secret with her, and generates a corresponding public key, which is shared with the world. Any payments made by the user are made using the private key but any payment to be received is sent to the public key, known to the world.[10]

It is important to note that the entire transaction process does not need any centralized authority, much less a government body. If most people in a country (or indeed the world) start using cryptocurrencies, there is no need to rely on the currency issued by the central bank. The bank would lose the sole authority to print money and with that, would lose a very significant power to control the money supply and liquidity in the market. This, in turn, would significantly hamper the ability of the bank to ensure the macroeconomic stability of the country.

III

The RBI Surgical Strike

There were several worries about cryptocurrencies. Primary among them were the issues of security, investor protection and monetary stability. As regards security, there was a concern that cryptocurrency could be used for terror financing. This was because while the original purchase (or indeed creation/mining) of the currency could be traced, any subsequent transaction was extremely difficult to detect.[11] Though investor protection was not the mandate of RBI, there were concerns that speculative investments in cryptocurrencies could adversely affect innocent investors.

The effect of cryptocurrencies on the power and authority of central banks was potentially immense. A report by the Bank of International Settlements noted that 'a widespread substitution of bank notes with digital currencies could lead to a decline in Central banks' non-interest paying liabilities and that if the adoption and use of digital currencies were to increase significantly, the demand for existing monetary aggregates and the conduct of monetary policy could be affected.'[12]

These kinds of statements must have struck fear in the hearts of the denizens at RBI. Faced with this emergent technology, as is often the case in India, a flurry of activity commenced.[13] Committees, sub-committees and working groups were formed. Each of these entities gave multiple reports, guidelines and suggestions. However, as was par for the course, the various committees constituted gave contradictory views. Some recommended banning cryptocurrencies with some others recommending their use after regulation.[14] Predictably, there was very little room for public consultation and most of the discussion on matters pertaining to regulation happened behind closed doors.

These multiple rounds of negotiations ultimately culminated with the government taking the view to severely curb the use of cryptocurrencies. RBI issued a circular on 6 April 2018 stating that 'it has been decided that, with immediate effect, entities regulated by the Reserve Bank shall not deal in VCs [virtual currencies] or provide services for facilitating any person or entity in dealing with or settling VCs. Such services include maintaining accounts, registering, trading, settling, clearing, giving loans against virtual tokens, accepting them as collateral, opening accounts of exchanges dealing with them and transfer/receipt of money in accounts relating to purchase/sale of VCs.' The ban was immediate and, not unlike a surgical strike, gave virtually no time to users and companies to organize their affairs.

Though the circular did not ban cryptocurrencies per se, the effect of the circular was to cut off the use of cryptocurrencies from the normal banking channels. One could theoretically purchase cryptocurrencies, but they could never be encashed in the form of money in a bank or traded in an exchange without that exchange itself being excluded from the banking system. In practice, the circular resulted in a ban on the use of cryptocurrencies. The irony of banning what was touted as a replacement of the banking system by denying it the use of the very system was not lost on many people.[15]

IV

The Judgment

The circular was challenged before the Supreme Court by way of writ petitions. In fact, the Court was already examining the legality of cryptocurrencies in some petitions that had been filed prior to the ban. These were matters filed in the public interest by individuals seeking a ban on cryptocurrencies. When the matter in relation to the RBI circular first came to the Court, the government indicated that it had constituted an inter-ministerial committee to look into the issue of the legality of cryptocurrencies. Hoping that the government would be able to resolve the issue, the Court adjourned the matter to await the report of the committee. The initial view of the committee was that a ban would be difficult to implement and might have an undesirable side effect of driving the operators underground. This, the committee believed, might encourage the use of cryptocurrencies for illegitimate purposes. However, this seemingly pragmatic view was short-lived and ultimately, after the intervention of the deputy governor of RBI, the committee did a somersault and decided that virtual currencies would be banned and that a law to this effect would be passed.[16]

The Court was thus left with no option but to determine the validity of the RBI circular. The petitioners raised several contentions before the Court justifying why the ban on cryptocurrencies was illegal. However, two main questions were considered by the Court. The first was the question of whether RBI had the power to regulate cryptocurrencies at all. The second question was, if RBI did indeed have the power, had that power been rightly used so as to ban cryptocurrencies? If the answer to either of these queries was in the negative, the circular issued by RBI would have to be set aside.

Of course, each of these questions was hardly straightforward and encompassed issues ranging from economics to history, with legal analysis strewn in between. For instance, as regards the first question, the Court was required to undertake a three-fold exercise. First, the Court was required to examine the extent and nature of RBI's powers. Second, the Court was called upon to determine what the true nature of cryptocurrencies was. Only after determining these two issues could the Court rule on whether RBI's powers extended far enough so as to be able to regulate cryptocurrency.

As regards the powers of RBI, an extensive historical review of central banks was undertaken—from considering the establishment of the Bank of England under a royal charter in 1694 to the establishment of the Indian Central Bank in 1920 by the Imperial Bank of India Act, 1921. After considering the history, the Court examined the functions that RBI was required to perform in modern times and came to the conclusion that one fundamental role was the supervision of monetary policy. As per the preamble of the Reserve Bank of India Act, 1934 (as amended in 2016), the primary objective of monetary policy was to maintain price stability while keeping in mind the objective of growth.[17] The Court also considered other statutory enactments[18] to conclude that RBI had extremely wide powers to operate the currency and credit system of the country, including the sole right to issue bank notes that would constitute legal tender. In fact, RBI had a special place in the economic system of the country, which even enabled it to exercise functions that were essentially legislative in nature.[19]

However, even if RBI did have wide powers to regulate the financial system, that power could not be used to regulate cryptocurrencies if they were mere commodities—ordinary articles of commerce. If they were not something akin to money, RBI could no more regulate virtual currencies than it could the price of edible oils or grains. The task before the Court was to flesh out the essence of cryptocurrencies to examine the validity of the petitioners' contention, i.e., that they were not 'money' as understood in the legal or the social sense.

The Court undertook an exhaustive analysis of how various other countries and regulators across the world had treated virtual currencies. The judgment contained an exhaustive table showing the different definitions of the term 'virtual currency' adopted by regulators around the world. The judgment also considered the definitions of the term adopted in legislation and other statutory instruments in almost thirty jurisdictions. As a result of this rather intensive exercise, the Court reached the conclusion that 'there is unanimity of opinion among all the regulators and the Governments of various countries that though virtual currencies have not acquired the status of a legal tender, they nevertheless constitute digital representations of value and that they are capable of functioning as (i) a medium of exchange and/or (ii) a unit of account, and/or (iii) a store of value.'[20] The Court also noted that though the various governments had refused to recognize cryptocurrencies as legal tender, it did not detract from the position that such currencies did in fact perform 'some or most of the functions of real currency'.[21] In the opinion of the Court, a failure to recognize the obvious would not change the situation on the ground. Hence, the Court ruled it was 'not possible to accept the contention of the petitioners that Virtual Currencies are just goods/commodities and can never be regarded as real money.'[22]

Thus the Court ruled that the powers of RBI were extremely wide and also that cryptocurrencies were something very similar to money. Hence, it was not a surprise when the Court ruled that RBI did, in fact, have the power to regulate cryptocurrencies. In the judgment of the Court, RBI was required to address all issues that are perceived as risks to the monetary, currency, payment, credit and financial systems of the country. In other words, RBI was not to be a mute spectator and only determine interest rates. Since by their very nature virtual currencies had the potential to interfere with those matters that RBI had been tasked to monitor, the Court had 'no hesitation in rejecting the first contention of the petitioners that the impugned decision is ultra vires.'[23]

The judgment thus far seemed to have swung the way of the government, and had that been the end of the matter, the RBI circular would have been upheld.[24] However, the petitioners in the case had another argument up their sleeve. They argued that the circular was violative of the right to free trade and business guaranteed under Article 19 (1) (g) of the Constitution. Access to the banking system was imperative for any business and hence, the petitioners urged, a complete ban on accessing those services imposed an unreasonable restriction on their right to carry on their trade. The loss of freedom by way of the ban was disproportionate to any interest that RBI had in regulating cryptocurrencies. In particular, the exchanges on which virtual currencies were traded pleaded that the RBI circular completely stalled their hitherto booming business.

To decide whether the contention of the petitioners had any merit, the Court relied on the doctrine of proportionality.[25] In particular, the test that the government had to meet was whether their actions were the least restrictive measures possible. The Court thus had to examine whether the ban was the best method to deal with the public interest argument raised by RBI, or whether regulation without a ban would have been possible or desirable. In doing so, the judgment referred again to how other countries had dealt with the issues raised by virtual currencies.

Internationally, the view in the developed world was that cryptocurrencies were best regulated rather than simply being proscribed. The view in India was muddled at best. The Court noted that the stand of RBI had hardly been consistent in the matter of recommending a ban. It had, in fact, been content with recommending regulation rather than prohibitions at various points in time. In fact, even the circulars did not ban cryptocurrencies but merely denied the exchanges access to the banking system. There was also no evidence to suggest that the exchanges had been indulging in any illegalities or were contrary to the public interest.[26] There was a palpable sense of frustration expressed by the Court when it held that 'When the consistent stand of RBI is that they have not banned VCs and when the Government of India is unable to take a call despite several committees coming up with several proposals including two draft Bills, both of which advocated exactly opposite positions, it is not possible for us to hold that the impugned measure is proportionate.'[27]

The Court thus held that since the government had not been able to show that there was any loss to the public interest by the issuance of the circular, any curtailment of the rights of the virtual currency exchanges was disproportionate, and hence violative of Article 19 (1) (g) of the Constitution. The circular was thus held to be unconstitutional and struck down. This conclusion was like a sting in the tail because the entire preceding discussion in the judgment had seemed to go in favour of the Court upholding the ban. In the end, however, the Court ruled to set aside the ban albeit with a rather abrupt reasoning. The ambivalence of the Court itself was apparent when it recorded that the judgment had a 'nail biting finish.'

Conclusion

Though the Court might have been lukewarm about the status of the ban, the result of the judgment was to open up the cryptocurrency markets once again. RBI was a rather sullen loser. The RBI governor made statements warning of the dangers of cryptocurrencies.[28] The effect of these statements was that banks kept on dissociating themselves from the crypto markets. Even though the ban had been struck down, in practice not much changed.

If it was believed that the fear of RBI would spur the government to act, the hope was misplaced. There was some movement with apparently the government proposing an enactment banning virtually all cryptocurrencies. The corridors of power were rife with rumours that the Cryptocurrency and Regulation of Official Digital Currency Bill 2021 would be introduced in the Lok Sabha in the winter session of Parliament in 2021.[29] However, the bill was never introduced. No bill has, as of the date of writing this chapter, been presented before Parliament for consideration. Rather than banning the use of cryptocurrency, the Union Budget of 2022 introduced a tax of 30 per cent on the profits earned through the trading of such currencies. This was, in the view of some analysts at least, a tacit admission of the legality of cryptocurrencies.[30]

In the midst of the policy uncertainty, the biggest victims might end up being the citizens of the country. Like the proverbial Nero who fiddled while Rome burnt, the government has yet to enact legislation regulating cryptocurrencies. The dangers of speculative investments in cryptocurrencies are as real as they were when the circular was passed.[31] A ban may not be the best option, but failure to regulate is an abdication of responsibility. Status quo and inertia can surely never be good economic policy.

Notes

[1] In spite of the Constitution guaranteeing the right to freedom of trade and industry under Article 19 (1) (g), the Courts have evolved the doctrine of *res extra commercium*, which literally means 'things outside the normal course of commerce', and permitted banning of such items. See *Khoday Distilleries v. State of Karnataka* (1995) 1 SCC 574. This ban has ranged from alcohol to online gaming, e-cigarettes and certain food items. For an interesting critique of this doctrine, see Arvind P. Datar, 'Privilege, Police Power and "Res Extra Commercium"—Glaring Conceptual Errors', *National Law School of India Review*, Vol. 21, No. 1 (2009), pp. 133–48.

[2] (2020) 10 SCC 274.

[3] Martin A. Powell. 'Money in Mesopotamia', *Journal of the Economic and Social History of the Orient*, Vol. 39, No. 3, pp. 224–42.

[4] An account of how debt was initially used to facilitate trade can be found in David Graeber, *Debt: The First 5,000 Years* (Melville House Publishing: NY, 2011).

[5] A lay discussion on the historical evolution of money can be found in Jacob Goldstein, *Money: From Bronze to Bitcoin, the True Story of a Made Up Thing*, Atlantic Books, 2020.

[6] *The Collected Writings of John Maynard Keynes*, 'A Treatise on Money in Two Volumes', Cambridge University Press, 1930.

[7] The bank could only print money to the extent of the gold reserves that it had in its vaults. The gold standard was revived after the end of the Depression in the form of the Bretton Woods agreement, but was finally abandoned in 1971.

[8] N. Gregory Mannkiw. 'Macroeconomics', 7th Edition, Worth Publishers (2009).

[9] FATF is an inter-governmental organization set up in 1989. It issued a report titled 'Virtual Currencies—Key Definitions and Potential AML/CFT Risks' in June 2014.

[10] Anthony Lewis. *The Basics of Bitcoins and Blockchains* (Mango, 2021).

[11] 'Emerging Terrorist Financing Risks', Report by the Financial Action Task Force in October 2015.

[12] 'Digital Currency', Report by the Committee on Payments and Market Infrastructure sub-group within the BIS, November 2015.

[13] The Cryptocurrency judgment notes that the RBI ban was the 'culmination of a flurry of activities by different stakeholders, nationally and globally, over a period of about 5 years'.

[14] These reports are discussed in some detail in paragraphs 5 to 26 of the Cryptocurrency judgment.

[15] In paragraph 142 of the Cryptocurrency judgment, the Court noted that 'it is ironical that virtual currencies, which took avatar (according to its creator Satoshi) to kill the demon of a central authority (such as RBI), seek from the very same central authority access to banking services so that the purpose of the avatar is accomplished'.

[16] In a prescient article, the author criticized the recommendations of the committee suggesting that it would be held to be unconstitutional. 'The Case for Regulating Crypto Assets', Jaideep Reddy, 'A Constitutional Perspective', *The Indian Journal of Law and Technology* (2019), p. 379.

[17] Para 3 of the Preamble to the Reserve Bank of India Act, 1934.

[18] The Banking Regulation Act, 1949 and The Payment and Settlements Act, 2007.

[19] The Court was dealing with the argument that though RBI may have the power to regulate, it did not have the power to prohibit cryptocurrencies. The Court held 'the difference between other statutory creatures and RBI is that what the statutory creatures can do, could as well be done by the Executive. The power conferred upon the delegate in other statutes can be tinkered with, amended or even withdrawn. But the power conferred upon RBI under Section 3(1) of the RBI Act, 1934, to take over the management of the currency from the Central government, cannot be taken away.' See Para 147 and 192 of the Cryptocurrency judgment.

[20] Para 110 of the Cryptocurrency judgment.

[21] Para 113 of the Cryptocurrency judgment. The Court also went on to add a fourth test that currencies had to fulfil to qualify as money—that of being a final discharge of debt or standard of deferred payment.

[22] Para 137 of the Cryptocurrency judgment.

[23] Para 139 of the Cryptocurrency judgment.

[24] Many other subsidiary points were raised by the petitioners, all of which were rejected by the Court. However, a detailed examination of each of those points would be more appropriate in a legal journal than a book such as this.

[25] The test for the doctrine has been comprehensively discussed in the case of *Modern Dental College v. State of MP* (2016) 7 SCC 353.

[26] In fact, academic work suggests that it is highly unlikely that cryptocurrencies will be able to replace central banks. See 'Cryptocurrency and the Problem

of Mediation', Cameron Hardwick (Spring 2016), *The Independent Review*, pp. 569–88.

[27] Paragraph 224.

[28] Rajiv Kapoor. 'RBI Lost Case on Crypto in Supreme Court, It Must Stop Behaving Like Sore Loser', News18, 18 September 2021.

[29] 'Why Is the Indian Government Cracking Down on Cryptocurrency?', DW.com, 16 December 2021.

[30] 'Budget 2022: Did FM Just Make Cryptocurrencies Legal by Taxing Them?', *The Economic Times*, 1 February 2022.

[31] There have been grave risks associated with investments in cryptocurrencies. See a recent example in 'How a Trash Talking Crypto Founder Caused a 40-Billion-Dollar Crash', *New York Times*, 18 May 2022.

Acknowledgements

This book concerns itself with subjects that are substantially different from what I have written before. It concerns itself with finance, the economy and the law. These are topics I regularly deal with in my practice of law. Yet I had, till now, found myself writing largely on issues concerning gender and sexuality. My friend, Rukmini Chawla, and my editor, Milee Ashwarya, egged me on to write something different, something that eventually became this book. There was also an extensive amount of research that was required, for which I must thank my research assistant, Shreiya Maheshwari.

Finally, a substantial part of this book was written during the lockdown due to the Covid-19 pandemic. As was probably the case with most people, living in close proximity for such a long time tested the normal limits of love and affection. I must therefore acknowledge the patience that members of my family showed when sharing space with me during those times. My parents, my nephew, and my partner, Nicolas Germain Bachmann, were the long-suffering people who created the environment where I could write. But the greatest thanks go to those family members who will never read this book—my dogs Barolo and Margaux. Whenever I was stressed or doubted myself, I only had to look at their adoring faces to know that there were creatures who believed I was capable of accomplishing anything I wanted to do. It is to them that I owe the greatest debt of gratitude.